AF394730

# BRITAIN'S ARMAMENTS INDUSTRY INDUSTRY in the SECOND WORLD WAR

## Fighting Fit

# BRITAIN'S ARMAMENTS INDUSTRY INDUSTRY in the SECOND WORLD WAR

## Fighting Fit

### ANDREW RAWSON

Pen & Sword
**MILITARY**

AN IMPRINT OF PEN & SWORD BOOKS LTD.
YORKSHIRE – PHILADELPHIA

First published in Great Britain in 2026 by
Pen & Sword Military
An imprint of
Pen & Sword Books Ltd
Yorkshire - Philadelphia

Copyright © Andrew Rawson, 2026

ISBN 978 1 03613 612 3



Typeset in INDIA by IMPEC eSolutions
Printed and bound in the England by CPI Group (UK) Ltd, Croydon, CRO 4YY

The Publisher's authorised representative in the EU for product safety is Authorised Rep Compliance Ltd., Ground Floor, 71 Lower Baggot Street, Dublin D02 P593, Ireland.
www.arccompliance.com

For a complete list of Pen & Sword titles please contact:

PEN & SWORD BOOKS LIMITED
George House, Units 12 & 13, Beevor Street, Off Pontefract Road,
Barnsley, S71 1HN, UK
E-mail: enquiries@pen-and-sword.co.uk
Website: www.pen-and-sword.co.uk

or

PEN AND SWORD BOOKS
1950 Lawrence Rd, Havertown, PA 19083, USA
E-mail: Uspen-and-sword@casematepublishers.com
Website: www.penandswordbooks.com

# Contents

# Acknowledgements

After spending a year researching and writing about Britain's munitions industry in the First World War, I decided to turn my attentions to the nation's armaments industry during the Second World War.

Professor Gary Sheffield, President of The Western Front Association, taught me many lessons about researching when I studied for my master's degree at the University of Birmingham. Professor John Bourne, Vice President of The Western Front Association, has encouraged me for many years, as I have worked my way through my various projects. He gave me many words of encouragement during the writing of this book. My brother, Fraser Rawson, a chemical engineer, checked the chemistry in the section about the explosives industry.

My research was made far easier by the unknown members of the Berkley Library at the University of California in the United States, who went to the trouble of digitally scanning the volumes of the History of the Second World War, United Kingdom Civil Series and putting them on the website: https://www.archive.org. This website is a treasure trove of rare and out of print books, which have been made available to the public.

Any book needs a good editor if it is to succeed and I would like to thank Heather Williams at Pen & Sword Books, who headed the team which guided me through the process. I would also like to thank Lori Jones, who copy edited the manuscript.

I dedicate this book to my grandfather, Edward Rawson, who sailed over 200,000 miles with the Merchant Navy during the Second World War. He survived the sinking of the RMS *Empress of Canada* in the Atlantic Ocean on 14 March 1943; one of over 3,300 ships sunk during the war. Many of his friends lost their lives and have no known graves. They are remembered on the Tower Hill Memorial in the centre of London.

Andrew Rawson, 2026

# Introduction

My journey learning about Britain's Second World War industry started five years ago, when I began looking at what my home city did during the First World War. With the help of the website Graces Guide: https://www.gracesguide.co.uk, 'the leading source of historical information on industry and manufacturing in Britain', I discovered that the number of men and women making munitions in Sheffield's steel industry had increased six times. So, while the well-known recruitment poster that asked the question, 'What did you do in the war daddy?' was meant to encourage men to enlist, many would have been able to answer, 'I repaired warships, I made howitzers, I assembled tanks or I built aircraft engines.' Women would have answered, 'I made fuses, I filled shells, I assembled gas masks or I made aircraft wings.' Many of those children would have been able to give a similar answer to their children some thirty years later, after the Second World War.

After completing a book on the work of the Ministry of Munitions during the First World War, *Britain's Munitions Industry in the First World War*, (also with Pen & Sword, 2024), I turned my attention to the work of the three supply departments, the collective term for the organisations making armaments for the armed forces: the Admiralty, the Ministry of Aircraft Production (MAP) and the Ministry of Supply during the Second World War.

A study during the early months of the conflict estimated that it needed 78 men and women working in the munitions industry[1] to support 100 servicemen in the armed forces by the end of the First World War. Technological advances between the wars meant that military hardware was more sophisticated by the end of the 1930s. There would also be far more tanks, aircraft and warships deployed in the Second World War. So, the same study believed that 112 men and women would be needed by Britain's armaments industry to support every 100 servicemen. This book charts the story of those men and women; their recruitment, their work, and how it was all organised and managed.

There is an Official History about their work and several volumes (listed in the Bibliography) form part of the History of the Second World War, United Kingdom Civil Series; the majority of which were published in the 1950s. The volumes cover various aspects of industry and civil defence and they are available for free on the website https://www.archive.org, if you want to do any further reading.

A lot has been written about the men and the battles that British troops were engaged in and we often see the words 'forgotten' or 'overlooked' being used. I use the words 'taken for granted' when speaking about the armaments industry. Students of the Second World War know that armaments were made but they take little notice of how or where they made; this book changes that. Without the efforts of hundreds of thousands of men and women, the soldiers would have had nothing to fight with, the air crews would have had no aircraft to fly and there would have been no ships to fight on the oceans or to import everything from food to oil.

This book is a condensed version of the struggle the supply departments faced to arm Britain's armed forces. It also covers the iron ore, coal and steel industries, and the hundreds of thousands of miners and foundry workers who dug the raw materials and forged the steel. It looks at the struggle for manpower, which had to be balanced between the armed forces and industry, and the reintroduction of women in large numbers into male dominated factories.

Britain could not have won the war on its own and the narrative looks at the contribution made by the armaments industries of the United States and Canada. It discusses the difficulties encountered in negotiating the export of huge amounts of imports, especially after the United States went to war with Japan. We then see how the enormous task of shipping millions of tons of oil, raw materials, armaments and food across the Atlantic Ocean was overcome. The difficulties of keeping industry functioning during the aerial Blitz by the German *Luftwaffe* are also examined.

The reader will find out how hard the British government and industry experts had to work on many levels to arm the Royal Navy, the Royal Air Force (RAF), the British Army, and their Allies. Prime Minister Winston Churchill said 'I have nothing to offer but blood, toil, tears and sweat' when he made first speech on 13 May 1940. This is an insight into the story of the hundreds of thousands of men and women who gave theirs, working in Britain's factories during the Second World War.

*Chapter 1*

# Rearmament

## Before the Munich Crisis[1]

Hopes for a long peace throughout the 1920s meant the British armed forces were run down, as budgets were cut to the bone. The Committee of Imperial Defence (CID) even went as far as to state that there would be 'be no major war for ten years.' Most national factories had been sold off after the First World War, leaving only a few to support the Royal Ordnance Factories. Many private companies had closed or merged, while the rest were making domestic goods.

The worldwide international depression that followed the Wall Street Crash, when the stock market crashed in October 1929 added to the nation's woes. It had increased unemployment to 2.7 million or 25 per cent by 1932. Shipbuilding was hard hit and unemployment was particularly high around Glasgow and Newcastle-upon-Tyne, where half the shipyards had closed. The coalfields were also struggling because new machinery required fewer men underground and while some factories were using other fuels, many ships were powered by oil.

The fledgling aircraft industry had expanded rapidly to meet the challenges of the First World War but it then disbanded, leaving the Air Ministry relying on a small number of private companies to make its aircraft. Meanwhile, the chemical firms had amalgamated into the Explosive Trades Limited in 1918, so they could share their knowledge. Imperial Chemical Industries Limited (ICI), a company formed to supply synthetic chemicals, took over them in 1932.

The British government continued to monitor rising tensions across Europe and around the world throughout the 1930s. The CID changed its prediction following the Japanese invasion of Manchuria, in the Republic of China, in September 1931. Prime Minister Ramsey MacDonald's government then launched an investigation into Britain's armaments industry, following Adolf Hitler's appointment as the Chancellor of Germany in January 1933.

The Defence Requirements Committee (DRC) and the CID reported that the nation's capacity to make armaments was lower than it had been in 1914 and most of them were being exported. They thought that private firms would be able to step in if there was an emergency but there would still be widespread shortages. They also thought there would be competition for raw materials, steel, components and subcontractors. They predicted that it was going to be a challenge to balance home production and imports.

The DRC and the CID also wanted to reduce any shortages (known as deficiencies) the British armed forces had as quickly as possible. A group of industrialists were appointed at the end of the year and they confirmed that the years of depression had left the British armaments industry in a poor state. So, they suggested building new factories, because they could be prepared without interfering with domestic production. They would be built to modern designs and run by staff provided by experienced armaments firms. The idea was adopted and they would become known as shadow factories.

In November 1934, the DRC and the CID cautioned the British government that there could be war with Germany. The Right Honourable Winston Churchill MP also warned that it was arming 'secretly, illegally and rapidly'. They all continued to warn to against appeasement as both Germany and Italy became more aggressive.

The experience of the First World War had highlighted that there needed to be a manpower balance between the armed forces and the labour force. Rapid technological advances since the First World War, particularly with tanks, aircraft, radios and electrical equipment, meant that industry would have to be more involved.[2] The threat of air attack also meant that civil defence would have to be organised, while vulnerable factories would have to be dispersed to safer areas.

In January 1936, Prime Minister Stanley Baldwin's government appointed the industrialist William Weir (later Viscount Weir) to find out how the three armed forces proposed to deal with rearmament. He learnt that the Admiralty used its own dockyards and a few private shipyards,[3] while the Air Ministry relied on private companies. The War Office worked with the Royal Ordnance Factories and a handful of experienced private contractors.

The CID set up the Ministry for Coordination of Defence (MCD), to look at what would be needed to achieve rearmament. Sir Thomas Inskip drew up 'deficiency programmes', which listed what the armed forces would need to bring them up to strength. He then evaluated how industry could make everything. However, he had to double his estimate for the RAF and half it for the British Army, after it was estimated that the *Luftwaffe* might be able to carry out more air attacks than previously thought.

The CID then assessed what materials, plant and labour were needed, so that the MCD could plan rearmament. The Principal Supply Officers' Committee (PSOC) was checking which firms could make armaments when its duties were taken over by two boards. The Board of Trade Supply Organisation started looking for raw material sources, while the Supply Board dealt with planning. Vice Admiral Sir Harold Brown, the Royal Navy's Engineer-in-Chief, was also appointed Director General of Munitions Production and he formed two directorates: one to plan the expansion of industry and the other to monitor the progress of production.

Events around the world continued to deteriorate as Germany remilitarised the Rhineland, defying the Treaty of Versailles. Meanwhile, Italy invaded Abyssinia and Japan expanded its navy. Baldwin's government responded by doubling the military budget and approved a slow rearmament, hoping it would act as a deterrent without upsetting the British economy. The Admiralty was allowed to renovate the Royal Navy's warships, while the War Office worked on the British Army's deficiencies. However, most of the money was directed to the Air Ministry's Scheme F, a plan to increase the number of aircraft for the RAF. Prime Minister Neville Chamberlain's government took matters a step further by approving a huge rearmament loan in 1937.

Meanwhile, unemployment remained high because few had the skills to make armaments. Contracts were also being shared out unevenly because everyone relied on the firms they knew. Following the lessons learned by the Ministry of Munitions during the First World War, it was decided to make all the armaments factories 'controlled establishments', to get the best out of them.

Managers would not be able to declare lockouts in controlled establishments, while the government would set wages, working hours, prices and profits. Workers would be banned from striking and trade union demarcation rules would be lifted, so workers could do any task while unskilled labour could be used. Meanwhile, the Ministry of Labour pledged it would be a fair and impartial employer, using arbitration to maintain industrial peace.

The Minister of Labour, Ernest Brown, wanted to avoid the chaos caused to industry by unregulated enlistment at the start of the First World War. He suggested that Britain should distribute its labour between the armed forces and the armaments industry, according to the scale of the fighting. So, it was decided that the armed forces would rely on young volunteers if there was a minor war but every man of military age would be conscripted if there was a major war.

Brown started to consider how to make the best use of the large numbers of unemployed in 1937. However, his manpower plan had to be revised after the Air Raid Precautions (ARP) Department (later the Civil Defence Service) said it would need a lot more staff to defend the country from air attack. Reports about the Luftwaffe's recent bombing of Guernica in northern Spain had demonstrated how devastating a bombing raid could be. So, it asked for tens of thousands of staff to man the anti-aircraft (AA) guns and searchlights, as well as medical staff to deal with the injured and homeless.

## After the Munich Crisis[4]

Britain's plans had to change following the Munich Crisis in September 1938. Although Prime Minister Neville Chamberlain declared that there would be 'peace in our time' when he returned to Britain, the threat of war was increasing. Germany would not be content with occupying the Sudetenland area of Czechoslovakia; it wanted to occupy the whole country. So, Britain's annual military budget was increased to over £800 million (£31.5 billion today) and factories were instructed to give armament orders priority over civilian ones. None of these steps deterred Nazi Germany.

While 500,000 men enrolled in the ARP services, the Manpower Control Subcommittee was anxious to keep skilled men at their jobs, rather than let them volunteer for the armed forces. National Service Committees were set up in January 1939 to provide information about enlistment, while recruiting offices were opened across the country. Handbooks explained what the different services did, to help men decide what their best option was.

A Schedule of Reserved Occupations explained who should not enlist but there was still a successful recruitment campaign. Over 300,000 had enlisted in the armed forces, while another 1.25 million had joined the Civil Defence

Service by the end of August. The only downside to the approach was that it limited recruitment into the Territorial Army.

The Munich Crisis had also promoted the Cabinet to ask for a survey of the nation's defences and the results were concerning. The Admiralty reported shortages of warships and incomplete coastal defences.[5] The Air Ministry had just started work on Scheme L, a new plan to provide even more aircraft for the RAF. However, only a few fighter squadrons had been equipped with the modern Spitfires or Hurricanes, while the first Wellington bombers were just leaving the factories. Only 25 per cent of airfields were ready, while very few AA guns and searchlights were in position. The fact that the number of aircraft the *Luftwaffe* possessed had been overestimated by 25 per cent, made the situation look far worse than it was. However, the British Army faced the biggest difficulty because most of its Regular units were still equipped for colonial warfare, the sort it expected to face across the Empire. Most Regular Army units were short of everything, while Territorial Army units were equipped with obsolete weapons dating from the First World War.

Following Germany's occupation of the rest of Czechoslovakia in March 1939, a newly appointed Manpower Policy Committee suggested that Britain might need to send an expeditionary force to the Continent. A Military Training Act was also introduced, requiring all men of military age to register for six months training, so they would be ready to join up if the nation went to war.

A Ministry of Supply was set up under The Right Honourable Leslie Burgin MP in August 1939. The plan was to coordinate what the factories could make, so they satisfied all three armed forces. However, the Admiralty successfully argued to remain in charge of making weapons, equipment and ammunition for the Royal Navy, while the Air Ministry did the same for the RAF. Both of their armaments programmes had been given a recent financial boost, so firms were more willing to take on their orders, even though profits were subjected to an Excess Profits Tax.

A National Service Act superseded the Military Training Act on the outbreak of war, while the Ministry of Labour was renamed the Ministry of Labour and National Service, to recognise that manpower was needed for both the armed forces and for industry. It then revised the Schedule of

Reserved Occupations to include workers supporting the armaments industry. Meanwhile, Chamberlain's War Cabinet set up three committees to organise war production:

- A Military Coordination Committee made sure industry supported military strategy.
- A Priority Committee decided which armaments had priority and distributed resources accordingly.
- An Economic Policy Committee coordinated the activities of all the departments involved with the war economy.

The Supply Board estimated what raw materials and other items the armaments factories would require. The Board of Trade Supply Organisation worked out where to source them from, while noting what Britain's civilian requirements were and what other nations used. A Contracts Coordinating Committee tried to prevent competition but the Munich Crisis had sparked panic buying, resulting in many shortages. A combined approach between the three armed forces would have helped but the Admiralty and the Air Ministry successfully argued to keep their supply departments separate.

The Director General of Munitions Production was working out how to rearm the British Army when plans to increase it to thirty-two divisions were announced in August 1939. The Ministry of Supply was set up to coordinate the supply of military equipment just before German troops invaded Poland on 1 September 1939. Britain declared war on Germany two days later.

As the *Wehrmacht* and *Luftwaffe* advanced, it became painfully clear that Britain's defensive measures were incomplete. The number of AA guns defending the nation may have doubled and there were radar stations covering the south and east coast. The RAF also had nearly 2,000 first line aircraft organised into twenty-six squadrons. However, the *Luftwaffe* demonstrated its power as it carried out devastating bombing attacks. The British Army had just five regular divisions, while the *Wehrmacht* had deployed sixty-six divisions in its march on Warsaw. The outbreak of war would speed up the building of new factories but the British armaments industry had a lot of catching up to do.

## Employment Before the War[6]

The Ministry of Labour had departments covering employment, unemployment, training and industrial relations. The Ministry opened a Military Recruiting Department in the spring of 1939, to deal with the 240,000 new recruits required to serve for six months under the Military Training Act. It also drew up a Schedule of Reserved Occupations identifying those who were doing essential work. The two steps were implemented because the government was anxious not want to make the same mistake that had been made in 1914, when uncontrolled volunteering had resulted in 20 per cent of skilled men enlisting.

The Ministry of Labour published a revised Schedule of Reserved Occupations based on skills instead of industries and occupations. Nearly 5 million men were covered and while many were of military age, some would be transferred to armaments factories when war was declared. However, the list was incomplete and many reservists with key skills were still called up over the months that followed. For example, the Air Ministry had to stop 15,000 aircraft employees being called up for military service on the outbreak of war.

The prolonged depression between the wars had resulted in many factories closing and mass unemployment. While the trade unions were anxious to get their members back to work, the highest unemployment levels were in the shipyards in the North. Meanwhile, there was shortage of workers around the aircraft factories in the Midlands and the South and the aircraft firms were prepared to pay high wages for skilled labour.

The Munich Crisis may have speeded up Britain's economic mobilisation but it was too little too late. Government investment in depressed areas and rearmament was then disrupted by a trade recession in the United States in 1938. It meant that unemployment started to rise again and there were still 1.25 million unemployed across Britain in September 1939.

The Air Ministry was going to require a lot of semi and unskilled labour to build the extra aircraft planned for the RAF. There had been many issues about dilution during the First World War and the government was anxious not to upset the trade unions. Firms also reported that shift work made it difficult to find enough labour, particularly skilled workers and supervisors. So, subcontracting was used to increase the production of parts and components. The Ministry of Labour also discretely advised the Air Ministry to start upskilling the workforce it was relying on.

The production lines in the new shadow factories were designed to divide complicated tasks into many simple ones. However, they still needed skilled workers from other industries to supervise the large numbers of unskilled workers required to operate them. While the Ministry of Labour refused to enforce dilution, the Amalgamated Engineering Union finally agreed to it in August 1939, with a guarantee that working practices would be restored when the emergency (and then war) ended. However, dilution only targeted men to begin with, because unemployment was so high in many industrial areas. Employing women in the shadow factories would eventually be considered in the summer of 1941, after male unemployment had fallen to a low level.

## Finances Before the War[7]

The Cabinet set Britain's military budgets while the Chancellor of the Exchequer agreed them with the three supply departments who worked for the armed forces. The departments then tendered for the best price and quality, buying what the supply branches needed. The Finance Department checked they were getting value for money.

Britain's defence expenditure had been small during the depression years but it increased in line with the rearmament programme, starting in 1936. For example, the Defence Loans Act of 1937 authorised £400 million (£15.7 billion today) to be spent over five years but it was doubled to £800 million (£31.5 billion today) just before the outbreak of the Second World War.

While the government was concerned about the deteriorating situation in Europe, it was also worried that expanding the armaments business too quickly could destabilise the nation's economy. It was equally concerned that it could undermine domestic industry because high spending in the armaments factories would result in labour and materials shortages in other ones. The large quantities of imports required for rearmament would also affect the nation's currency and its financial reserves.

Even so, worries about the situation in Europe resulted in the Air Ministry's financial limits being removed in 1938, so that aircraft production could be expanded to fulfil Scheme L. Financial constraints were also removed from the Admiralty and the British Army the following year. While the three supply departments had permission to buy what they required, the Treasury was concerned that it would not have enough gold or cash to pay for all the raw materials and imports required.

Military budgets may have increased significantly for the RAF but they were insufficient to turn the Royal Navy and British Army into modern fighting forces. For example, the annual cost of warship repairs was just £340,000 (£13.4 million today) in 1934, while it would rise 130 times to £44 million (over £1.5 billion today) by 1943. Although the British Army's annual budget increased from £7 million (£275 million today) in 1934 to £68 million (£2.7 billion today) in 1939, all it had done was to reverse the deficiencies created by twenty years of underfunding.

A credit system was introduced on the outbreak of war, so the supply departments could buy what they needed without having to get their budgets authorised in advance. While the ordering process was accelerated, the Treasury made regular checks on expenditure and stepped in to stop any unnecessary purchases.

The increase in expenditure lowered unemployment but it also caused inflation to rise. Higher employment meant people had more money to spend and some luxury goods were being imported from the United States. While the improved economy helped Britain's balance of payments, it did take up shipping capacity which was required to import items for the armaments industry.


## Supplying the Royal Navy[8]

The Washington Naval Treaty, or Five-Power Treaty, had been agreed in 1922, to prevent a naval arms race between the British Empire, the United States, France, Italy and Japan. It limited the annual tonnage of warships each nation could make. It also set the maximum displacement for each class of capital ship and fixed the largest calibre of gun each class could be armed with.[9] The London Naval Treaty would add restrictions for smaller warships and submarines in 1930. At the time, Britain's only naval threat came from Japan in the Far East and while the Royal Navy could match the Imperial Japanese Navy in numbers of warships, many were outdated.

The worldwide depression that followed the Wall Street Crash in 1929, resulted in the Royal Dockyards repairing old warships rather than building new ones. Out-of-date construction methods, a lack of investment and restrictive working practices resulted in inefficient work in many yards. The Admiralty had relied on private shipyards for much of its work but the recession meant that many had merged or closed. The number of men working in the industry had halved since the First World War, leading to high unemployment and rising tensions between employers and the trade unions. It would require a lot of money to bring the fleet up to date but Britain's shipbuilding industry was in decline and time was running out.

The situation across Europe deteriorated when Germany violated the Treaty of Versailles and the Locarno Treaties, by sending troops into the Rhineland in March 1936. Britain was also alarmed when Germany and Japan signed the Anti-Comintern Act in November 1936. To make matters worse, the CID reported that the German *Kreigsmarine* was rearming at an alarming rate, as the London Naval Treaty came to an end.

Prime Minister Stanley Baldwin's government wanted to rearm the Royal Navy but warships were expensive and most of the limited military budget had to be spent on aircraft, to defend Britain from air attack. So, the Admiralty received a 'rationed' budget spread over three years and it was far less than what was needed to bring the Royal Navy up to date. Meanwhile, the Shipbuilding Consultative Committee was instructed to look at how the shipbuilding industry would cope if the nation went to war.

Capital ships took several years to build, so the Admiralty only ordered one battleship, and that would not be finished until after the war had ended. While two destroyer flotillas were also ordered, money was spent on a fleet of small warships, fast craft and submarines, to protect Britain's coastal waters and merchant shipping.

The Royal Navy had replenished its ammunition stocks by 1938 but it was struggling to get specialist equipment. Many companies had shut down, while others were busy working on orders for export. AA guns and fire control equipment were also in short supply because the War Office was buying them all up for air defence. Meanwhile, a shortage of armour plate was causing a construction bottleneck because the naval treaties had severely reduced demand. While some came from Britain's steel foundries, large amounts were imported from Czechoslovakia until German troops moved into the Sudetenland in October 1938. Shortages developed as all the services increased their demands until they all found it difficult to acquire anything.

While the Admiralty was considering how to increase its strength, the government instructed it to plan how to move large parts of its staff out of London because it did not want air raids to disrupt their work. Many departments were sent to Bath on the outbreak of war, making it difficult to run the Admiralty. The split site situation became known as 'Bathmanship'.

## Supplying the Royal Air Force[10]

Aircraft production was a specialised industry that had struggled to survive between the wars. The RAF worked with sixteen private firms but they only built around seventy-five aircraft a month between them. The Air Ministry relied on the following directorates to work with them:

- The Scientific Research and Technical Development Directorates looked at design and development.
- The Equipment Directorate dealt with production, maintenance and repair.
- The Aeronautical Inspection Directorate inspected all the components and assemblies.

First World War era biplanes continued to be built well into the 1930s, while Germany and Italy were trying out modern designs over the battlefields of Spain. Meanwhile, budgets were so low that the number of squadrons the RAF had was falling.[11]

The Defence Requirements Committee wanted to match the number of aircraft the *Luftwaffe* had but the financial restraints limited expansion. The Air Ministry was also anxious to arm its squadrons with the new monoplanes the aircraft firms were designing. However, the Secretary of State for Air, Phillip Cunliffe-Lister, Viscount Swinton, was aware that accepting new aircraft designs before they had been fully tested could interrupt production. So, the RAF was left flying out-of-date aircraft until the prototypes were ready.

The early 1930s were a time of innovation, as monoplanes made from lightweight alloys started replacing the wooden and canvas biplanes. The Air Ministry issued specifications for new designs and while companies could change them, they lost their money if their modifications were rejected. The new designs incorporated many inventions, including cantilevered wings, variable pitch air screws, improved engine efficiency and retractable undercarriages. So, the changing nature of aircraft design required three new directorates:

- The Armament Development Directorate dealt with weapons and bombs.
- The Aeronautical Production Directorate focused on production.
- The Repair and Maintenance Directorate scheduled repairs and maintenance.

The Air Ministry wanted a monoplane to replace the Bristol Bulldog fighter biplane, which had been in service since 1929. Reginald Mitchell of Supermarine Aviation Works Limited submitted a cantilever design powered by a Rolls-Royce Goshawk II engine in 1934. Discussions with the Air Ministry resulted in the wing shape being changed, the cooling system being improved and a retractable undercarriage being added. The redesigned Spitfire was powered by the Rolls-Royce P.V. 12 engine, which was later named the Merlin engine. Meanwhile, Sydney Camm of Hawker Aircraft Limited had his first design rejected, but a revised prototype was accepted as the Hurricane in 1936.

Cunliffe-Lister announced a new aircraft production programme in February 1936. The Air Ministry's increased budget would be used to equip the RAF with modern aircraft, to create an air force capable of defending the nation from air attack.

Scheme F was introduced in 1936 and the plan was to increase production from 3,800 aircraft over two years, to 8,000 aircraft over three years. Cunliffe-Lister planned to start three types of government financed factory programmes and the Air Ministry set up a Factories Directorate to supervise them:

- An extension programme built extensions to existing factories.
- An agency programme built new factories in areas safe from bombing to be run by aircraft firms.

- A shadow programme built new factories in areas safe from bombing to be run by engineering firms.

The Air Ministry announced that the Austin Motor Company Limited would make aircraft at its Longbridge factory near Birmingham and run a shadow factory in Bromsgrove. Rootes Limited, another car company (Humber Limited), would make aircraft at its Ryton factory near Coventry and manage a shadow factory in Speke near Liverpool.

The Committee of Imperial Defence believed that the RAF would be heavily engaged from the start of the war. It also noted that the Germany industry had increased aircraft production soon after Scheme F was announced. Adolf Hitler had also ordered troops into the Rhineland in March 1936, breaking the Treaty of Versailles and the Locarno Treaties.

The Air Ministry monitored the *Luftwaffe*'s expansion as Scheme F fell behind programme and the shock of German troops marching into Austria in March 1938, known as the *Anschluss* (union), prompted the issuing of a new aircraft production plan. The new Secretary of State for Air, The Right Honourable Sir Kingsley Wood MP, announced Scheme L; a plan to make 4,000 aircraft by the summer of 1939 and another 8,000 over the following year. However, they could only be made if the promised factories were completed and enough labour could be found.

Prime Minister Neville Chamberlain's Cabinet agreed the armaments industry would have to be given all the money it needed. Britain would have to restructure its economy to keep up with Germany, as financial limits were lifted. The government also approved of the Air Ministry's plan to let the aircraft factories work at maximum output with no financial limits on the following approved models for the next two years:

- Hurricane, Spitfire and Defiant fighters.
- Whitley, Blenheim, Battle, Hampden and Wellington bombers.

Meanwhile, a survey of the industry by Ernest Lemon, the new Director General of Production, reported a labour shortage in the aircraft factories. So, he convinced the aircraft companies to hand over around one third of their work to hundreds of engineering workshops. It meant they could make everything from alloy airframes to engines, for the main factories to assemble. The move quickly expanded the output of armaments and without additional expense.

Air Marshal Sir Wilfrid Freeman was appointed the head of Development and Production while Air Commodore Roderic Hill became the head of Technical Development. Four new production directorates were also set up:

- The Materials Directorate dealt with the companies making alloy parts.
- The Aircraft Directorate organised the companies making airframes.
- The Engines Directorate dealt with the engine companies; mainly Rolls-Royce and the Bristol Aeroplane Company.
- The Armament and Equipment Production Directorate sourced other components.

Four auxiliary directorates and a committee were also established:

- The War Production Planning Directorate matched production with the Air Ministry's strategy.
- The Factories Directorate discussed factory design, machine tools and labour.
- The Subcontracting Directorate worked with subcontractors.
- The Supply Committee checked firms' estimated output and dealt with order problems.
- The Statistics and Planning Directorate collected data and reported on progress.

As we have seen, Scheme L increased the number of aircraft to be built to 17,500. Meanwhile, the Air Ministry's Production Department was confident that the industry could be making 2,000 aircraft per month within just 18 months. However, the rapid increase in production caused balance issues, because far more airframes were being made than engines. So, the Production Department formed companies into assembly groups which made all the thousands of parts, large and small, needed to build an aircraft in the right proportions. Although the problems were being addressed one by one, time was running out.

While the Air Ministry was busy working on Scheme L, it was instructed to look at how to move its staff out of London. The Cabinet did not want bombing raids against the capital to disrupt how it functioned. So, a plan was made to move some of its departments to Harrogate in North Yorkshire, close to many of the RAF's airfields. The move was made on the outbreak of war, making it harder to coordinate work with the rest of the armed forces. Its staff would be back in London in the spring of 1940, just in time for the Battle of Britain.

The Air Ministry was anxious to follow up Scheme L in 1939, so it could maintain the arms race with the *Luftwaffe*. However, the War Cabinet was more concerned about how to reduce the potential damage to factories from air raids. Work had started on ten new factories, while extensions to existing structures was expected to increase production by 60 per cent. Three more shadow factories were also being built, so experienced firms could help engineering companies build complete aircraft:

- Handley Page helped the English Electric Company Limited assemble Halifax bombers in Preston.
- Avro helped Metropolitan-Vickers make Manchester bombers in Trafford Park near Manchester.
- Supermarine planned to help the Nuffield Organization build Spitfires in Castle Bromwich.[12]

The new plan was to increase the aircraft industry's workforce to 60,000 in just two years. However, it would take time to find enough skilled workers to train the thousands of unskilled ones needed to operate the assembly lines.[13]

On the outbreak of war, the Air Council estimated that production was still only 780 aircraft a month. While the Air Member for Development and Production wanted to increase the number to 3,000 per month as quickly as possible, it was too many for the aircraft companies to deal with. So, the number was reduced to 2,250 made in British factories, with another 250 being produced in Canada. This new target became known as the Harrogate Programme and it would become the basis for planning aircraft production during the early months of the war.

## The Royal Ordnance Factories (ROFs)

The Royal Arsenal in Woolwich and the Royal Small Arms Factory (RSAF) in Enfield made rifles but they were unable to make larger items. ROF Nottingham made artillery pieces and while a few private firms made larger armaments, they were all barely ticking over between the wars:

- William Beardmore and Company Limited and G. & J. Weir Limited, both in Glasgow, made guns and worked on heavy engineering projects.
- Vickers-Armstrongs in Newcastle-upon-Tyne made guns, small arms and light engineering projects.
- Greenwood & Batley made small arms ammunition in Leeds.
- Birmingham Small Arms Company Limited (BSA) worked on light engineering projects in Birmingham.
- Projectile and Engineering Co. Limited made shells in London.
- ICI Limited made explosives at several sites.

The Royal Gunpowder Mills in Waltham Abbey also made small amounts of explosives. Only three national factories dating from the First World War were still operating and they only employed 8,000 workers between them:

- ROF Irvine made explosives in Ayrshire.
- ROF Birtley made armaments near Newcastle-upon-Tyne.
- ROF Hereford filled shells in Herefordshire.

A committee headed by the industrialist William Weir, Viscount Weir, had recommended building new ROFs as early as 1935, believing it would be easier than expanding existing firms. So, a Director of Industrial Planning was appointed to coordinate the growth of the ROF network. The Director of Army Contracts decided what quantities of weapons and ammunition to make, while the Director of Ordnance Factories controlled production.

The War Office decided to expand production at the Royal Arsenal but it also wanted the government to finance private firms, either by expanding their works or building new ones for them to run. Three new armaments companies were also set up to deal with specific shortages:

- Nuffield Organization (part of Morris Motors Limited) made tanks and Bofors AA guns.
- British Manufacturing and Research Company made Hispano 20-millimetre guns and ammunition.
- New Crown Forgings (part of Stewarts & Lloyds) made shell forgings.

Steel came from two large conglomerates. The English Steel Corporation Limited had been formed from a merger of Vickers, and Cammell Laird & Co. Limited, both of Sheffield, and Whitworth of Newcastle-upon-Tyne in 1928. Firth Brown Steels had been formed when John Brown & Company, and Thomas Firth & Sons Limited, both of Sheffield, merged in 1930.

The Weir Committee located the new ROFs away from coast, so as not to interfere with shipbuilding labour. However, some were placed in the south and east, an area that would soon be in danger from air raids. There would be three types of ROFs, each supervised by a deputy director:

- Engineering factories which made guns, tanks and shells, rifles, bullets and tools.
- Explosives factories which made the cordite propellants and TNT explosives.
- Filling factories which filled the shells and bullets with the propellants and explosives.

There were three types of engineering factories and while those making artillery pieces used standard machine tools, the ones making shells and small arms required specialist equipment.

## Supplying the British Army[14]

The Royal Navy was seen as the most important service, while the RAF was more seen as the most impressive, resulting in the British Army being treated as their poor cousin. It received less than 10 per cent of the meagre military budget between the wars and most of it was spent lorries, so units could be motorised. It meant there was left little to spend tank development, while the infantry had to train with obsolete weapons.

The British Army had just four regular divisions in 1934 and while the Army Council regularly discussed their needs with the Secretary of State for War, budget constraints meant little happened until 1936. The Chief of the Imperial General Staff were supported by four senior officers, who were responsible for supplying the British Army with weapons, equipment and ammunition:

- The Master General of the Ordnance was the supplier.
- The Quartermaster General stored and issued items.
- The Chief of the Imperial General Staff was the user.
- The Adjutant General dealt with the administration.

Three directorates decided what weapons, equipment and ammunition the British Army required, according to where it was expected to fight:

- Operations and Intelligence decided what type of warfare was expected and how much opposition could be expected.
- Staff Duties decided the Order of Battle, the weapon specifications and the quantities needed.
- Military Training prepared the troops according to the chosen tactical doctrine.

Four directorates helped the Master General of the Ordnance with design and manufacture:

- The Contracts Directorate dealt with the ordering process, contractors and finance.
- The Artillery Directorate dealt with artillery and tank guns.
- The Mechanisation Directorate worked with armoured fighting vehicles and transport.
- The Ordnance Services Directorate organised ammunition, inspection and storage.

The Quartermaster General dealt with transport, storage and the issuing of items, until a new Director General took over in the summer of 1936.

The War Office worked to two types of armaments programmes:

- Deficiency programmes made sure units were armed with their full complement of weapons and ammunition.
- Rearmament programmes were then used to arm the reserves that would be needed when units deployed.

Army programmes may have been small compared to those of the Admiralty and Air Ministry but the infantry, artillery, tank and transport units needed many different items. Most of them could be made by general engineering factories and the Supply Board picked suitable contractors from the Capacity Register, which was also known as List 392. Inspectors then confirmed a firm had the skills to do the work and assessed whether it could expand. Contracts were then issued, along with an instruction manual explaining how to make the items.

The limited budget between the wars meant that it took many years to design arms and equipment. For example, the Bren gun took twelve years, the No. 4 Rifle took eleven years and the 3.7-inch AA gun took ten years. The 25-pounder was made by converting First World War era 18-pounder guns to save money on designing a new one. Design times would be halved in wartime because more money was made available.

The Cabinet cancelled a planned expansion of the British Army in April 1937, in favour of expanding the RAF. Meanwhile, the Director General of Munitions Production said that he wanted more factories built, even though there was sufficient manufacturing capacity. His reasoning was that imports from Europe would be cut if there was a war with Germany. So, money was made available to finish the building work on the new Royal Ordnance Factories, resulting in extra capacity being ready when war broke out.

The Director General of Munitions Production took over from the Master General of the Ordnance at the beginning of 1938, as the War Office considered reorganising how it supplied the British Army. He wanted to involve as many engineering companies as possible, so he asked them to make small amounts of items, known as 'educational orders'. In doing so, he found out which firms were suitable and it gave them experience of armaments work. He also over ordered 5 per cent of each item, in case the War Office increased its demands.

The situation in Europe deteriorated when Germany formed a union or *Anschluss* with Austria in March 1938. The Munich Crisis and the annexation of the Sudetenland, on Czechoslovakia's western border, in October 1938, increased concerns. France asked Britain for assistance and Prime Minister Neville Chamberlain accepted that the British Army would require extra divisions, so it could deploy an expeditionary force to France.

The government decided that conscription would be required to increase the British Army to six Regular divisions and twenty-six Territorial divisions. However, the Ministry of Supply said the that armaments industry could not increase its output sufficiently to arm them all in time. Instead, it suggested reducing the number of Territorial divisions to fourteen.

When the British Army's budget was finally increased, the extra money was spent on improving the nation's anti-aircraft defences, rather than on tanks, artillery or transport. What little money was spare was spent on equipping the Territorial Army with modern weapons and equipment. The War Office was finally given enough money to reorganise its mobile division into two mechanised divisions in 1938.

Following Germany's occupation of the rest of Czechoslovakia in March 1939, the DRC considered how to organise the Regular Army divisions into an expeditionary force ready to serve in France. It also considered what was needed to equip the Territorial Army ready to defend Britain. However, its plans to increase the size of the British Army to five Regular divisions and twelve Territorial divisions were hindered because most the budget was still being allocated to the RAF and the Royal Navy.

The Ministry for Coordination of Defence then stated that France was not expecting any help and that the Regular Army should be used to defend the British Empire instead. Meanwhile, the CID said it was planning for a 'limited liability' war and that troops would only be deployed to the Continent for defensive purposes once they had been re-equipped. Meanwhile, the Prime Minister and the Cabinet were still focused on increasing the size of the RAF, to defend the country. So, all that the War Office could do when war broke out in September 1939, was to promise to send as many divisions as possible to France.

## The Tank Factories[15]

Tanks had been introduced to the battlefield during the First World War but interest in new designs waned when the conflict ended. A limited budget meant only one prototype could be considered every year, while the League of Nations had limited the weight of a tank to just 16 tons. The Design Superintendent's Tank Department eventually closed in 1930, leaving it to the War Office's Mechanisation Directorate to work with the Royal Arsenal and Vickers-Armstrongs. Work on tank guns was also handed over to the Director of Artillery.

The British Army only had a single tank brigade in 1930 and it was equipped with two small models, designed to police colonies across the Empire. The A4 light tank was armed with just a Vickers machine gun, while the A6 medium tank had a 2-pounder gun. The brigade was also equipped with a tracked tankette for reconnaissance work.

By 1936, the War Office noted that France's new Char tanks and Germany's new Panzer tanks had thicker armour. Meanwhile, Woolwich's Research Department had worked out how to weld hardened steel plates together. A tough nickel-chromium-molybdenum steel alloy was also being used.

Following the alliance between Germany and Italy in October 1936, the Research Department started considering three designs with different roles:

- Infantry Tanks: slow heavily armoured tanks armed with guns which could knock out bunkers.
- Cruiser Tanks: medium speed, lightly armoured tanks armed with anti-tank guns for exploitation and pursuit.
- Reconnaissance Tanks: fast, lightly tanks armed with machine guns for scouting and policing duties.

The British Army did not have a suitable infantry tank until the Matilda II was ordered in the summer of 1938. However, four engineering firms had been contracted to build small numbers of light tanks:

- Vickers-Armstrongs Limited in Elswick near Newcastle-upon-Tyne.
- Harland and Wolff in Belfast, Northern Ireland.

- Birmingham Railway Carriage and Wagon Company in Smethwick near Birmingham.
- Metropolitan-Cammell Carriage and Wagon Company[16] in Saltey near Birmingham.

Orders for cruiser tanks were given to Nuffield Organization, a new company set up by William Morris, Lord Nuffield, the owner of Morris Motors Limited. It opened factories in Coventry and Oxford in 1938, ready to design and build tanks. It was joined by the London, Midland and Scottish Railway (LMS) workshops and a locomotive firm. The Metropolitan-Cammell Carriage and Wagon Company of Birmingham was contracted to make Cruiser, Valentine and Matilda tanks in 1939. Edwin Foden Sons & Company of Sandbach, Cheshire, and Leyland Motors Limited of Leyland and Chorley, Lancashire and Kingston-upon-Thames also made them.

# Chapter 2

# The Administration

## War Planning[1]

Both urgency and priority had to be considered to get the best out of the armaments industry. Urgency involved solving a short-term problem, to prevent or end a delay. The Ministry of Supply identified what labour, plant and materials were required to keep the factories busy. A few items were required immediately to restart work, while others were required by a certain date to avoid future delays. Some were just preferred items that would ease an issue.

Priority involved deciding what to do first, to achieve the maximum output in the long-term. The Central Priority Department prioritised what would be made first and how many, so that the available labour, plant and materials could be allocated accordingly.

The government appointed a Priority Committee on the outbreak of war and it was given control of key materials, such as iron and steel. It prioritised the demands made by the Admiralty, Air Ministry and Ministry of Supply through licensing, purchasing and distribution systems. The Ministry of Aircraft Production would take over from the Air Ministry when Winston Churchill was appointed Prime Minister in May 1940.

The Priority Committee appointed a Materials Priority Subcommittee in the spring of 1940, to cover the other raw materials and components associated with the armaments industry. The Principal Priority Officer and Raw Material Control used List 392, a list of 7,000 factories, to source what was required. However, it took time to work out how to allocate materials fairly, to limit stockpiling and reduce waste. The Priority Committee would take over the buying of plant and machine tools in the summer of 1940; it also started deciding which order to build factories in.

Arthur Greenwood joined the Ministry of Labour as head of a Production Council in May 1940 and it took over from the Ministerial Priority Committee. He prioritised armaments into the following categories:

- Category 1A: aircraft, bombs and small arms ammunition.
- Category 1B: field guns and ammunition.
- Category 2: naval equipment, infantry support weapons, tanks and transport.

The categories would change in line with the strategic plans. But new items kept being added to the priorities list, slowing the Production Council's work down until the supply departments asked for the system to be streamlined. So, the Production Council set up six committees to help turn the armed forces' demands into production plans:

- The Joint Materials and Production Priority Committee calculated what materials were required to meet the supply departments' needs.
- The Manpower Requirements Committee evaluated how much labour was required.
- The Manpower Priority Committee worked out where to place labour to meet the priorities.
- The Industrial Capacity Committee assessed what factories were available.
- The Works and Buildings Priority Committee decided what order to build new factories in.
- The Industry Location Committee chose the best place to build new factories based on advice given by the Labour Supply Branch.

A Building Construction Controller started coordinating building projects in 1941 and the post was renamed the Building Executive when he started approving and prioritising them as well.

The Production Council still struggled to balance the ever changing requirements for materials, plant and labour. While materials could be supplied quickly, plant took time to source and labour took even longer to train. Meanwhile, the supply departments were focused on meeting their targets, rather than their long-term labour requirements. Armaments and building projects always needed to be completed as quickly, which resulted in materials and labour being used unwisely or wasted.

The American Neutrality Act had banned the sale of armaments since 1935. However, President Franklin D. Roosevelt allowed them to be sold to Britain and France, starting in November 1939. A British Purchasing Commission was then set up in Washington DC, to talk to American manufacturers. The Neutrality Act ended in September 1940, when America transferred fifty destroyers to Britain, in exchange for bases in Newfoundland and the British West Indies.[2]

## The Admiralty[3]

The government set Britian's naval policy while the Admiralty decided what warships it required and planned the production programme to build and maintain them. Private companies did most of the shipbuilding while the Royal Dockyards did repairs and maintenance. The Admiralty was run by a board of four Sea Lords:

- The First Sea Lord decided what ships were needed after studying other countries' navies.
- The Second Sea Lord dealt with personnel.
- The Third Sea Lord organised construction, engineering, ordnance and repairs.
- The Fourth Sea Lord dealt with the stores, except for armaments, fuel, medicines and food.

Admiral Sir Dudley Pound was a First World War veteran who later served as the Second Sea Lord. He joined the Mediterranean Fleet in 1933 and commanded it as tensions with Germany and Italy increased. Pound was appointed First Sea Lord in June 1939 and was promoted to Admiral of the Fleet. He commanded the Royal Navy through the difficult early months of the war, as it tried to help Norway before supporting the British Expeditionary Force (BEF), as it escaped from Dunkirk. The Royal Navy then protected Britain's coastal waters and tried to keep the Atlantic convoys safe. It then suffered setbacks, when the Imperial Japanese Navy sank several capital ships in the Far East.

Pound chaired the British Chiefs of Staff until his health declined and he was succeeded by Field Marshal Alan Brooke in March 1942. Three months later Admiral Sir Charles Kennedy-Purvis became his deputy, taking over many of his administrative duties. Pound's health deteriorated after his wife died and he resigned in September 1943, dying only a month later.

Admiral Sir Andrew Cunningham replaced Pound and he was another First World War veteran who had been appointed Rear Admiral of Destroyers in 1933. He became the deputy of the Mediterranean Fleet in 1936 and was appointed Deputy Chief of the Naval Staff in December 1938. He returned to the Mediterranean as Commander-in-Chief in June 1939 and participated in the battles for Malta, Taranto and Cape Matapan, before evacuating the garrison from Crete. He was also Naval Commander of the Allied Expeditionary Force, which invaded North Africa in November 1942.

Cunningham was appointed First Sea Lord in September 1943, as the Royal Navy gave support to the Allied campaigns in the Mediterranean. It then covered the invasion fleets, which landed troops in Normandy in June 1944 and on the south coast of France in August. Preparations for fleet operations in the Pacific were cancelled when the war with Japan ended in August 1945.

One third of the Admiralty's construction work was the building of ship's hulls, while two thirds was the making of armament and equipment. In many cases, it used the same factories as the other armed forces, so it relied on the Ministry of Supply to discuss their shared needs.

## The Air Ministry and the Ministry of Aircraft Production[4]

The Air Ministry's Supply Committee regularly discussed the aircraft production programme from September 1939 to March 1940. It set up a capital division to deal with financing of the new aircraft factories while four other divisions looked after raw materials, airframes, engines and armaments.

The Air Member for Development and Production controlled technological advances through the following directorates:

- The Armament Development Directorate looked at weapons and bombs.

- The Communications Development Directorate dealt with radio and radar.
- The Aircraft Equipment Production Directorate organised the aircraft instruments.
- A Radio Production Directorate was created in February 1940 to deal with radios.

The Ministry of Aircraft Production (MAP) took over responsibility for aircraft design, development, construction, inspection, storage and repairs from the Air Ministry on 17 May 1940. Max Aitken, Lord Beaverbrook, was at its head and he appointed Air Vice Marshal Arthur Tedder as the Director General of Research and Development. Tedder set up directorates to organise scientific research and the development of technical and communications equipment, as well as armament and inspection. Another eleven directorates dealt with different aspects of production.

Churchill said that Beaverbrook was full of 'vital and vibrant energy', while he chose businessmen who were prepared to share responsibilities and do what was necessary to get the job done. While his team increased aircraft production during the Battle of Britain, the rest of the armaments industry suffered, because the MAP grabbed more than its fair share of labour, plant and materials.

Patrick Hennessy of the Ford Motor Company organised the raw materials and lightweight metal alloys required to make the airframes and aero engines. Meanwhile, Sir Charles Craven of Vickers-Armstrongs Limited organised the factory construction programme and the labour and machine tools required to meet it. Sir Frank Smith, a retired director of the National Physical Laboratory, was appointed the Controller of Telecommunications Equipment and his staff worked on aircraft radio and radar equipment. Trevor Westbrook of Vickers-Armstrongs Limited dealt with maintenance programmes and aircraft repairs. He also looked at how factories could be defended from air attack.

Hennessy replaced Craven in November 1940, while Westbrook took over airframe production. Once the Battle of Britain ended in October 1940, Hennessy was able to make a structured aircraft programme. The MAP then added new directorates to cope with the large number of engines and airfield equipment required to expand the RAF.

Lieutenant Colonel John Moore-Brabazon took over the MAP on 1 May 1941 and while he was first and foremost a pilot, he introduced an organised management approach. He organised directorates for materials, aircraft and equipment, while forming a Supply Council to advise on programmes, delivery and repairs. The Council also gave firms advice on how to recruit labour and how to dilute work, so the aircraft industry's workforce could increase to 1.7 million. Moore-Brabazon also had to coordinate production with the American aircraft programme and work out how to supply the Soviet Air Force with aircraft.[5] Meanwhile, a Controller of Research and Development ran directorates covering scientific research and the development of engines, armament, radio and radar.

Moore-Brabazon was forced to resign in February 1942, after stating that he wanted Germany and the Soviet Union to destroy each other. He was replaced by Colonel John Llewellin who worked with Air Chief Marshal Sir Arthur Harris, as Bomber Command worked out how to bomb German industry, alongside the United States Army Air Force (USAAF).

The Right Honourable Sir Richard Cripps MP was appointed the Minister of Aircraft Production in November 1942. He fully supported the RAF's strategic bombing campaign stating;

> the more we can destroy from the air the industrial and transport facilities of the Axis, the weaker will become his resistance. The heavier our air attack, the lighter will be the total of our casualties.[6]

Cripps appointed controllers to improve the organisation of production, labour, maintenance and repairs. Other controllers coordinated the import of American and Canadian aircraft. A Controller of Research and Development also oversaw the work on the jet engine and other facilities involved in research schemes. Cripps served as Ministry of Aircraft Production until the end of the war, during which time the RAF dealt a devastating blow to German industry.

## The Ministry of Supply[7]

There had been a Supply Board in existence since 1927. Some wanted a Ministry of Supply to avoid the shortages of munitions experienced at the start of the First World War. However, the idea was rejected because more objected, concerned it could interfere with domestic trade. The British Army compiled a deficiency programme in 1936, which listed what was needed to arm all its units with up to date weapons and equipment. Manufacturing them all was soon causing problems, so there were discussions about setting up a Ministry of Supply to deal with supplies and stores for the three armed forces. The War Office agreed to use its services but Admiralty and the Air Ministry objected and they would continue to rely on their own staff to organise the items they required.

The Ministry of Supply was eventually set up on 1 August 1939, to deal with the British Army's expansion to six Regular and ten Territorial divisions.[8] The Right Honourable Edward Burgin MP had served as the Minister of Transport before he was appointed the first Minister of Supply. He added two production divisions on the outbreak of war and while one dealt with explosives and chemicals, the other looked after tanks and transport. The Mechanisation Directorate reported to the Director General of Tanks and Transport, while the Industrial Planning Directorate was closed.

They checked to see if firms had the necessary experience and then gave them advice on what buildings, plant, labour and materials. The Contracts Division placed the orders, while the production divisions monitored progress and gave advice. They also became involved with controlling the rail network over the winter of 1939–1940. Burgin was replaced when Prime Minister Neville Chamberlain stood down in May 1940.

Prime Minister Winston Churchill chose The Right Honourable Herbert Morrison MP to organise the rearming of the British Army following the BEF's escape from Dunkirk. The armaments industry also had to arm the 1.5 million men who had volunteered for the Local Defence Volunteers (known as the Home Guard after August 1940).[9] The Ministry of Supply had become involved with many industries and building projects, so it set up production divisions to deal with the manufacture of many products from design to delivery.

Morrison was appointed as Home Secretary in October 1940, and his knowledge of London served him well during the Blitz of the capital. The Morrison air raid shelter was named after him and he appealed for more fire watchers and guards in December with the appeal, 'Britain shall not burn'. He served as Home Secretary until the end of the war in Europe.

The Right Honourable Andrew Duncan MP, the Chairman of the British Iron and Steel Federation and President of the Board of Trade, replaced Morrison as the Minister of Supply in October 1940. He made sure the Civil Defence Service was armed with enough anti-aircraft guns and searchlights during the Blitz. He also continued to oversee the rearming of the expanding British Army. The Contracts Division would help after an armaments factory was damaged by an air raid, either helping the company rebuild or relocate.

The Right Honourable Lord Beaverbrook continued Duncan's work in June 1941, expanding the Ministry of Aircraft Production's control of the manufacture, import and distribution of machine tools and small tools in the autumn 1941. Beaverbrook often argued with the Ministry of Labour over labour, so the Royal Ordnance Factories struggled to equip the British troops in North Africa and the Far East.

By 1942, the Ministry of Supply was dealing with all departments and all aspects of armaments, from research to output. The Production Directorate took control of many aspects of industry, ranging from production delays to bulk purchases of materials and plant. It was also involved with Operation Bolero, providing accommodation and facilities for the 3 million US military personnel heading to Britain.

Duncan was reappointed Minister of Supply in February 1942 and he would stay in the post until the end of the war in Europe.

The raw materials' organisers were transferred to the new Ministry of Production early in 1942. Meanwhile, ammunition production was split between two director generals, with one covering artillery shells and the other covering bullets. An Armoured Fighting Vehicle Division (AFV) was created in September 1942 to deal with concerns about tank design and production. The Director General of Tank Supply studied component design, considered tank assembly and organised supplies. Meanwhile, the Director General of Fighting Vehicle Production monitored factory capacity and manufacturing issues.

Additional director generals for artillery design and scientific research were appointed in the summer of 1943. The roles of the two directors general dealing with tanks were combined at the same time, because many difficulties relating to tank design and production had been overcome.

The final reorganisation of the Ministry of Supply into five directorates was made at the end of 1943:

- The Director General of Raw Materials supervised deliveries of materials.
- The Senior Military Advisor collected the feedback from the fighting units.
- The Chairman of the Armoured Fighting Vehicle Division dealt with tanks.
- The Controller General of Munitions Production covered shells and bullets.
- The Senior Supply Officer made sure the factories made what the fighting units needed.

The British Army's demand for tanks, artillery, transport and ammunition had levelled out by the end of 1943. After seven years hard work, its deficiency programmes had finally been completed.

Work on new models and modifications continued but the demand for ammunition was reduced to maintenance levels, while there was enough field data to predict consumption. The Ministry of Supply continued to expand during Duncan's administration, and his staff were eventually dealing with 80,000 contracts a year. However, production started to slow down at the end of 1944 and large numbers of the workforce were laid off as factories closed.

The Ministry's work would be cut to a minimum at the end of the war. Duncan had successfully organised the supply of the British Army during its campaigns in Burma, across North Africa and Italy and through France into Germany.

## The Ministry of Production[10]

Britain had worked out how to control its armaments industry by December 1941. However, the Production Executive was struggling to coordinate the recommendations of its four committees, which controlled materials, labour, capacity and building, because they were responsible to different ministers. The Prime Minister also wanted to coordinate Britain's actions with the United States now it was at war and that required a representative of ministerial status. So, Max Aitken, Lord Beaverbrook was appointed the Minister of Production in February 1942, with instructions to coordinate the work of the three supply departments and the Ministry of Labour and National Service. He was also supposed to link what British industry made and American imports to Allied strategy.

Unfortunately, Aitkin immediately fell out with the Minister of Labour, Ernest Bevin, and resigned. So, Oliver Lyttelton took over as Minister of Production and he worked with Sir Walter Layton to coordinate the many aspects of strategy, industry and manpower. Lyttelton appointed a Joint War Production Staff to decide priorities and distribute materials, labour and plant to meet them. He also set up a Combined Production and Resources Board in Washington DC to synchronise British industry with America's.

Unfortunately, the three supply departments objected to their work being duplicated. The appointment of a Munitions Management and Labour Efficiency Committee, known as the Five-Man Board, only made things worse. However, a Progress Division did start to produce useful forecasts, providing information on unbalanced programmes and companies which failed to deliver.

It took Lyttelton time to work out how coordinate his Ministry's work with the Ministry of Labour's work and he focused on seeing that factories had enough materials, machine tools and components. The Joint War Production Staff and the Programmes and Planning Division kept Lyttelton informed about the strategic situation. He, in turn, advised the Chiefs of Staff about production possibilities, so they could plan future operations.

The Ministry of Production also helped the Regional Boards remove bottlenecks from the supply chains in their areas. The Boards continually reported on their local situation, helping the Ministry to decide where new orders should be placed. An Industry Location Committee was given the power to stop, start or transfer production according to the labour situation in a region. The Ministry also helped firms sort out their problems, linking them though a scheme called Mutual Aid by Technical Experts, so large ones could share their expertise with smaller ones.

The Ministry of Labour continued to deal with labour demands through its Preference Committee and Labour Coordinating Committee. By the end of 1941, the Defence Supply Committee was pinpointing which items needed to take priority, so the Preference Committee could direct labour to where it would be needed. The Minister of Production became involved in February 1942, using its national knowledge to help make local decisions.

The US War and Naval Departments had been inflating their needs since America entered the war in December 1941, leaving Britain short of what it required. It made it impossible for the Combined Raw Materials Board and Combined Munitions Assignments Board to meet the demands of the British Chiefs of Staff. Lyttelton eventually visited America in June 1942, to explain Britain's manpower problems and discuss the havoc the German U-boats were causing amongst the supply convoys. His Supply Mission presented the list of items British industry needed to equip the nation's armed forces.

Lyttelton returned to head the Joint War Production Staff, which matched the programmes of the three supply departments with available raw materials and manpower. A Munitions Management and Labour Efficiency Committee implemented the Joint War Production Staff's recommendations but the U-boat attacks had caused serious shipping shortages. It left the Joint War Production Staff having to work out how to cut Britain's monthly imports by 350,000 tons.

A Combined Production and Resources Board had been set up to deal with armaments supplies to the American and British armed forces. It started by asking the Combined Chiefs of Staff to predict how much was needed for their planned operations. The Joint War Production Staff then looked at how to coordinate American and British supplies, so their industries could meet the demands. An American Requirements Committee decided how everything would be allocated and the British War Supplies Committee reported back to London. Lyttelton would have to return to Washington DC in November 1942 to discuss the next round of supplies.

Lyttelton served as the Ministry of Production until the end of the war, working hard to coordinate the Britain's industrial plans with the Chiefs of Staffs' strategic plans. He also asked that American imports topped up what British factories could not make. His staff made sure that regional action complimented the government's plans and helped the Ministry of Labour provide enough manpower for the armed forces and industry during the final months of the war.

## Roads and Railways

### Inland Transport[11]

Britain's railway companies played an essential part in keeping the nation's civilians and armed forces fed, warm and armed. They had been pushed to the limit by the movement of materials and munitions during the First World War, so the Ministry of Transport identified bottlenecks on the network and looked at road haulage before the war. Studies were also made into how much shipping could be diverted to the west coast ports, so ships did not have to sail through the English Channel. But it was difficult to estimate what would be required and demands often failed to match the actual capacity.

A Railway Control Officer was appointed to coordinate the work of the 'Big Four' railway companies,[12] helping them to cope with the large-scale military mobilisation and civilian evacuation during the early months of the war. Freight increased as passenger services were cut and while petrol rationing limited road transport, coastal shipping was busy taking supplies to the BEF on the Continent. Cold weather at the beginning of 1940 increased the amount of coal required in London and extra shipping had to be requisitioned to prevent a crisis.

The railways had to change how they operated following the Fall of France in June 1940. The sudden end of exports to France left thousands of wagons of coal having to be diverted to London. Air raids by the *Luftwaffe* then started to interrupt rail traffic and rail junctions soon became prime bombing targets, disrupting rail traffic. Attacks by the *Kreigsmarine* also divert shipping to the west coast ports of Glasgow, Liverpool and Bristol. The combined effects halved the amount of coal reaching London at times, which caused concerns during the winter months.

The Mines Department formed a Standing Diversion Committee to work out how to improve the distribution of coal around the rail network. It opened dumps north of London, so local trains, lorries and barges could take coal into the capital between air raids. After a difficult winter, Lord President John Anderson, Viscount Waverley, said the crisis had been overcome by 'a variety of expedients and some narrow squeaks.'[13]

A Central Transport Committee was set up to coordinate all forms of transport, while the Ministry of Transport and the Ministry of Shipping merged to form the Ministry of War Transport in May 1941. Its Railways Division coordinated work of the rail companies, while a Railways Inspectorate dealt with inspections and safety issues.

A new Controller of Railways started working out how Britain was going to get through the winter of 1941–1942. The amounts of armaments and troops were increasing, while the number of railway staff were being reduced; the rail network was also deteriorating under the extra traffic. There was also a shortage of freight locomotives and wagons but the companies that usually built them were busy making tanks. It meant that rolling stock was being used beyond its working life, resulting in expensive repairs, late trains and many cancellations.

Eventually, 400 engines were imported from the United States, while another 600 were used on Britain's railways before they were forwarded to other countries. Despite all the shortages, the train companies were learning how plan their journeys better and use their rolling stock more efficiently. A publicity campaign also reduced civilian traffic by asking potential passengers to consider, 'Is your journey really necessary?'

The Central Transport Committee started moving as much freight as possible by coastal shipping and canals, after taking control of them in July 1942. The Road Haulage Organisation saw to it that companies made the most economical use of their vehicles, even taking over several uncooperative businesses.

Fortunately, the winters of 1942–1943 and 1943–1944 were mild but Britain's transport system still struggled to move sufficient coal to build up enough reserves during the summer months. Meanwhile, freight increased, as shipping delivered increasing amounts of fuel and armaments for the US Army and the USAAF to Britain's ports. The rail network did, however, manage to move 100,000 American and British troops around the country every month.

A lot of new track had to be laid to the southern ports ahead of D-Day, resulting in track maintenance being neglected elsewhere. The buildup required an extra 1.2 million tons a month to be moved during the early months of 1944. Many coastal ships were kept busy moving goods south for the invasion, resulting in other goods having to be moved by rail from the northern ports. Train watchers were deployed to all the bottlenecks on the network to make sure deliveries were made to the ports on time, so the invasion ships could be loaded according to strict timetables.

The rapid Allied advance across France and Belgium in the autumn of 1944 forced the *Kreigsmarine* to move its bases back into Germany, so Allied shipping could gain use the English Channel. The *Luftwaffe* also retreated into Germany, so air attacks against the British rail network ended. After five difficult years, the rail companies were able to get on top of the distribution of goods. While life returned to normal in Britain in the summer of 1945, there was a lot of repair work to be done before British Rail took over the 'Big Four' railway companies in January 1948. The neglect during war years would contribute to the closure of many unprofitable lines in the years that followed.

# Chapter 3

# Research, Design and Development

## Research

### The Scientific Research Directorate[1]

There had been little coordination between the scientists and the armed forces between the wars and there was even less money to research, design or develop anything. Scientists also focused on researching how things worked rather than what they could be used for. Research scientists were often reluctant to hand over their inventions to the engineers and the engineers had to hand them back if new ideas emerged during development. Meanwhile, all three armed forces encouraged everyone to be inventive and think of new ideas that could be passed onto the scientists. They, in turn, tried to build practical prototypes.

A Scientific Research Directorate was eventually established in 1938 to bring together science, design and development, and it had three deputies covering armaments, aircraft and radar. They sent scientists to the research establishments to study everything from weapons to bombs and radar to jet engines. The Directorate's Research Committee was later renamed the Specification Committee.

Over time, the scientists, engineers, technicians and industrial experts were brought together to share their ideas and expertise. The scientists continued exploring new ideas in the hope of finding something new but they rarely discovered anything practical. Meanwhile, the armed forces just wanted the scientists to improve their existing weapons, to keep one step ahead.

One successful example to illustrate how the relationship worked was how the experience of the Blitz resulted in a change in specification and strategy. The RAF's 500-pound bombs had been designed for precision bombing but the *Luftwaffe*'s attacks proved that larger bombs destroyed factories and lowered the morale of the workforce. The specification for the new Lancaster bomber meant it could carry 14,000 pounds (6,350 kilograms), while the B-17 could only carry a 4,000 pounds (1,814 kilograms) payload. It meant that the USAAF carried out precision daylight bombing raids with their lighter bomb loads, while the RAF did night-time area bombing.

## Coordinating Research and Development[2]

The Scientific Research Directorate combined the research, design and development work of all three armed forces before the war but the Artillery Directorates and Mechanisation Directorate maintained independent control. The Ministry of Supply took over research, design and experiments of armaments in April 1939 and it appointed Directors of Scientific Research, Artillery and Mechanisation. It also took control of the Ordnance Board, a Research Department and a Design Department, as well as fourteen research and experimental establishments around the country. A Scientific Advisory Council was added in 1940, followed by a Central Scientific Office in Washington DC in January 1941.

The Minister of Supply, The Right Honourable Leslie Burgin MP, appointed Air Vice Marshal Arthur Tedder as Director General of Research and Development in charge of the research, design and development branches. However, random suggestions to the Ministry of Supply for new or improved armaments started to interfere with production. So, Burgin asked the General Staff to draw up a design and development programme at the start of 1942.

A new Scientific Advisory Council reported that the Research and Development Departments still had a disorganised approach in the summer of 1942. So, Dr Henry Guy, appointed Professor Lennard-Jones FRS, the Chief Superintendent of a new Armaments Research Department with instructions to coordinate the work of the Ordnance Board, the Research Department and the Armaments Design Department.

Three officers were appointed to divide up design and development work in a logical fashion:

- The Controller General of Armaments Production organised artillery and mechanical development, as well as scientific research.
- The Chairman of the Armoured Fighting Vehicles Division dealt with tank development.
- The Senior Supply Officer controlled other armaments.

Many academics and scientists joined the Ministry of Supply, to speed up how it dealt with the armed forces' requests. Heads of the Research and Design Establishments and the Scientific Advisory Council looked at new weapons, improved existing weapons and shared knowledge between the supply departments. A theoretical research branch also began experimental work in September 1943. A Joint Committee of Research and Development Priority improved coordination in the summer of 1944. Even the research and production teams responsible for designing and building new tanks were united, improving liaison between the scientists, the factory owners and the tank crews.

## Design and Development[3]

The research, design and development of weapons became reactionary in wartime. The process started with the troops reporting problems with their own weapons or noting trends with enemy ones. Occasionally, they retrieved captured ones to study. Six directorates worked closely with industry, looking at new specifications, reviewing prototypes, organising tests and advising on production:

- The Naval Construction Directorate designed warships.
- The Tank Design Directorate worked on tanks.
- The Armament Development Directorate designed guns and bombs.
- The Communications Development Directorate worked on radio equipment.
- The Engine Development and Production Directorate helped firms with their designs.
- The Technical Development Directorate advised firms on their designs.

They all tried to balance technical improvements with how quickly factories could make new or improved items.

## The Research Establishments[4]

The Admiralty needed assistance with the many design and research issues which were unique to naval combat. The Naval Research Institute and the Scientific Research Board coordinated their work through five establishments:

- The Research Laboratory coordinated research and design.
- The Naval Construction Directorate designed ships.
- The Technical Development Directorate advised private shipyards firms about designs.
- The Experiment Works tested model ships in Torquay.
- HMS *Excellent* (a shore establishment) tested guns near Portsmouth.
- HMS *Vernon* (another shore establishment) worked with mines, torpedoes and submarines near Portsmouth.
- The Signals and Radar Establishment was also near Portsmouth.

The Admiralty added an Operational Research Department and a Miscellaneous Weapons Development Department during wartime. It then opened a Naval Construction Research Establishment in Rosyth, Scotland, to investigate the effects of underwater explosions on ships' hulls, following the sinkings of HMS *Prince of Wales*, HMS *Repulse* and HMS *Ark Royal*. There was also an Engineering Laboratory, which worked on mechanical and electrical equipment in West Drayton and a Compass Observatory based at Slough.

The Air Ministry used the Aeronautical Research Committee to work on research and design issues unique to aerial combat. It reopened the Royal Aircraft Establishment (RAE) in Farnborough, in Hampshire, so the Performance Test Squadron could test prototypes. Meanwhile, the Armament Squadron tested weapons at the Aeroplane and Armament Experimental Establishment in Martlesham Heath, Suffolk.

A Technical Development Directorate monitored armaments' improvements across the country and abroad, sharing useful ideas across the directorates. Meanwhile, the Telecommunications Research Establishment (TRE) worked on offensive and defensive radar equipment. Power Jets (Research and Development) Limited was set up to develop the jet engine and it worked with the National Gas Turbine Establishment and the Airborne Forces Experimental Establishment.

The General Staff submitted suggestions about weapons from the three armed forces to the Ministry of Supply, many of which had arisen from battle experience. The Ordnance Board turned useful ideas into specifications and the Armaments Design Department produced drawings for engineering companies to work on.

The Master General of the Ordnance worked with the Mechanisation Directorate during the research and development of weapons, ammunition and explosives. The Mechanisation Board helped it design armoured fighting vehicles and transport, while the Royal Engineer and Signals Board dealt with engineering problems and signals equipment. The Chemical Warfare Committee was renamed the Chemical Defence Committee when it started focusing on defensive measures.

Radar was developed at Bawdsey Manor in Suffolk but the Research and Development Establishment had to move to Christchurch in Dorset and then Malvern in Worcestershire, to avoid air attack. A Signals Research and Development Establishment was added in 1943, to work on military signalling.

## Warship Design and Development

### Building Warships[5]

The Admiralty's specification of a warship dictated its speed, armour, weapons, endurance, stability and accommodation. The Naval Construction Department turned the requirements into designs but it took two or three years to prepare drawings for a capital ship. Scale models were then tested in water tanks at the Admiralty Experiment Works near Portsmouth. Large warships could then take another five to seven years to build. These are the classes of warship and what they were used for:

- Fleet carriers carried a full complement of aircraft for offensive purposes.
- Light aircraft carriers carried around half the number of aircraft.
- Escort carriers were made by converting a merchant ship and were used to escort convoys.
- Battleships were the largest warships and were armed with batteries of large calibre guns.
- Battlecruisers were faster than battleships but they had less armour and smaller calibre guns.
- Heavy cruisers were defined by the London Naval Treaty as ships armed with guns up to an 8-inch calibre.

- Light cruisers were defined by the London Naval Treaty as ships armed guns up to a 6.1-inch calibre.
- Destroyers were defined by the London Naval Treaty as ships armed guns up to a 5.1-inch calibre.
- Frigates were designed to escort convoys and were often engaged in anti-submarine activities.
- Corvettes were designed for coastal patrols but they were also used as convoy escorts.

Work on a warship started with the Naval Construction Directorate checking the Admiralty's drawings before a shipyard was contracted. Each shipyard had large lofts, where scaled down parts of the ship were marked out using wooden moulds or by cutting scaled down shapes out of scrive boards laid on the floor. The dimensions were then scaled up, so steel plates could be ordered from foundries such as William Beardmore and Company Limited near Glasgow, Vickers-Armstrongs Limited near Newcastle-upon-Tyne and Vickers, John Brown & Company, and Cammell Laird & Co. Limited in Sheffield.

The flat plates were then bent into shape, trimmed and drilled, before they were transferred to the shipyard by train. Many plates were reinforced before the keel was assembled on building blocks laid along a slipway. Cranes lifted the huge steel plates into place, so plating gangs could rivet or weld them together. Caulking gangs then hammered iron strips into the seams, to make the hull watertight. Once the hull was complete, cradles and dog shores (wedges) took the weight off the building blocks, so it could be launched. Once in the water, tradesmen started work on the accommodation, galleys, water tanks, fuel storage, boilers and engine rooms. The funnels, conning tower and masts completed the superstructure.

Most of the large calibre guns were made by Vickers-Armstrongs Limited and the largest could weigh over 100 tons and take over a year to make. Gun turrets were complicated structures weighing up to 300 tons and they could take up to two years to assemble in the factory. They were then dismantled and the parts were taken to the shipyard, so the turret could be rebuilt on the ship.

Weeks of inspections followed and gangs were on hand to deal with any problems. The ship could then be put through exercises, testing the engines and rudders before the ship was put through speed trials. The turrets, barrels and shell handling equipment were checked before firing tests were carried out. Only then could a warship be commissioned for service.

## The Dockyards

An Admiral Superintendent or Captain Superintendent ran the Royal Dockyards at the following locations:

- Scarpa Flow on the Orkney Islands.
- Rosyth near Edinburgh on the Firth of Forth.
- Pembroke in southwest Wales.
- Portsmouth in Hampshire.
- Devonport next to Plymouth.
- Chatham in Kent built submarines.

Several small dockyards were used for repairs and refits:

- Portland in Dorset.
- Sheerness in Kent.
- Dover in Kent.

Private shipyards carried out most of the construction work on warships but the workers were supervised by Admiralty overseers and inspectors. Assistant Naval Construction Directors coordinated all the shipbuilding contractors working across their district.

A huge amount of rearmament and conversions had to be carried out at the start of the war, resulting in a shortage of qualified staff at the dockyards. The shortage of private shipyards around Britain meant that some ships had to be dealt with overseas.

## Battleships and Aircraft Carriers

Devonport Dockyard and Portsmouth Dockyard commissioned three battleships each before the war. The following private shipyards commissioned large warships on the River Clyde:

- John Brown & Company commissioned two battleships and two aircraft carriers.
- Fairfield Shipbuilding and Engineering Company Limited commissioned two battleships and one aircraft carrier.
- William Beardmore and Company Limited commissioned one battleship and converted one old aircraft carrier.

The following private shipyards commissioned large warships on the River Tyne:

- Swan, Hunter & Wigham Richardson commissioned one battleship and one aircraft carriers.
- Armstrong Whitworth converted three old aircraft carriers and commissioned one new aircraft carrier.
- Vickers-Armstrongs Limited commissioned three battleships and four aircraft carriers.
- Palmers Shipbuilding and Iron Company Limited of Hebburn commissioned one battleship.

The following shipyards also commissioned warships:

- Vickers in Barrow-in-Furness commissioned one battleship.
- Blyth Shipbuilding & Dry Docks Company Limited in Northumberland had launched one aircraft carrier during the First World War which was recommissioned for the Second World War.
- Harland & Wolff in Belfast commissioned five aircraft carriers.
- Cammell Laird & Co. Limited on the River Mersey commissioned two battleships and two aircraft carriers.

Five merchant ships were also converted into aircraft carriers by adding flight decks; they were called MV class or MAC carriers.[6] A captured German merchant ship was also converted into one. Another forty-six aircraft carriers, many of them Bogue class ships, were built in American shipyards and transferred to the Royal Navy under the Lend-Lease programme. The small

escort carriers supported convoys and were known as Woolworth carriers
(after the high street chain store).

## Naval Armament[7]

The downturn in the shipping and steel industries between the wars, meant
that only a few companies continued to work for the Admiralty. The decision
to rearm the Royal Navy meant the Admiralty could start offering financial
help to shipbuilding firms in 1935. William Beardmore and Company Limited
near Glasgow and the Vickers, and Cammell Laird & Co. Limited's foundries
in Sheffield made armoured plate; John Brown & Company, also near Glasgow,
hardened Cammell Laird's plate steel. However, the Admiralty still needed more
armour plate than the foundries could supply, so large amounts were imported
from Czechoslovakia until the Germans seized the Sudetenland in October 1938.

The Royal Arsenal made guns, while Harland & Wolff and the English Steel
Corporation Limited built gun mountings; William Beardmore and Company,
and Vickers-Armstrongs Limited made both. Barrels were complicated affairs
which started with the inner lining being forged as an octagonal bar. A hole
was drilled through the centre and a hollow mandrel[8] was inserted and then
cooled with water, as it was reheated and squeezed into a round tube. The
lining was then planed, smoothed and heated before it was put into an oil bath
to temper (harden) the steel.

Spirals of wire were wound around the inner lining and then squeezed,
giving increased strength for less weight. The tube was tempered again before
it was rubbed smooth. The outer jacket was then formed in the same way as the
inner jacket before it was reheated and slid over the lining. The rifling, which
made the shell spin in flight, was then slowly carved into the inner lining.

The Admiralty extended its propellant and cordite making facilities before
the war. ROFs, including one at Birtley near Gateshead, and several agency
factories managed by ICI Limited, were making explosives and cartridge
cases by 1939. ROFs had also started making guns in Dalmuir, Leeds and
Nottingham.

## Naval Ordnance Directorate[9]

The Naval Ordnance Directorate dealt with the Royal Navy's weapons. The
Armament Supply Department contracted locomotive builders to make large

gun mountings and engineering works to make smaller ones. It had to employ more companies in 1942, because the mountings were taking longer to make than hulls. The Admiralty sent it shells to the Royal Ordnance Factories to be filled and they used cordite because seawater did not affect it.

The Torpedoes and Mining Department made torpedo parts and sent them to private firms to assemble. It also made anti-torpedo nets and mines. Thousands of mines would be laid between the Orkney Islands, Iceland and Greenland, to stop German ships and U-boats reaching the Atlantic Ocean. However, the Northern Barrage was difficult to maintain and it was abandoned in July 1943 after Admiral Sir Bruce Fraser, the new Commander-in-Chief of the Home Fleet, called it 'the least profitable voluntary major undertaking of the war'.

## Electrics, Electronics and Acoustics[10]

The Admiralty's Electrical Engineering Department dealt with every type of electrical equipment on ships apart from radio and radar. It sent inspectors to the factories where the equipment was made and to the dockyards where it was being installed. The department fitted degaussing equipment to ships, which stopped them attracting magnetic mines.[11] It also equipped them with guard loops and indicator loops to detect submarines. A Boom Defence Department organised physical barriers to protect anchorages from U-boats.

The Anti-Submarine Warfare Division dealt with the Anti-Submarine Detection Investigation Committee (ASDIC) equipment,[12] which was used to locate submarines and the depth charges which were used to destroy them. It also equipped warships with counter-measures against torpedoes. It was renamed the Anti-U-Boat Division in 1943.

Ships required equipment for visual signalling, ultraviolet, infra-red, waves and electro-magnetic waves. The Radio Equipment Department and the Signal Department decided what communications equipment was required, where it would be made and how to install it.

## Landing Craft[13]

Landing craft were required for the amphibious operations planned in the Mediterranean and Normandy. Engineering companies made the prefabricated steel sections and they were assembled in derelict shipyards which had reopened in Glasgow, Stockton, Middlesbrough and Chepstow. By the summer of 1943, over eighty firms were involved in making them.

The Landing Craft Tank (LCT) was simple to build and experience soon halved the manufacturing and assembly time. However, other types of landing craft were more complicated to make. Shipyards did not have enough room to build all the large Landing Ship Tank (LSTs) required, so the majority were made in American yards. The demand for landing craft continued after D-Day because they were required for landings on the Dutch coast and for the war against Japan. British shipyards had assembled over 4,100 landing craft by the end of the war.

## Naval Aircraft[14]

Before the war the Admiralty ran the Fleet Air Arm, while the Air Ministry developed special designs for it. Naval aircraft operated over long distances and required two crew. They had to take off from and land on carrier decks, while their wings needed to fold, so they could be stored in the hangars below.

Differences of opinion over aircraft design caused problems, so a Fifth Sea Lord and Chief of Naval Air Services were appointed to control the Royal Navy's airpower in May 1938. The Ministry of Aircraft Production took over from the Air Ministry in April 1940; however, it was busy building aircraft to fight in the Battle of Britain for the next six months. While the delay gave the Royal Navy the opportunity to decide what type of aircraft it wanted, its requirements were often misinterpreted or ignored.

# Aircraft Design and Development

## Research Establishments[15]

The Royal Aircraft Factory Research Establishment in Farnborough had closed at the end of the First World War. It left the Air Ministry dependent on sixteen aircraft firms and four aero-engine firms, so it kept giving them experimental projects, to keep their staff busy. A lot of research was done by universities and while fighter design was usually determined by its armament, bomber design was often decided by its bomb load. Despite the lack of investment, design continued briskly and aircraft evolved from slow, wooden and canvas biplanes, into fast metal monoplanes during the 1930s.

The Royal Aircraft Establishment (RAE) researched and developed aircraft and equipment design, in accordance with the Aeronautical Research Committee's programme. It was assisted by the Scientific Research Directorate, the Technical Development Directorate and the Engine Development Directorate. The National Physical Laboratory and several universities also worked with the Aeronautical Research Committee. The RAE's staff helped the private firms with their design problems and testing, so they were familiar with an aircraft before it went into production.

## Coordination of the Directorates[16]

The aircraft firms only had limited hangar facilities before the war because they spent most of their time designing rather than building. They relied on a few skilled craftsmen to handmake the small number of aircraft ordered by the Air Ministry. The rapid expansion of production during the rearmament period meant that their technical staff were busy training an expanding workforce, while their draughtsmen switched from design drawings to production drawings.

Designers and developers combined their ideas to produce new prototypes and while the factories added their production experience, the air crews gave their feedback. Specifications had to consider what speed and range an aircraft would fly at, as well as which weapons it would be armed with or what size of bomb load it had to carry.

The Air Ministry helped the companies pool their staff to speed up the design work and it acquired photographic equipment to help reproduce the drawings. A design would then be checked by testing mocks ups and a prototype. While there was good cooperation between the Operational Requirements and Technical Development Directorates, it would be compromised when many of the Air Ministry staff moved to Harrogate in 1939.

The Ministry of Aircraft Production (MAP) took over from the Air Ministry in May 1940 and the Development and Production Department was at the heart of its organisation. It had two directorates and while Air Vice Marshal Arthur Tedder supervised research and development, Ernest Lemon dealt with production.

Economical designs aided assembly, while modern machine tools and jigs made work even easier. The coordination between the design and production teams would eventually result in well-designed aircraft that were quick to assemble and easy to fly. Aircraft firms were grouped together, so they could discuss how to coordinate the assembly of the engines, the airframes and the rest of the aircraft parts. The MAP encouraged them to exchange plans and while most pooled their ideas, some refused resulting in work being duplicated.

An Operational Requirements Directorate was formed to discuss the impact of modifications on production. A Joint Production and Development Committee was added early in 1941, resulting in better coordination between the Air Ministry and the MAP. A Controller of Research and Development took over in June and it helped the RAF switch its focus from a defensive fighter force to an offensive bomber force over the winter of 1941–1942. However, the relationship between the Air Ministry and the MAP would deteriorate when the post of Controller General was terminated in June 1943.

## New Aircraft Designs[17]

Aircraft firms were encouraged to do their own research, based on their experiences and the feedback they received. The Air Ministry and then the MAP provided officers to help develop their ideas into designs before mock ups and prototypes were built. They tested the speed, manoeuvrability, ceiling and armament of fighters and they tested the speed, range, bomb load, ceiling and sturdiness of bombers. Pairs of designs were developed in tandem, in case one turned out to be unsuitable problem. For example, the Hurricane and Spitfire fighters were developed at the same time, as were the Wellington and Hampden bombers.

The Air Ministry and the MAP also sent officers to the factories to solve any production problems. Once an aircraft was in service, intelligence officers debriefed the air crews on their flying experiences and forwarded the information to the Operational Requirements Directorate, so modifications could be made to future aircraft.

Each company focused on one type of plane and they worked to the Ministry's specifications; these are the men who designed the RAF's fighter aircraft:

- Sydney Camm designed the Hurricane, Typhoon, Tempest and Sea Fury at Hawker Aircraft Limited.
- Reginald Mitchell designed the Spitfire at Supermarine until he died in 1937. Harold Payn continued his work.
- Frank Barnwell (killed in a flying accident in 1938), Archibald Russell and Leslie Frise designed the Beaufighter at the Bristol Aeroplane Company.
- Ronald Bishop designed the Mosquito at de Havilland Aircraft Company Limited.

These are the men who designed the RAF's bomber aircraft:

- Frank Barnwell, Archibald Russell and Leslie Frise designed the Beaufort and Blenheim at the Bristol Aeroplane Company.
- Rex Pierson and Barnes Wallis designed the Wellington at Vickers.
- George Volkert designed the Halifax at Handley Page.
- Roy Chadwick designed the Manchester, Lancaster, York and Lincoln at Avro.
- Roy Chadwick also helped Cyril Lipscombe design the Stirling at Short Brothers.

Fairey designed the Battle fighter and the Swordfish and Firefly naval aircraft. Blackburn Aircraft Limited also designed naval aircraft. William 'Teddy' Petter designed the Lysander liaison plane and the unsuccessful Whirlwind fighter at Westland. Meanwhile, Sir Arthur Gouge designed the Sunderland flying boat at Short Brothers.

Two men were responsible for the engines which powered many of the RAF's planes. Sir Roy Fedden developed the Hercules and Centaurus engines at Bristol Aeroplane Company, while Ernest Hives designed the Merlin engine at Rolls-Royce.

The MAP started financing private research work, when it took over the aircraft industry in May 1940. It issued specifications which outlined an aircraft's operational purpose, the main features it needed to have and the minimum requirements it had to meet. An Advisory Design Conference checked the overall design, while the Operational Requirements

Directorate and the Equipment Installation Department looked at the crew accommodation, aircraft controls and equipment layout. The MAP eventually started asking private firms to check design ideas.

Companies could suggest changes to specifications and both Supermarine and Hawker improved the Spitfire and the Hurricane respectively. Vickers and Handley Page also designed four-engined variations of their Wellington and Halifax bombers, to accommodate a different engine design. In doing so, they doubled the weight of bombs they could carry. Good engineering practices suggested by private companies were often adopted by the MAP and then shared with other companies. Occasionally private designs, such as the Mosquito (designed by de Havilland), were approved.

## Private Designs[18]

The Bristol Aeroplane Company was producing the Bristol Bulldog biplane fighter for the RAF, when it offered the Air Ministry a radical design for a fast monoplane in 1935. The alloy airframe was covered with a metal stressed-skin and it had a retractable undercarriage, to improve its aerodynamics. Wing flaps improved its manoeuvrability, while variable-pitch propellers increased the airspeed. The Air Ministry added a powered gun turret to the original design, known as Britain First, and the design was adopted in 1937. It was known as the Blenheim bomber.

Bristol Aeroplane Company then combined the specifications for a bomber, a reconnaissance aircraft and torpedo carrying plane to design the Beaufort in 1939. It went onto design the Beaufighter, a fighter variation of the Beaufort which could be equipped with cannons or radar equipment.

Handley Page's Halifax bomber and Avro's Manchester bomber were going to be powered by two Rolls-Royce Vulture engines. However, the engine was underpowered and suffered from reliability issues, so both companies designed four-engine variations based on the Rolls-Royce Merlin engine. The Halifax retained its name but the modified Manchester became known as the Lancaster.

De Havilland had focused on civil aeroplanes in peacetime and it was left short of orders when war broke out. So, Sir Geoffrey de Havilland designed a fast unarmed aircraft, which received the backing of Sir Wilfrid Freeman,

Air Member for Development and Production. The Mosquito initially carried out reconnaissance missions and was then armed with machine guns in July 1940, turning it into a long-range fighter. It was used by pathfinders who marked targets ahead of the bomber streams after 1941 and even carried out precision bombing raids.

## Airborne Forces[19]

Churchill demanded enough transport aircraft for 5,000 parachute troops after he was appointed Prime Minister in May 1940, having seen the recent *coup de grâce* missions German paratroopers had carried out in Norway and the Netherlands. Armstrong Whitworth Aircraft Limited's Whitley bomber was the only suitable aircraft and the RAF only had enough to carry 800 men, so aircraft companies were asked to design gliders, because they were quicker to build than powered aircraft.

General Aircraft Limited's eight-seater Hotspur was used for training while Airspeed Limited's thirty-seater Horsa was used for operations. Horsa gliders were built by Austin Motor Company Limited in Christchurch, Hampshire, and by Harris Lebus, a London furniture manufacturer. They would be towed to the drop zone by a mixture of Wellington, Stirling, Albemarle and Whitley bomber aircraft. General Aircraft also designed the larger Hamilcar glider which could carry a light tank, a gun and towing vehicle, or engineer equipment. They were towed by Halifax bombers.

Around 2,000 American Douglas C-47 Skytrain transport aircraft (produced by the Douglas Aircraft Company) were given to the RAF under the Lend-Lease programme and they were renamed the Dakota. They were used to carry paratroopers and to tow Horsa gliders.

## Aircraft Quality[20]

The RAF required top quality aircraft if it was to win the battle for the skies and keep the morale of its air crews high. That meant reducing production at times, when improvements needed to be made and problems had to be corrected. However, the emphasis changed to quantity when Winston Churchill's government took over in May 1940. The MAP was told to make as many fighters as possible after the BEF was rescued from Dunkirk. Work on new aircraft designs was halted because every plane and pilot were needed to defend Britain. It meant that the aircraft factories started working around the clock to make Hurricane and Spitfire fighters.

Quality resumed once the Battle of Britain was over and a new production programme was produced. Colonel John Moore-Brabazon continued the policy in May 1941 but the Prime Minister's demands for extra bombers at the end of 1942, meant that the MAP had to limit the development of new models and focus on proven ones, like the Wellington, Halifax and Lancaster.

## Aircraft Modifications[21]

The design and development of new aircraft always took far longer than estimated and sometimes ended in disappointment. So, the Air Ministry and then the MAP often relied on improved designs, recognising that the ability to modify an aircraft was the sign of a good design.

A Modifications Committee coordinated the Local Technical Committees, which worked with each aircraft firm. Some modifications resulted from feedback given by the air crews' flying experiences. Some were suggested by the ground crews who serviced and repaired the aircraft. Others were recommended by the factories, who wanted to facilitate production. Modifications could involve everything from replacing engines and redesigning structural members to installing new equipment or safety features.

A major modification resulted in the aircraft being given a new mark and the Hurricane had twelve marks as well as several variations. However, radical changes required a new name and the Manchester was renamed the Lancaster when the number of engines was increased from two to four. The Typhoon became the Tempest when its wings were redesigned, to improve high altitude flying.

Modifications were introduced as soon as they were approved but they could interfere with the assembly lines and production targets. Eventually, an Aircraft Modifications Committee was set up to assess how urgent modifications were and how much they would affect output. It also decided if changes were only required on new aircraft or if operational ones had to be upgraded as well. Modifications were classified as follows:

- Class 1: implemented immediately for safety reasons.
- Class 2: an urgent modification to carried out as soon as practicable.

- Class 3: applied to all new aircraft but optional for operational aircraft.
- Class 4: could be carried out without interfering with production.

The Controller of Research and Development could stop production if a modification was required to prevent accidents but he never called for aircraft to be scrapped.

The first Mark I Spitfires took 330,000 man hours to build but after five years' experience and many production improvements, the time had been reduced to 62,000. Over 1,000 modifications had been made and the aircraft had gone through 24 marks between 1938 and 1945. The airframe had been remodelled to accommodate different engine designs, while the wings had been redesigned to improve manoeuvrability. In doing so, the top speed was increased from 350 to 460 miles per hour and the service ceiling was increased from 10,485 metres (34,400 feet) to 13,560 metres (43,000 feet). Many improvements had also made to the cockpit, the controls and the weapons.

## Design Problems[22]

Designing new fighters often resulted in delays and disappointments because most failed to meet expectations. Westland Aircraft's Whirlwind fighter was delivered eight months late, while its twin Rolls–Royce Peregrine engines were slower than single engined models. The Hawker Tornado was eventually cancelled due to problems with the Rolls–Royce Vulture engine.

Hawker Aircraft Limited had more luck with the Typhoon, which was powered by the Sabre engine (produced by D. Napier & Son Limited), but it was still delayed by twelve months. Even then it flew slower and lower than promised, so it was used to attack ground targets, while the improved Spitfire was used for aerial combat. The Tempest was also a disappointment because the Spitfire and the American P51 Mustang III were better aircraft. Both the Typhoon and Tempest would be used to counter the V-1 flying bombs. Westland Aircraft introduced the Welkin, another twin engined fighter in September 1943, however, few were built because the single engined Mosquito (designed by de Havilland) was faster.

There were similar problems with new bomber designs. Vickers had been working on the Wellington and Handley Page had been developing the Hampden since 1932. However, the Chief of the Air Staff, Sir Cyril Newall, wanted a bomber capable of carrying heavier loads over longer ranges in 1936. Two specifications were issued and six companies were asked to submit a design:

- Hawker designed the P.13/36, but it was rejected.
- Avro designed the two-engined Manchester but it had engine problems.
- Vickers designed the Warwick but it was obsolete by the time its engines were ready.
- Supermarine designed the B.12/36, but the prototype was destroyed during a bombing raid in September 1940.
- Short designed the successful four-engined Stirling.
- Handley Page designed the H.P.56, which became the successful two-engined Halifax.

Rolls-Royce switched to the Merlin engine after problems with its Vulture engine. Scheme L then called for 3,500 heavy bombers in 1938 and while no changes were made to the Stirling, the Halifax and Manchester were improved.

The first four-engined heavy bombers appeared in 1941 and while the Halifax kept its name, Avro called its new design the Lancaster. Vickers had also started work on the four-engined Warwick but it was obsolete before the design was complete. The target number of heavy bombers set in 1938 was finally reached in the spring of 1943.

Bristol Aeroplane Company designed the light Buckingham bomber but it performed poorly and there were problems with the Centaurus engine. Meanwhile, de Havilland's faster wooden framed Mosquito, which could carry a similar bomb load, so it was adopted.

The delay to new aircraft designs resulted in the Air Ministry using stopgap orders, which involved continuing with obsolete aircraft until their replacements were ready. For example, the Air Council had wanted to replace the slow Fairey Battle bomber but 3,100 had to be made to meet the requirements of Scheme L. Over 200 were lost in the battle for France but it was October 1940 before it was replaced by the Wellington. Battles were then used as trainers and target tugs.

Armstrong Whitworth Aircraft Limited's Whitley bomber were made obsolete when bomb loads were increased. However, 1,800 had been made by the time the Lancaster and the four-engined Halifax had been developed. Whitleys were then used for glider towing, paratrooper dropping and reconnaissance for Coastal Command.

The American Liberator Mark III bomber was better than the Blenheim, so British factories switched to making Lancasters and Halifaxes. However, the Blenheim continued in service until the summer of 1943. Several factories continued to build obsolete models for a wide range of tasks, including transport, training, rescue, glider tows, mine laying and coastal protection. They also continued to make Hurricane fighters after they had fallen out of favour, including nearly 3,000 for the Soviet Union.

## Aircraft Programming[23]

In 1938, the Air Ministry's Scheme L planned for 4,000 aircraft in the first year and 8,000 in the second. But that meant the RAF needed many more airfields and hangars, as well as trained air crews and ground crews. While the aircraft manufacturers said they could meet the targets, their limited experience meant they were often over optimistic. Close monitoring of production and manhours by the Air Ministry, resulted in a far more accurate programme being published in January 1940.

Initial planning focused on making the airframes, which included the fuselage, wings, tail assembly and undercarriage. Too little attention was given to casting the alloys needed to make them and the rest of the components, such as the engines, weapons and radios. The result was stoppages on the assembly lines and late deliveries.

Lord Beaverbrook took charge of aircraft production in May 1940 and he wanted 'all that can be done' to increase production. He relied on people who would get results and the MAP churned out as many of the five chosen models of aircraft as possible; they were the Spitfire and Hurricane fighters and the Wellington, Whitley and Blenheim bombers. Once the Battle of Britain ended Lord Beaverbrook's assistant, Patrick Hennessy of the Ford Motor Company, checked how many aircraft each factory could make under normal conditions. His optimistic programme gave figures to aim for and while it was known as the 'target programme' or the 'carrot programme', bomb damage to factories and the dispersal of work during the Blitz meant the numbers had to be reduced.

Colonel John Moore-Brabazon took over from Lord Beaverbrook in April 1941 and he relied on a structured organisation to get the best out of everyone. He appointed Professor John Jewkes, an expert of Social Economics, to link aircraft production to the Air Ministry's strategy and the RAF's requirements. He also revised the bomber programme because the airframe programmes were based on unreliable estimates, while engines were taking longer to get into production than promised.

Jewkes published an accurate programme in January 1942, making it possible to estimate what materials, tools and labour the factories needed. The MAP could then compare firms' performance and share information to solve problems. Jewkes approach finally brought order to aircraft production.

By 1944, the workforce involved in aircraft production peaked at over 1.7 million men and women. The next problem faced was how to scale down the number of aircraft made, to match the changing predictions about the defeat of Germany and Japan. On the one hand, the MAP did not want to stop making aircraft too soon, or there would be a shortage. On the other hand, the Air Ministry did not want a post-war surplus.

## Design to Production[24]

It was a complicated process taking a design from the drawing board into production. It sometimes took so long that the aircraft was obsolete by the time it reached the RAF. Four examples were:

- Boulton & Paul's Defiant fighter
- Westland's Whirlwind fighter
- Vickers' Warwick bomber
- Bristol's Buckingham bomber

In peacetime, it took around four years to just get from inception to ordering and there were three phases:

- The Inception Phase involved deciding the new aircraft's purpose.
- The Formulation Phase saw the Air Ministry draw up the specification.
- The Tender Phase involved deciding which company would be contracted.

The length of time from design to order during peacetime were:

- Hurricane fighter: forty-eight months
- Spitfire fighter: forty-eight months
- Beaufighter heavy fighter: nineteen months
- Blenheim light bomber: twenty-two months
- Wellington medium bomber: eighty-four months
- Stirling heavy bomber: forty-six months
- Manchester heavy bomber: forty-nine months
- Halifax heavy bomber: fifty months

The procedure was accelerated during wartime, because the RAF kept having to meet new challenges. Companies were initially over optimistic about how quickly a prototype would be ready, which disappointed everyone. In wartime, the competitive tender stage was dropped and designs were ordered off the drawing board, reducing the design to order times:

- Tempest fighter: twenty-five months
- Typhoon fighter: forty-three months
- Mosquito light bomber: seven months
- Lancaster heavy bomber: thirteen months

Once a contractor had been appointed, there were another four phases to pass through before full production was reached:

- The Prototype Phase involved building a prototype.
- The Royal Aircraft Establishment took the prototype through the Test Phase.
- The Development Phase let the factories get organised while building a small number.
- The Production Phase involved the factories increasing production to peak output.

Contractors were sometimes allowed to fly their own prototypes under supervision, to speed up testing. However, modifications during the development phase were kept to a minimum because they caused delays, as did problems with aero engines. The following list shows how long it took to take each model from the prototype to peak production:

- Hurricane fighter: thirty-two months
- Spitfire fighter: fifty-six months
- Beaufighter: thirty-seven months
- Typhoon fighter: thirty-eight months
- Mosquito bomber: thirty-seven months
- Wellington bomber: forty-five months
- Blenheim bomber: thirty-seven months
- Stirling bomber: fifty-eight months
- Halifax bomber: sixty months
- Lancaster bomber: thirty-four months

It took a factory a long time to switch production between different aircraft. Sometimes managers slowly introduced a new model while phasing out the old one. However, this proved to be complicated, so they set up new assembly lines on spare floor space instead, ready to make a straight swap.

## Aircraft Components

### Ordering Components[25]

The Air Ministry had relied on bulk ordering until the increase in aircraft production during the rearmament period caused problems. The MAP set up a Planning Section in May 1940, which was supposed to order equipment and spares according to the Scheme A aircraft programme. However, it often made urgent demands for bulk deliveries, causing problems for the factories. So, an Aircraft Equipment Directorate was formed in July to organise the delivery of parts to the factories, to keep the assembly lines moving. It also sent them to the Aircraft Storage Units and airfields, so they could carry out repairs and maintenance.

Scheme B was linked to monthly estimates after May 1941, reducing the number of aircraft waiting for parts. The problem was how to match up what the factories could make with what the Air Ministry and the RAF wanted. Scheme B was eventually dropped as it became too difficult to predict and orders were calculated by multiplying everything by a factor of 1.5 instead, copying the RAF's planned expansion. Over time, the MAP and the Equipment Directorate reduced the expansion factor down to 1.25 and then 0.8, as the RAF contracted.

A Direct Delivery Plan was also implemented to send equipment directly from the manufacturer to the factory but the ordering of parts was still referred to as 'unnecessarily frequent and often hysterical.' Forecasting was eventually refined as the war ended; a remarkable feat considering that the number of aircraft rolling off the assembly lines had increased from 700 to 3,275 a month.

## Alloy Components[26]

Biplanes were chiefly made from wood and canvas, so the aircraft industry had only required 2,500 tons of aluminium a month between the wars. It required four tons of bauxite to make one ton of aluminium, so half of what was required could be mined in Britain. However, the new aircraft designs had lightweight alloy airframes covered with thin metal sheeting. It meant the demand for aluminium increased to 6,500 tons a month and the extra bauxite had to be imported from Canada. While the quantity of alloys required peaked at 24,500 tons in 1944, two thirds of them were made by melting down crashed aircraft.

Half a dozen firms across the Midlands and South Wales cast the alloy sheets and strips, which made up large parts of the aircraft. However, a new factory was opened in Falkirk in Scotland in 1942 when an extra 1,000 tons of sheeting a month was required by the bomber programme. Subcontractors were employed to make as many small parts as possible but specialist companies had to be employed to press the spars, which attached the wings to the airframe, into shape. The wingspan of the various Spitfire marks was only around 12 metres (38 feet) but the Lancaster bomber required two huge spars to create its 31-metre (102-feet) wingspan.

## Turrets, Guns and Bombs[27]

Aircraft weapons were ordered from a range of firms. Hurricanes and Spitfires were initially armed with Browning machine guns before they were upgraded to 20-millimetre cannon, after the *Luftwaffe* fitted their aircraft with armour. Eventually, 3-inch rockets were mounted onto rail projectors and fixed onto the wings of Hurricanes. A 6-pounder was the largest gun mounted on an aircraft and it was fixed in the fuselage of a Mosquito.

The Air Ministry and then the MAP bought the gun turrets and they were issued to the aircraft manufacturers. The Daimler Company Limited and Brockhouse Engineering made them for the Bristol Aeroplane Company, while Boulton & Paul Limited made French turrets under license. Frazer Nash also used French ideas to design the turrets made by Parnall Aircraft Limited. More companies became involved in making them but work had to be dispersed during the Blitz.

The air crew needed help to aim their weapons, as the speed of aircraft increased. A deflection ring fitted to the sight helped a gunner pick his lead on a target, while tracer bullets helped him fine tune the shot.[28] A gyroscopic sight with a pneumatic control was introduced to increase accuracy at the end of 1940. Aiming devices continued to improve and new ones were introduced for rockets. Remote control weapons were added to bombers in 1944, increasing their firepower without adding the weight of an extra crew member.

The Ministry of Supply ordered gun ammunition for aircraft but the MAP ordered bombs direct from the engineering firms. Bomb cases had to be cast, then forged and finally welded, with many being made by Hadfields Limited of Sheffield. They were filled with explosives at agency factories working for ICI, while specialist firms filled incendiary bombs with magnesium. The standard incendiary bomb only weighed 1.8 kilograms (4 pounds) and while the nose was made from cast iron or steel, it had an aluminium–magnesium alloy body. The filling of thermite incendiary pellets burned for several minutes after the bomb hit the ground. A 14 kilogram (30 pound) version that was dropped with a parachute was introduced towards the end of the war. Lancaster bombers alone dropped around 55 million incendiary bombs.

## Undercarriages[29]

Airframe manufacturers had made the fixed undercarriages used on their biplanes. However, retractable ones were used on modern designs, to improve the aerodynamics. They used hydraulic systems made by the following companies:

- Armstrong Whitworth made them for the Whitley bomber.
- Fairey Aviation Company Limited made them for the Battle, Firefly and Albacore.
- De Havilland made several types, including one the Mosquito.
- Vickers Aviation made them for their own aircraft, Supermarine and other firms.
- Vickers made undercarriages for many fighters and bombers.

Eventually, sixty shadow firms and subcontractors became involved and an Undercarriage Directorate was formed in 1942 to organise them all.

## Aero Engines and Propellers[30]

Aero engines could cost as much as an aircraft's airframe. Some engines were developed following an official initiative, while others were private ventures. Production was increased in three ways:

- Aero-engine factories were expanded.
- New agency factories were built for the aero engine companies to run.
- Shadow factories were built, for car engine manufacturers to manage under guidance from the aero engine companies.

Four firms designed engines:

- Rolls-Royce
- Bristol Aeroplane Company
- D. Napier & Son Limited
- Hawker Siddeley Aircraft Company

They eventually ran twenty large engine factories between them, with the new ones being far more efficient because they were purpose built and equipped with new tools. Many small engineering companies made parts, while larger subcontractors made assemblies. For example, British Thomson-Houston and Rotax made the magnetos that started the aircraft engines.

The Air Ministry and later the MAP accepted an engine design and the details were then worked out. Prototypes were tested at the Aircraft and Armament

Experimental Establishment on Boscombe Down. The design departments then looked at modifications, to see if they could improve performance.

The 158,000 men and women employed by Bristol Aeroplane Company and Rolls-Royce made most of the 250,000 engines used by the RAF. Both companies designed the mountings with the aircraft manufacturers, making sure the engines could be easily maintained and repaired. The Ministry for Aircraft Production bought the engines and issued them to the aircraft manufacturers.

Bristol Aeroplane Company made over 100,000 engines and Roy Fedden designed the three main types:

- The Taurus for the Beaufort and Albacore.
- The Hercules for the Beaufighter, Stirling and Halifax.
- The Centaurus for the Tempest.

Bristol Aeroplane Company set up an aero-engine factory in Accrington in Lancashire, while Austin Motor Company Limited set one up next to its factory in Longbridge, Birmingham. Ten firms formed two shadow groups to make components and sub-assemblies for. They were assembling 250 engines a month at the start of the war. Daimler Company Limited and Rootes Securities Limited[31] paired up, as did the Rover Company Limited and Standard Motor Company Limited, and the Singer Manufacturing Company and Wolseley Motors Limited. The pairs of factories mirrored each other, so work could continue if one was bombed.

H.M. Hobson Limited opened a shadow factory in Oldham and Bristol Aeroplane Company opened an agency factory in Accrington, increasing the output of Bristol Aeroplane Company's engines to 3,000 a month. Bristol Aeroplane Company also opened an underground factory in Corsham, Wiltshire in 1942 but it had cost too much and had taken too long to complete.

Ernest Hives designed the Rolls-Royce Merlin, Peregrine, Vulture, Kestrel and Griffon engines. However, the Merlin was the most popular and 110,000 would be made for the following aircraft during the war:

- Bombers: Handley Page Halifax, Avro Lancaster and the de Havilland Mosquito.
- Fighters: Hawker Hurricane and Supermarine Spitfire.

They were made at the company's factories in Derby and Crewe, while an agency factory was opened in Hillington near Glasgow. The Ford Motor Company ran a shadow factory in Trafford Park near Manchester, while the American Packard Motor Car Company started making them in Detroit, Michigan. Between them, they ended up making 4,650 engines a month.

Frank Halford designed D. Napier & Son Limited's Sabre engine in 1940 but it proved difficult to adapt it to assembly line work. The company had factories in Luton and Acton near London, as well as an agency factory near Liverpool. However, production problems meant that the English Electric Company was instructed to take the firm over in 1942. Hawker Siddeley made the Cheetah engine for the Oxford and Anson training aircraft in Coventry.

The Air Ministry and then the MAP bought propellers and issued them to the aircraft firms. Fixed pitch propellers with metal blades were made by Fairey in Hayes, Middlesex. However, most were variable pitch propellers which changed angle as the aircraft's speed increased, to improve fuel consumption. De Havilland had made the first variable pitch airscrews at Edgware and Hatfield, London, and in Lostock, Lincolnshire. Rolls-Royce and Bristol Aeroplane Company had formed Rotol Airscrews before the war and it was making 1,600 airscrews a month in Gloucester, Cheltenham and Worcester by 1941. Sixty firms were involved in making parts for propellers and airscrews by 1943.

## Jet Engines[32]

Dr Alan Griffith had written about turbine design as early as 1926; however, the Royal Aircraft Establishment had not recommended his theory to the Air Ministry. Meanwhile, Flight Lieutenant Frank Whittle was injecting fuel into compressed air, which made a thermal jet and created thrust. He patented the idea in 1930 and the government set up the company Power Jets (Research and Development) Limited in Lutterworth, Leicestershire, in 1936, so he could continue his experiments. Meanwhile, the aeronautical engineer Hayne Constant was developing Dr Griffith's theory.

The RAE was working on an axial flow turbine[33] with Metropolitan-Vickers, while Whittle focused on a simpler single-stage turbine. Hawker Siddeley, C.A. Parsons & Company Limited, and Fraser & Chalmers all worked on parts of the engine. Sir Henry Tizard, Chairman of the Aeronautical Research

Committee, arranged tests at British Thomson-Houston's works in Rugby in 1937 and the Air Ministry eventually bought Whittle's single-stage jet engine in the summer of 1939. While it contracted the Gloster Aircraft Company Limited and Power Jets to design a super-fast fighter, there were arguments over patents and manufacturing rights.

The Air Ministry and the MAP told Churchill that the jet engine could be a war winner, when he was appointed Prime Minister in May 1940. However, the urgencies caused by the Battle of Britain meant that the idea was shelved until the winter. Whittle continued with his design and his work received a boost when Sir Henry Tizard joined the Air Council in June 1941. He gave an order to the Gloster Aircraft Company, ending the arguments between Power Jets and Rover. It meant that experimental flights could be flown and other firms could become involved, resulting in many engineers pooling their ideas as the Gas Turbine Collaboration Committee.

The RAE checked the engine's design and looked at how it would work with an airframe. Details of the W.2.B. (produced by Whittle), the F.2 (produced by Metropolitan-Vickers) and H.1 engines (produced by de Havilland and known as the Goblin) were also shared with the General Electric Company in America. However, progress stalled because the Whittle W.2.B engine failed to produce enough power. Power Jets and Rover were also struggling to complete the engine and airframe, because there were so many new features. Modifications eventually resulted in the W.2.B/23 engine.

The Meteor was powered by the W.2/500 engine (produced by Power Jets (Research and Development) Limited) or the de Havilland H.1 engine. Both gave high speeds but the aircraft could only fly for short distances, so they were only suitable for home defence. It meant the RAF had little use for them, because it was on the offensive over Europe.

Rolls-Royce took over the Barnoldswick factory in April 1943, a move welcomed by Power Jets. The MAP also appointed Dr Roxbee Cox as Deputy Director for the research and development of turbine engines. While the changes slowed development down, they produced a better quality engine.

Power Jets and Rolls-Royce continued to develop a gas turbine engine for a short range interceptor fighter and a long range bomber. Meanwhile, Gloster was busy building Tempest fighters ready for the Normandy campaign, while a few Meteor I's had been deployed to combat the V-1 rockets aimed at

London. The Meteor II was equipped with the de Havilland H.1 engine but the war was nearly over by the time the Derwent Series I engine was ready to be fitted into the Meteor III.

Power Jets would eventually be reorganised as the National Gas Turbine Establishment. While D. Napier's and the Bristol Aeroplane Company continued developing the jet engine after the war, the production budget was cut in line with all military spending.

## Tank Design and Development

### The Design Process[34]

Tanks had to keep evolving, to satisfy the British Army's demands and to keep up with the arms race. For example, anti-tank guns needed to be upgraded to pierce the armour protecting an enemy tank. Design agencies would suggest how to modify existing weapons and help firms make the changes. Their objective was to see that changes were made quickly, without upsetting production.

The Design Superintendent focused on the tank's fighting compartment: the small space occupied by the crew, gun and ammunition. Meanwhile, several private companies looked at the design of the body and the suspension, including the American company J. Walter Christie. The railway industry focused on assembling hulls and turrets, while the car industry designed engines and transmissions. Lightweight aero engines had to be used after vehicle engines were found to be underpowered.

Every new tank design went through three stages. The first stage turned a concept into a specification, complete with drawings. This could take several years during peacetime because of the limited budgets. The second stage involved putting the design out to tender and the Superintendent of Design competed with private companies, to see who had the best ideas. Unfortunately, the manufacturers had been excluded from the design stage, which slowed down the final stage, which involved testing the prototypes. For example, it would take four years to complete the Covenanter tank and the Crusader tank and they both had serious problems when they finally rolled off the assembly line in November 1940.

Rearmament accelerated the design and development processes and several prototypes would be made, to speed up testing. But it still took five years of design, development and testing before the Matilda II was delivered in September 1939. The urgency of war accelerated the process and the Ministry of Supply helped companies increase production. While the Mechanical Equipment Directorate considered new designs, the Tank Design Department dealt with modifications.

The BEF had to abandon all its armour in France, when it was evacuated from Dunkirk in June 1940 and it had to be re-equipped with the accepted designs, ready to fight off an invasion. Churchill's new administration formed a Tank Board and Sir Alexander Roger's team set about identifying the design problems with all the tanks.

Twice as many firms were involved in assembling tanks by the end of 1940 and they were now allowed modify the designs, to speed up assembly, and pass on their experiences to others. Combat experience meant that improvements were required as soon as a problem arose, so the competitive design process was suspended, while issues which arose on the battlefield were solved as quickly as possible.

Improved designs saved time while companies became more proficient at manufacturing components and assembling tanks through trial and error. Later designs were much easier to build than the early ones, however, ordering tanks off the drawing board led to problems, such as with the Covenanter, Crusader and Churchill tanks.

Accelerating the tank design and development process caused a reliability crisis in 1941 and then interrupted tank supply ahead of the Second Battle of El Alamein of October 1942. The first 1,000 Churchill tanks off the assembly line needed modifications to their transmission, steering and suspension before they could be sent to North Africa. Even then, many required further work after failing endurance tests. Manufacturers also learnt that ordering tanks off the drawing board made it impossible to calculate how many spares required, resulting in maintenance problems in the field.

A compromise between speeding up the design process, while limiting production issues was resolved by building six pilot models. They were subjected to a 2,000-mile-endurance test, so modifications could resolve problems. A handful of production vehicles were then tested, while the factory dealt with any assembly line issues.

Combat tested tanks to their limits and a problem with just one faulty part could bring many tanks to a halt, especially on the harsh North African landscape. Experience proved how long parts lasted and some had to redesigned to make them more durable. The Ministry of Supply sent officers into the field, to get feedback from British Army units; they also examined any enemy designs that had been captured. However, it was 1942 before their feedback on tanks was acted on appropriately.

The Tank Design Department became the main tank designer in the final months of the war. Unfortunately, it again restricted how much input the tank firms could have and the factories often found it difficult to incorporate the many modifications.

## Designing the Cruiser Tank

The Vickers-Armstrongs' Light Mark VI tank had no gun and its armour was too thin, so the company designed the Mark VII, which was armed with a 2-pounder gun. However, Metropolitan-Cammell Carriage and Wagon Company had only made a few, when the battle for France started in May 1940. It was reported that more cruiser tanks were needed to face German armour and while Vickers-Armstrongs worked on a new design, their Mark VIII (A25) did not appear until the summer of 1943.

Sir John Carden had designed the A9 Mark I Cruiser Tank in 1936 and while it had a rotating turret made by Nash & Thompson, it also had thinner armour to increase its speed. Only a few had been delivered by the start of the war and they had reliability issues. The A10 Cruiser Mark II tank took until 1938 to design after Carden was killed in a plane crash. However, it was complicated to build and the thicker armour slowed it down.

Demand for a faster tank was inspired after seeing what Red Army tanks could achieve during trials. However, the A13 Cruiser Mark I tank designed by Morris Motors Limited was slow and unreliable. The A13 Mark II Tank was a poor compromise between speed and armour, so few were made. London Midland and Scottish Railway designed the A13 Mark III Tank body, while the Nuffield Organization designed the turret. It was powered by a new Meadows DAV flat-12 engine, while the Christie suspension allowed it to travel faster. However, the radiators had been mounted at the front resulting in both the engine and the fighting compartment overheating, so they could not be deployed to North Africa. It was, however, the first British tank to be given a name: the Covenanter.

The Nuffield Organization then designed the A15 Mark VI Tank, which was called the Crusader. It was powered by a Liberty engine and while the Marks I and II were armed with a 2-pounder gun, the Mark III was upgraded to a 6-pounder. The armour was still too thin and it struggled in the desert terrain but 5,300 Crusaders were still made because it took so long to find something better.

The Ministry of Supply asked companies to design a new cruiser tank based on existing designs and four companies responded. Vauxhall Motors suggestion to reduce the armour of the A22 Churchill infantry tank was rejected. Mechanisations and Aero Limited's attempt to convert the Crusader into the A24 Cavalier was a failure. English Electric built the A27L Cruiser Mark VIII Centaur but the weaker Liberty engine was too weak to power it. Meanwhile, Leyland Motors and the Birmingham Railway Carriage and Wagon Company created the A27M Cruiser Mark VIII, and it was powered by Rolls-Royce's Meteor engine, a version of their Merlin engine. London, Midland and Scottish Railway, Leyland Motors and Morris Motors built what became known as the Cromwell tank. Many Cromwells were deployed in Normandy but only a handful of Centaurs saw action.

The Birmingham Railway Carriage and Wagon Company also designed the Challenger A30 Cruiser Mark VIII, which required a large turret to house the 17-pounder gun required to fight the heavier German tanks. However, only a few were made because it proved easier to mount the large gun in converted Sherman tanks, known as Fireflies. The Birmingham Railway Carriage and Wagon Company also designed the low profile Comet A34 Cruiser Tank, which was armed with the 77-millimetre high velocity gun. It was the last cruiser tank designed during the war.

## Designing the Infantry Tank

Sir John Carden of Vickers-Armstrongs completed the design of the A11 Infantry Tank Mark I in 1935. However, the Matilda was slow, had a cramped crew compartment and was only armed with a machine gun. Meanwhile, the Royal Arsenal and the Vulcan Foundry Limited (a railway company near St Helens in Lancashire) designed the A12 Infantry Tank Mark II or Matilda II, which was in production by the start of the war. It was also slow but it was armed with a 2-pounder gun.

Vickers-Armstrongs finished designing the Infantry Tank Mark III in 1938 and it was known as the Valentine. Early ones were armed with a 2-pounder gun, while later marks had a 6-pounder gun; some were armed with a 3-inch howitzer. The Valentine would become the most produced tank of the war, peaking at eighty a month in 1943.

The War Office was concerned there could be a repeat of the sort of trench warfare seen during the First World War. So, the Special Vehicle Development Committee and William Foster & Co. Limited of Lincoln[35] worked on the TOG I and TOG II, while Harland & Wolff of Belfast made the A20, which had two 2-pounders mounted in side sponsons. Development was abandoned after Dunkirk because it was clear that tanks were going to be involved in fast moving battles rather than trench warfare.

Vauxhall Motors of Luton, Bedfordshire, was given a new specification to work on in June 1940, so the factories already making tanks could re-equip the British Army after Dunkirk. The company quickly designed the A22 Churchill and they were ordered straight off the drawing board, bypassing the usual testing procedure. While the first ones rolled off the assembly line in June 1941, they had many problems. Production had to be halted in the spring of 1942 and 700 were recalled, so Broom and Wade of High Wycombe could help Vauxhall modify their transmission, steering and suspension.

The experiences in Dieppe in August 1942 and El Alamein in October 1942 resulted in the Churchill's 2-pounder gun being upgraded to a 6-pounder, while many other modifications were made. Later versions would be armed with the dual purpose 75-millimetre gun or the 95-millimetre howitzer ahead of the invasion of Normandy. Later Marks also had much thicker armour, to counter the heavier German tanks.

## Specialist Tanks

Several specialist tanks were built, such as the Mark VII Tetrarch light tank, to support airborne units. The A25 Light Mark VIII Harry Hopkins tank was designed by Vickers-Armstrongs Limited to accompany airborne infantry into battle. Metropolitan-Cammell made a few but they were never used in battle. While cordite powered flame throwers were mounted on Valentine tanks, a gas pressured version mounted on the Churchill Crocodile was preferred. Several types of rollers were experimented with for detonating mines but the chain type flails mounted on Sherman tanks were more successful and they were known as the Crab. A few variations were made to help troops exit the Normandy beaches; they were nicknamed Hobart's 'Funnies'.[36]

## Transport[37]

The British Army had to motorise many of its units before the war, which required a lot of transport. The War Office rejected Vickers' design for a tracked vehicle and switched from 6 x 4 wheeled lorry vehicles to a 4 x 2 wheel design. It meant that commercial vehicle manufacturers such as the Associated Equipment Company (AEC), Albion Motors Limited, Austin Motor Company Limited, Bedford Vehicles and Morris Motors could make them.

The Morris 4-wheeled 15 hundredweight (cwt) lorry was used as a stop gap vehicle because some firms were busy making parts for tanks and aircraft until 1940. Many vehicles were imported from America and Canada and while their designs were faster and able to carry more weight, the War Office continued to order British models, in case there were import issues. New plant allowed heavier vehicles to be made and 600,000 lorries had been built by the end of the war.

Orders for the Vickers Universal Carrier and the Loyd Carrier, two turretless tracked vehicles, were given to engineering firms because they were easy to make. Over 45,000 had been made by a variety of firms by the end of the war:

- Sentinel Waggon Works Limited was a railway wagon company in Shrewsbury, Shropshire.
- Aveling-Barford made road rollers in Grantham, Lincolnshire.
- Wolseley Motors was a car manufacturer in Birmingham.
- Ford Motor Company was another car manufacturer in Dagenham, London.
- John Thornycroft Limited was a commercial vehicle manufacturer from Gerrards Cross, London.

- Vivian Loyd and Company of Camberley, Surrey, made small-tracked vehicles.
- Dennis Brothers Limited made commercial vehicles in Guildford, Surrey.

Daimler Company Limited and Humber Limited made the engines and transmissions for wheeled armoured cars and scout cars, while engineering firms made the hulls and turrets. The AEC armoured car was an improvement on them. The American T.17E1, Staghound was used instead of the Coventry vehicle, a design by Daimler and the Rootes Group.

## Radio and Radar

### Radio Equipment[38]

Around 43,000 men and women were making make parts for radio, radar and other communication instruments across Britain in the 1930s. The Air Ministry helped 250 electrical engineering companies open new factories, as an insurance against bomb damage, during the early months of the war. Eventually, a wide range of nautical, optical, electrical, radio and telephone manufacturers were involved but they could not keep up with the military's demand, so a lot of items were imported from America.

Radio proved to be an important asset for all the armed forces and its uses increased as technology improved. The Ministry of Aircraft Production produced valves and components for all the supply departments, but a shortage of skilled labour resulted in arguments over how many each service received. Typically, the Royal Navy required 33 per cent, the RAF wanted 40 per cent, the British Army needed 20 per cent, and 7 per cent were used for other purposes.

The BEF's experience in France over the winter of 1939–1940 demonstrated the need for better radios, so companies redesigned their sets and began to mass produce them. The workforce was increased to 120,000 and while skilled staff made the specialist parts, semi and unskilled workers made the rest.

The demand for extra equipment meant that valves became the limiting factor, while new uses for radar increased the numbers required. They were made under 'crash' programmes involving the General Electric Company,

EKCO, EMI Group Limited, Mullard Limited, Cosmos Engineering Co. and A.C. Cossor Limited. They eventually made 3.75 million valves a month but another 1.25 million a month still had to be imported from America.

## Radar Origins[39]

Radio waves had been used to track aircraft for several years, when Sir Henry Tizard and Robert Watson-Watt were asked if they could be used to counter bombing raids in 1934. They worked out how a line of stations could reflect radio pulses off aircraft, so their movements could be plotted. They carried out successful tests at the British Broadcasting Corporation's (BBC) Daventry station in February 1935 and then built a pulse transmitter in Slough. The Air Ministry's Scientific Research Directorate refined the equipment at Orford Ness in Suffolk, calling it Range and Direction Finding or RDF, and it operated on four wavelengths, in case the Germans attempted to jam the equipment. The Directorate's work impressed Prime Minister Stanley Baldwin's government so much, that it increased the scientists' wages.

Coastal RDF stations were built at 20-mile intervals between the River Tyne in the northeast and Southampton on the south coast, following the Munich Crisis in September 1938. They were handed over to the RAF in May 1939 and were called Chain Home stations; they were eventually extended as far north as Scapa Flow in the Orkney Islands.

Professor Marcus Oliphant, Dr John Randall and Harry Boot worked out how create a narrow radio beam, which would be difficult to jam, in the autumn of 1939. They worked with Dr Herbert Skinner and (later Professor) Philip Dee on a resonant cavity magnetron, so they could build centimetric radar devices which could detect smaller items, with much smaller antenna.

Tizard visited the United States to share their progress and it led to the Massachusetts Institute of Technology exchanging their research with the Telecommunications Research Establishment (TRE). Further improvements meant radar would change the face of aerial and naval warfare. The Air Ministry studied what methods the Germans were using while the TRE developed countermeasures, in a radar war which involved increasingly complex devices. Some transmitters jammed signals, while others interfered with the radar sets and a few even transmitted false signals to confuse the enemy radar.

## Fighting the *Luftwaffe*[40]

Gun Laying (GL) radar was introduced at the end of 1940 and it warned AA gun crews when aircraft were approaching, while continuously calculating the direction and range to them. The Mark II considerably reduced the number of shots required to down an aircraft, while the Mark III used a magnetron to increase the gun's accuracy. The equipment was soon replaced by the American made SCR-584, which could simultaneously scan and track targets.

Identification, Friend or Foe (IFF) devices at the Chain Home stations picked up signals transmitted by British aircraft and identified them as friendly. The Mark II notified early warning stations and AA guns, while the Mark III also gave the location of the aircraft or ship. A portable version codenamed Eureka became available in 1943.

The interception system was refined by four new radar devices in 1941. Air Interception (AI) equipment was an aerial scanner which helped bomber crews direct fighters towards incoming enemy squadrons. A Plan Position Indicator (PPI) electronically plotted enemy aircraft on a map, while Ground Control of Interception (GCI) equipment calculated an aircraft's height. Chain Home Low (CHL) stations were added to the system, to pick up low-flying aircraft. The new devices meant fighter pilots could accurately intercept enemy aircraft, day or night.

## Tracking the Bombers[41]

Bob Dippy devised a system called GEE which used pulse transmissions to guide pilots back to their bases, starting in the summer of 1940. A chain of GEE devices transmitted a lattice of pulses which could direct bombers to other airfields, if their own base was fog bound. The same network was used guided night fighters around their patrol patterns. Coastal Command aircraft and ships also used GEE for navigation.

Unfortunately, German night fighters soon learnt to use the GEE signal to track bombers. The Mark II device would switch wavelengths near the target, so the German pilots started using plane mounted radar devices to search for them instead. Bombers started to drop narrow strips of metallised paper, codenamed Window in July 1943 to confuse the *Würzburg* tracking system, which was guiding the German pilots to the bomber streams.

High-power jammers, codenamed Jostle were fitted into aircraft in 1944, while the Germans updated their AI devices. Fortunately, a German plane accidently landed in Britain and the new equipment was reverse engineered, so a new jammer could be built. German ground direction-finding stations countered the mistake by fixing on the transmissions made by bombers. The night fighters were then able to track the signal made by a device codenamed Monica, which had been fittcd to the bombers to warn their crews about threats approaching their rear.

## Obscured Targets and Mapping the Ground[42]

The Wireless Investigation and Development Unit worked out how the Luftwaffe guided their bombers to targets and located the transmitting stations in 1941. While the Chain Home Low stations measured the ranges and equipment codenamed Howler Chaser guided bombers to the stations, they failed to knock any out. Howler Chaser was nicknamed Oboe because of the sound it made.

Bomber Command wanted to hit targets obscured by industrial haze and smoke, such as the Ruhr factories, so radar direction equipment was tried. One radar directed the bombers to the target, while a second one released the bomb over it. The range could be extended by using aircraft mounted equipment to repeat the ground signals. However, pilots had to fly a steady course over the target for it to be accurate, which made it dangerous to use.

The Track and Release System[43] guided aircraft out to an agreed radius from one ground station while a second station released the bomb over the target. However, the Oboe signals could not handle many planes, so they guided the pathfinders instead, so they could drop coloured indicators over the target.

Watson-Watt devised a device that bounced radar signals off the ground and displayed the results on a screen, which the navigator could follow. Unfortunately, the aircraft carrying the prototype and the scientists crashed on 7 June 1942, hindering the development of the equipment. The H2S was first used in January 1943 and improvements meant that the equipment could eventually map towns, lakes and airfields. Unfortunately, the German scientists soon learnt how to detect and follow the H2S pulses, so they could direct night fighters towards a bomber stream.

### Radar and the Royal Navy[44]

A crude Air-to-Surface Vessel (ASV) detector was in use at the start of the war. The improved Mark II could spot surfaced U-boats by 1941 but U-boats were being fitted with a receiver that warned the crew they were being tracked. The Mark III was far more accurate, resulting in many U-boats being tracked and sunk in 1943.

Type 271s were radar devices that could guide convoys at night and they were fitted to escort vessels in the summer of 1941. They could also spot enemy aircraft and land based devices were used to watch the English Channel. Coastal Command also mounted H2S/ASV sets on their bombers, so they could monitor the coast.

Radar devices were used to hide the huge D-Day invasion fleet, as it approached the Normandy coast early on 6 June 1944. Aircraft mounted devices codenamed Moonshine jammed the German radar, while an airdrop of Window simulated another fleet miles from the real one. Other devices jammed the German radar stations across Normandy, while the RAF tried to knock them out. Radar beacons were also used to identify the landing zones for airdrops.

## Nuclear Weapons

### The Atomic Bomb[45]

The British scientist, James Chadwick, discovered the neutron, a sub-atomic particle with no electric charge, in 1932. Germany scientists Otto Hahn and Fritz Strassman then split a uranium nucleus in 1938; a process called nuclear fission. It enabled chain reactions to be triggered and they had the potential to create huge amounts of energy.

The Italian nuclear physicist and Nobel prize winner Enrico Fermi emigrated to America in January 1939, where he met the US Naval Department. President Franklin D. Roosevelt appointed the Advisory Committee on Uranium to determine if it was possible to create nuclear chain reactions, believing that the Germans could be doing the same. Meanwhile in Britain, the Committee for the Scientific Survey of Air Warfare appointed the MAUD Committee[46] under Professor George Thomson in April 1940. He would start sharing ideas with Professor Kenneth Bainbridge of the American National Defence Research Council in April 1941.

The Scientific and Industrial Research Department set up the Tube Alloys Directorate, a secret programme to supervise the making of a uranium bomb, under Wallace Akers, ICI's executive manager. Initially, the National Academy Reviewing Committee was more interested in atomic power than making a bomb, but a Top Policy Group soon decided it was a worthwhile military project.

The Quadrant Conference between Roosevelt, Churchill and their Chiefs of Staff agreed on a joint programme in August 1943, because the British team's research was more advanced, while the American facilities were better. Chadwick represented the British government in Washington DC, while British scientists became involved with a prototype scheme in Montreal, Canada. A plant to treat uranium deposits was also set up in Petawawa, Ontario. The British scientists were scattered across several laboratories until a central one was established in Los Alamos in New Mexico. Professor Robert Oppenheimer was appointed the director in October 1942.

Thousands of scientists ended up working on several atomic devices and the first bomb, codenamed Trinity, was detonated near Alamogordo, New Mexico on 16 July 1945. It was followed by the dropping of the Little Boy bomb on Hiroshima on 6 August 1945; it is thought to have killed between 90,000 and 166,000 people.[47] It was followed by the dropping of the Fat Man bomb on Nagasaki on 9 August, which killed between 60,000 and 80,000 people. The next bomb would be 'ready for delivery on the target on the first day of good weather after 24 August 1945.'[48] However, Emperor Hirohito announced Japan's surrender on the 15th and it was formally signed on 2 September 1945, ending the Second World War.

# Chapter 4

# The Fuel Industries

## Raw Materials[1]

Britain had to import most of its raw materials, so there were always concerns about shortages, particularly when German submarines started working together in what were known as 'wolfpacks'. They eventually sank over 2,800 merchant ships and Prime Minister Winston Churchill would later say that 'the only thing that really frightened me during the war was the U-boat peril.'[2]

By May 1941, imports had increased to a safe level. However, the Japanese entry into the war in December caused further concerns after they seized Malaya, the Dutch East Indies and the Philippines, cutting off the supply of many raw materials. It would take the Allies time to find new sources and develop them. America's entry into the war at the same time, caused further problems because the US War and Naval Departments increased their demands for everything, as they planned to rearm and expand.

Transport was a big issue because raw materials required a lot of shipping to carry them the long distances across the oceans. It was also difficult to find cargoes to fill the ships in both directions, because each material had its own storage requirements. The number of ships being sunk by U-boats continued to rise at an alarming rate so propaganda campaigns and rationing were introduced across Britain, to try and reduce consumption.

Import quantities had to be revised down until stock minimums, which only left enough to cover emergencies, had to be set at the end of 1942. Britain faced difficulties when had to make shipping available for the invasion of North Africa, codenamed Operation Torch in November 1942. For example, it still needed to import 1.63 million tons of iron ore, 630,000 tons of pig iron, 1.1 million tons of steel ingots and 640,000 tons of scrap steel every month to keep its armaments industry busy. Exploiting home sources of iron ore eventually reduced the amount needed to be imported from Spain by 650,000 tons a month.

Meanwhile, Churchill had to tell all three supply departments to cut the amount of imported raw materials they required. The Minister of Production still predicted shortages but three factors would save the country from critical shortages of raw materials:

- The Royal Navy started winning the Battle of the Atlantic in the spring of 1943.
- Success in North Africa and Italy reopened the shipping route through the Mediterranean Sea.
- The armed forces used less ammunition than expected.

The final problem to be overcome, was the strain put on shipping by Operation Overlord in the summer of 1944.

What follows is an explanation of the factors which affected the main raw materials required by the armaments industry. They were coal, iron ore, steel and the lightweight metal alloys used by the aircraft industry.

## The Coal Industry

### The Coal Industry Before the War[3]

The Royal Navy needed the best quality coal, which was anthracite mined in southwest Wales. The railways needed good quality bituminous coal for its trains, while poor quality bituminous coal was used to power factories and heat homes. Coking coal was required to heat the foundries to high enough temperatures make iron and steel. It was made by baking coal in an airless oven, to remove all the organic substances.

Britain had traditionally exported 20 per cent of its coal; half of it to France. However, the industry had suffered during the prolonged depression between the wars. The Coal Mines Act had introduced the maximum seven and a half hour working day in 1930 and while it allowed mine owners to set their quotas and prices, the country soon needed more coal. It meant miners were again working longer hours. However, irregular employment had made working underground unattractive and many had found different jobs, rather than follow their fathers down the pit.

In 1936, the Minister for the Coordination of Defence asked if coal production could be increased by 20 per cent if the country went to war, only to be told it could only rise 10 per cent. Although the amount of machine cut coal was increasing, huge investment was required to improve the machinery that carried it to the surface.

The Coal Act created the Coal Commission in 1938 and it put the nation's coal deposits in the hands of the State. Colliery owners would be paid compensation for what was extracted and the bill would eventually total over £66 million (£5.4 billion today). Meanwhile, a study into coal distribution noted that it would be difficult to transport sufficient coal from the northeast coalfields down to London, especially if the sea lanes were threatened or the rail network was damaged. It also estimated that the steel industry would require more high-grade coal during wartime, while less low-grade coal would be needed for domestic heating. The question was, could a balance in production be struck, without causing industrial unrest across the coalfields?

## The Opening Months of the War, 1939–1940[4]

The colliery owners were instructed not to raise their prices on the outbreak of war. The Mines Department put Supply Officers in charge of the coalfields, while Export Officers organised shipping and exports. Divisional Officers made sure the factories received their quotas of coal, while Local Fuel Overseers implemented rationing schemes to conserve stocks. The Mines Department also deployed Conciliation Officers to deal with issues that arose at any of the collieries. The government was anxious to stop any of the 800,000 miners joining the armed forces, as had happened at the start of the First World War, so few enlisted and the amount of coal dug did not fall over the winter of 1939–1940.[5]

Exports were reduced because the German and Polish markets had been closed to business, so surplus coal was delivered to Spain, in exchange for iron ore. Steps were also taken to increase the amount exported to France. The French Government would plead for more coal when the German *Wehrmacht* overran its coalfields in May 1940 but the country had surrendered before anything was organised. It left Britian with an excess of coal, so part of the

South Wales coalfield had to be closed temporarily. Meanwhile, the northern coalfields were told to keep digging and stockpile a reserve, to stop its miners seeking alternative work or enlisting.

In September 1940, the *Luftwaffe* started bombing the railway network, delaying the coal trains heading to London. Meanwhile, raids against the Thames dockyards and the mining of the sea lanes reduced the amount of coal that could be shipped from the northcast. The bombing also sparked an evacuation from the cities and the extra passenger trains often caused delays on the rail network. The combination of these factors slowed the delivery of coal to London down to dangerous levels, so the Lord President's Coal Committee was formed to resolve the problems. It reduced the delays, diverted trains from blocked tracks and established coal dumps north of London. It also made use of the stockpile of coal left in South Wales after to France's capitulation and the South Coast Coal Convoy was soon sending 200 trains a week to the capital.

Meanwhile, new schemes were implemented to encourage new workers into the coal industry. A Mines Medical Officer studied industrial diseases, while a Mines Medical Service administered first aid to injured miners. A Miners' Welfare Commission applied a levy on coal to fund rehabilitation centres and support convalescing miners. While a Pit Relations Division and Pit Production Committees resolved issues, the miners resented their interference in what they saw as the work of the Miners' Federation of Great Britain, which coordinated their miners' trade unions. Pithead baths were opened at many collieries but over half still did not have any. Pit canteens were also opened but few miners used them.

## Maintaining Production, 1941–1942[6]

Balancing the supply and demand of coal under wartime conditions was complicated. The Mines Department bought the coal from the seventeen mining districts, while Coal Supplies Officers found out where supplies were required and the Ministry of War Transport organised deliveries. A Fuel and Lighting Order limited energy use only to find that coal consumption was lower than expected, while the loss of the French markets had resulted in a surplus. A Fuel Efficiency Committee eventually started a propaganda campaign to further reduce domestic use and it was followed by the rationing of all forms of fuel.

The new armaments factories soon needed large quantities of coal, so more was dug over the summer of 1941, to build up reserves ahead of the winter. Unfortunately, many of the 80,000 miners laid off after the South Wales coalfields were closed had enlisted in the armed forces or found work in the armaments factories, where wages and conditions were better.

Meanwhile, morale up across the coalfields was falling and absenteeism was rising, reducing production. So, the Coal Production Council, Coal Production Advisers, District Production Committees and Pit Production Committees had to work together to deal with the issues. Wages were guaranteed and attendance bonuses were agreed, while persistent absentees were dealt with.

The Ministry of Labour made sure miners could not change jobs nor be made redundant without permission after May 1941. However, an appeal for volunteers failed to bring in many newcomers and while 100,000 ex-miners had been identified, many already had key jobs or were in the armed forces. Others failed the medical, their health ruined by years of working underground. Around 40,000 ex-miners were eventually recruited back into mining under the Miners' Registration Scheme but it took time to retrain them. Eventually, every man who was called up for National Service was offered the option to work underground but most preferred to join the armed forces instead.

## Unrest Across the Coalfields, 1942–1943[7]

A Ministry of Fuel and Power, headed by The Right Honourable Major Gwilym Lloyd George MP,[8] took over the coal industry in June 1942. He organised the country into eight coal-producing regions and set up directorates to deal with production, labour, distribution and industry finances. The mine owners remained responsible for their finances and pit managers continued to run the collieries but Pit Production Committees now advised them on how to improve production. Wilfred Greene headed a board dealing with wages and while it increased pay and attendance bonuses, productivity failed to increase, leading to a coal shortage over the winter of 1942–1943. So, Churchill had to give the Ministry of Labour and the Secretary for Mines, The Right Honourable Dai Grenfell MP, extra powers to deal with the problems.

Wages remained poor compared with the armaments industry, so there were frequent stoppages. Recruitment continued to be a problem and while thousands of older men were retiring every month, few young men were choosing mining as a career. Many pit owners were also concerned that the demand for coal would drop after the war, so most refused to invest in new machinery.

Morale across the coalfields continued to fall until many miners started to ignore their managers and their trade union officials. A new order eventually had to be introduced so that miners could be prosecuted if they went on strike, the same as all the other industries. Grenfell, Lloyd George and the Miners' Federation of Great Britain were all calling for full nationalisation but the government refused, concerned that such a major change would cause disruption. Instead, Churchill adopted a compromise, to appease the miners. Group Production Directors were given control of personnel and finances, while Regional Production Directors started running the pits. It meant that the state was running the coal industry but the owners still owned their collieries.

While problems in the industry continued, the planned invasion of Europe meant that the demand for coal was going to increase. The Ministry of Fuel and Power needed time, which meant that consumption had to be reduced until production was improved. So, trains carried exactly what coal each depot required, to eliminate any unnecessary stockpiling.

The Minister of Labour reported a manpower shortage in mining in the summer of 1943 but all adult males were either in the armed forces or doing essential war work by now. Few were entering the coal industry because it was dangerous work with poor prospects.[9] So, the Ministry of Labour introduced a lottery scheme in December, to select young men to work in mining. The Bevin Boys' Scheme (as it became known) was unpopular and so was the work. Boys were selected by comparing a randomly selected number with the last number on a man's National Service Act registration card. Over one third of those selected wanted to join the armed forces instead but most of their appeals were rejected.

Nearly 22,000 fit young men were selected, trained and allocated to a pit. Only 6,500 worked at the coal face, while the rest worked elsewhere underground or on the surface. Around 500 were prosecuted for failing to turn up for work and 143 were imprisoned. Most of the Bevin Boys left the industry as soon as they could.

## The Final Year of the War, 1944–1945

A publicity campaign further reduced consumption and the government was relieved that the winter of 1943–1944 was mild. The Allied forces preparing for the invasion of France were also using less coal than estimated. The combination of factors meant that supply met demand; but only just.

A National Conciliation Scheme headed by Samuel Porter, Baron Porter, raised the price of coal to fund a higher minimum wage, intending to stimulate recruitment and secure the industry after the war. However, the National Wages Agreement, which was announced in April 1944, was made without consulting the miners nor the Miners' Federation of Great Britain. It caused a widespread stoppage across the industry and it cost £11.5 million (£390 million today) to adjust the wage discrepancies and end the unrest. The increased pay scales moved the miners even further up the pay scales, creating resentment in other industries, especially as everyone was working hard to prepare for D-Day.

The stoppage resulted in 24 million tons of production being lost, leaving the nation with no reserve coal stocks ahead of D-Day. It meant that every spare ton had to be stockpiled along the south coast, ready for the invasion. Meanwhile, the Fuel Efficiency Committee had been encouraging factories to switch to different fuels and it eventually reduced industry's coal requirements by 40 per cent. However, nothing could be done to reduce the steel industry's and there was a shortage of coal for the coking plants. As D-Day got underway, the public was encouraged to use as little coal as possible, so any surplus could be used on military projects.

The total output of coal had dropped from 204 million tons in 1942 down to 184 million in 1944. However, the production per man had also fallen due to several reasons.[10] Many experienced managers had left the industry, resulting in poor working practices, while owners objected to government interference and rejected ideas from other areas. A plan to concentrate labour into the most productive pits was shelved in case it caused further unrest. The government also tried importing up-to-date cutting machinery from America, to speed up production, but it could not work in many narrow seams. Mine owners also continued to refuse to buy the machinery needed to carry the coal to the surface.

There were distribution problems over the winter of 1944–1945, due to bad weather and problems on the rail network. Despite the cold weather, the public continued to make the biggest cuts while the public utilities increased their consumption. But overall, national consumption was down by 10 per cent.

The Ministry of Works had spent two years surveying the coalfields and believed that 40 million tons could be dug by open cast mining methods. American excavation equipment was imported to dig it and load it into a fleet of lorries. Digging up vast tracts of land was unpopular and while only 15 million tons had been excavated across South Yorkshire by the end of the war, it had made up half of the national deficit. Unfortunately, huge amounts of money then had to be spent to restore the excavated areas.

In January 1945, the National Union of Mineworkers (NUM) took over from the Miners' Federation of Great Britain; it had a membership of over 380,000. As the war came to an end, demobilisation plans were put in place. However, it was deemed unwise to release miners early from the services, in case it caused unrest.

The events of the past six years had made the public painfully aware of how important the coal industry. Meanwhile, the colliery owners and the new National Union of Mineworkers looked to the future and nationalisation. It would be implemented when the Coal Industry Nationalisation Act created the National Coal Board (NCB) in July 1946. It took over on 1 January 1947 and would invest £550 million (over £17 billion today) in the nation's coal industry over the next ten years.

## Oil Imports

### The Oil Industry Before the War[11]

An Oil Board had been set up in 1925 to carry out annual reviews of Britain's oil and tanker requirements. The Petrol Department monitored the relationships with France and America, while the Sea Transport Department kept it informed about the tanker situation. Following the Nazis' seizure of power in Germany in 1933, the Oil Board prepared plans in case Britain went to war. The plan was to avoid the sort of oil shortages experienced during the First World War, especially as the armed forces had become motorised. It estimated how much oil would be required and then located enough supplies. It also checked shipping routes and sourced enough tankers to cover them.

Shell produced 40 per cent of Britain's oil needs, while the rest was bought from the Standard Oil Company and the Anglo-Iranian Oil Company.[12] The three companies owned most of the tankers and they agreed to share their railways, rolling stock and storage tanks on the outbreak of war. C.C. Wakefield and Company was the main motor oil importer and it traded under the name Castrol.

The Oil Board estimated Britain would need 850,000 tons a month to fight Germany or Japan. Most of it would be used by merchant shipping, the steel industry and agriculture. One third would eventually be imported from the Iranian oil fields, while a revision to the Neutrality Act[13] allowed American to sell oil to Britain after 1937, providing London organised the tankers.

The Oil Board correctly assumed that the shipping route through the Suez Canal and the Mediterranean Sea could be cut in wartime, so 150 whale oil and molasses tankers were converted, ready to cover the longer routes around Africa. However, government plans to stock up oil reserves for all three armed forces were undermined by a lack of tankers and British companies could not afford to buy any new ones.

The Oil Board was also concerned that the *Luftwaffe* would start bombing the terminals along the Thames Estuary, where London's oil was stored. However, companies refused to build new ones in safer areas and while some tanks were protected by earth, concrete and camouflage, it was slow and expensive work. There were also concerns that the *Kreigsmarine* would patrol along the English Channel and mine the Thames Estuary, so plans were made to offload oil at the west coast ports of Avonmouth, Swansea and Stanlow, on the River Mersey. Their facilities were upgraded, while the train and haulage companies were warned that they would have to transport oil across the country to London.

## The Phoney War, September 1939–April 1940[14]

An Overseas Supply Committee took over the sourcing of oil on the outbreak of war, while the oil companies pooled their supplies of fuel and lubricants. A Tanker Tonnage Committee organised the tankers, while the Ministry of Shipping licensed them. Shipping Control coordinated tanker movements with the Port and Transit Control authorities, to make sure they were unloaded quickly. The Petroleum Board controlled distribution, organising the rail tankers, lorries, ships and barges which moved the oil around Britain's network of installations and depots.

An Oil Control Board was set up in November 1939, only to discover that everyone was using far less oil than expected, which reducing oil demand by 70,000 tons a month. Civilian consumption had dropped by one third because a petrol shortage had forced thousands of vehicles off the roads. Dual-fuel ships[15] had started using coal because it was easier to buy than oil. Meanwhile, the BEF was using half of what had been estimated in France and Belgium. They would continue to do so throughout the period later known as the Phoney War.[16]

Germany was known to be using the Fischer-Tropesch process to produce synthetic oil from coal but Britain neither had the time nor the resources to build the new refineries needed to create a similar industry. So, different alternative fuel sources were tried, like burning creosote or using benzole, a byproduct from the coke ovens, as a motor fuel. A few vehicle owners even used coal gas stored in bags on the roof of the vehicle as fuel for short journeys. An attempt to set up a National Lubricant Reclamation Scheme also had limited success.

The Admiralty was surprised that the *Kreigsmarine* was able to sink two or three tankers a month, either with mines or U-boats. It was far more than they had expected and it made companies based in neutral countries wary of moving British goods. Norway refused to let its tankers carry British oil, until London threatened to stop selling it coal and fish. Around 130 Norwegian tankers then started transporting oil to British ports. Around fifty Dutch and Panamanian tankers were also chartered but all the owners charged high prices as danger money.

The dangers required new defensive measures and they increased the time that convoys took to cross the Atlantic Ocean. Tankers were escorted to a point 200 miles west of Ireland before they headed west to Halifax, Nova Scotia, travelling at the speed of the slowest ship. They then sailed down America's eastern seaboard to the Caribbean oilfields. A return trip took around sixty-five days and ships' captains loaded their bunkers with enough fuel for the round trip, to reduce the journey time. While the Oil Board considered shipping more oil from the Caribbean oilfields, in case the Mediterranean route was closed, it was wary of upsetting Iran. Caribbean oil was also more expensive.

An Anglo-French Oil Committee was set up to coordinate the two nations' policies and monitor what neutral and enemy countries were doing to source their oil. However, a failure to agree joint import programmes meant that little had been decided before Germany went back on the offensive.

## The Crisis, May 1940–February 1941[17]

The German invasion of Norway and Denmark in April 1940 and then of the Netherlands, Belgium and France in May, made Britain's oil situation worse. A new Trade Control Committee dealt with imports, while a new Petroleum Department coordinated activities with other countries.

The situation continued to deteriorate but several hundred ships had evacuated nearly 400,000 men from Dunkirk and across the Channel by the beginning of June 1940. Italy declared war on Britain and France on the 10th, effectively closing the Mediterranean shipping route. France then capitulated on the 22nd, which exposed shipping to sea and air attack from new German bases across occupied France. The only positive effect was that Britain now had access to the tankers which had escaped from occupied countries.

Britain now had to prepare to repel an invasion as the air battle intensified. Steps were taken to protect fuel supplies because it was known that the Germans had used captured fuel to cross France. Over 17,000 small depots were closed while troops were sent to protect 2,000 large depots, with orders to destroy them if necessary. Walls and earth bunds were built to protect tanks during bombing attacks, while many were emptied because they were too close together.[18] The invasion never came but the air attacks did, particularly against the storage tanks along the Thames Estuary. Although 500,000 tons were lost, it was only 5 per cent of oil stocks and far less than expected.

The threat of invasion also closed the English Channel to tankers, while merchant ships and large vessels were banned from sailing around Scotland and down the east coast to the Humber Estuary. Instead, they sailed around the north side of Ireland and into the Irish Sea, before heading to one of the west coast ports. However, the port approaches were easy to mine and they became congested, as captains waited for favourable tides. There was a shortage of large berths, while the lack of tugs meant that tankers had to dock in daylight. Frequent air raids put everyone on edge, which meant it took longer than expected to discharge the oil.

Oil stocks were running low by October 1940 because of delays, so the following procedures were implemented to accelerate off the offloading of oil.

- Many tankers were repaired in American dockyards.
- American tankers shuttled oil from the Caribbean to New York.
- Escorts were organised to accompany the convoys across the Atlantic.
- Fast tankers could sail up the Channel and into the Thames Estuary.

American shipping experts visited Britain to see if the tankers' turnaround time could be improved but there was little that could be done.

The Admiralty had taken control of every small ship to defend the coast, so lorries and canal barges were requisitioned to help the overworked railways move oil around the country. The main improvement was a new pipeline connecting Stanlow to Avonmouth. It could move nearly 3,000 tons a month, making it easier to balance stocks across the county. The Oil Control Board had also started building extra oil storage tanks.

A Tanker Advisory Committee started issuing licenses, authorising voyages and organising convoys in January 1941 but shipping losses increased as the weather improved. So, an appeal for help had to be made to the United States government. Tanker losses during the first two years of the war had peaked at over 100,000 tons in some months and Britain's shipyards was unable to replace it all. It was also increasingly difficult to secure charters.

## From Lend-Lease to Pearl Harbor, 1941[19]

Despite the heavy shipping losses, Britian's biggest problem by the start of 1941 was financial. It was running out of the money needed to buy the $33 million ($1.2 billion today) a month of oil it required. Britain had spent its gold reserve and while buying oil with Sterling would have saved over $4 million ($140 million today) a month, both the American and Dutch suppliers refused to accept it. Britain appealed to the United States government but the Republican Party objected to giving aid, so nothing could be done until the Democratic Party was re-elected in the November 1940 presidential elections.

President Franklin D. Roosevelt proposed a Bill to allow the United States to lend or lease articles to Britain, so it could defend itself. The Democrats voted overwhelmingly in favour, outweighing opposition from the Republicans, and the Bill was accepted on 11 March 1941. A British Petroleum Mission was set up in Washington DC and while it arranged to ship $150 million ($5.9 billion today) of oil bought by the US government, the first tankers would not reach Britain until the summer.

American owned tankers continued to shuttle supplies along the Eastern seaboard, while American shipyards started building tankers for British shipping companies. However, requests for oil industry equipment were refused because America did not want the British oil industry to gain an advantage. The President may have declared a state of 'unlimited national emergency' on 27 May 1941 but he refused to implement rationing across the United States, worried it would upset the people.[20]

A new Petroleum Coordinator started organising seized French and Danish tankers and he also arranged for Canadian, Panamanian and Norwegian tankers to be used. Sea bases were built in Iceland to service the convoy escorts while extra air patrols over Britain's Western Approaches. Meanwhile, American shipping companies were busy degaussing their tankers, ready to cross the Atlantic.

Britain had taken control of oil distribution across the Eastern Hemisphere, while America controlled it across the Western Hemisphere by the end of 1941. The new arrangements had restored the size of the tanker fleet to nearly 7 million tons and it would help Britain restock its reserve. The increase in imports coincided with additional rationing of oil, paraffin and lubricating oil across Britain. Petrol allowances were reduced while the number of inspectors was doubled, to counter the black market in petrol coupons. Steps were also taken to increase the use of alternative fuels, such as creosote-pitch and gas.

However, everything changed when the Japanese attacked Pearl Habor and the Philippines in December. Germany and Italy then declared war on the United States, prompting the Prime Minister to visit President Roosevelt in Washington DC.[21] They agreed to coordinate their sourcing and distribution of oil through a Combined Raw Materials Board. A new Combined Shipping Adjustment Board would organise the shipping.

British oil supplies were sufficient for the time being and while the Petroleum Mission merged with the British Merchant Shipping Mission, the Ministry of War Trasport and the War Shipping Administration worked together to organise the tanker fleet. It was a difficult task deciding how many tankers were needed, so joint organisations were set up in each area to judge local needs, while distribution facilities were pooled.

## A Difficult Year, 1942[22]

The Japanese attack against Pearl Harbor on 7 December 1941, resulted in Britain having to switch fifty tankers from the Atlantic to the Indian Ocean, to counter the threat to Burma and Mandalay. German U-boats were soon swarming the American coastal waters and it took time to implement a convoy system between the Gulf of Mexico and New York because of a shortage of escorts. Even then, the U-boats reduced the available tonnage from 650,000 tons a month down to 600,000 tons. It resulted in British stocks again falling below the safe level, prompting further petrol rationing.

Britain wanted another seventy tankers to increase its reserves but only forty-five were made available and they were known as the Red Gap assistance. Another fifty-four tankers shipped oil for the US troops stationed in Britain and they were known as the Blue Gap assistance. More tankers became available once the Plantation Pipeline connecting the Gulf Coast to North Carolina was commissioned.

British stock levels were again below their minimum levels after 30,000 tons of oil had to be diverted to support Operation Torch, the invasion of northwest Africa in November 1942. America had also withdrawn its fast Greyhound tankers from the Atlantic route because the convoys were too slow for them. It was too dangerous to let them sail across alone, so they were put to work moving oil from the Caribbean to New York.

America also formed the New York Navy Pool, allowing any company's oil to be stored in any company's tank. A new Intelligence and Movements Control Section started supervising the convoys but it had a disastrous start, when it sent nine tankers directly from the Caribbean to North Africa as an experiment. They were intercepted by U-boats and seven were sunk. However, a second attempt by faster Greyhound tankers on the same route was successful. While it would have halved the time the traditional route took, there were insufficient fast escorts and so most of the Greyhound tankers were transferred to the safer Pacific Ocean.

Despite the measures, Britain again had to introduce more rationing as it endured a bad winter. It had not gone unnoticed that the Americans were hoarding fuel and they were still not rationing. The difference in the two nations' attitudes to oil supplies was threatening to explode like 'political dynamite'.[23]

## Preparing for D-Day[24]

By the summer of 1943, Britain was being turned into a huge military base, as tens of thousands of US and Canadian servicemen arrived ahead of D-Day. Hundreds of USAAF and Canadian aircraft were also being deployed to join the bomber offensive. While pressure against Germany was increasing, the aircraft required fuel and that meant extra storage was required. The good news was, that the Thames Estuary oil tanks could be used once again, because the *Luftwaffe* threat was over. Extra tanks were being added next to the west coast ports as well. Huge oil depots were also being built in Misterton in Nottinghamshire, Sandy in Bedfordshire and Aldermaston in Berkshire.

American tanker superintendents reduced the tanker turnaround time at the ports, so the railways had to increase their movements. Meanwhile, pipelines were being laid from the ports to the new storage facilities. They, in turn, were connected to the airfields and to the south-coast ports, ready for the invasion of Europe. Another pipeline between Avonmouth and the Thames had been opened in November 1941 and it was able to deliver 180,000 tons a month to the capital.

Further cooperation between Britain and America over oil supplies stalled as the Chiefs of Staff focused on supplying their increasing commitment to military operations. It was October 1943 before the first United Nations (UN) Oil and Tanker Programme meeting took place and the next one would not be held until May 1944; just before D-Day.[25]

The Combined Shipping Adjustment Board had tried and failed to coordinate the tanker requirements of the US Naval Department, the War Shipping Administration, the Admiralty and the Ministry of War Transport. However, the British would not join a new Allied Tanker Coordinating

Committee until February 1944 because it was wary of handing control of oil shipments over to the US War and Naval Departments.

The U-boats had been defeated by improved convoy tactics and technical innovations by May 1943. Forty-three U-boats had been sunk while the number of tankers lost every month had dropped from ten down to two. Meanwhile, American shipyards were launching 500,000 tons of Greyhound tankers a month. While most were deployed to the Pacific Theatre, they did release the smaller, slower tankers for the Atlantic and Mediterranean routes. Meanwhile, the amount of oil available had been increased by shipments of crude oil from South America. Two pipelines called Big Inch and Little Big Inch were also transferring 1.7 million tons of crude oil a month from Texas to New York, reducing the number of tankers required on the eastern seaboard route.

Planning for Operation Overlord created the spirit of cooperation that the British had been asking for since Pearl Harbor. At long last, Allied Tanker Coordinating Committees were set up in Washington DC and London, to discuss the deployment of tankers. Planning the deliveries of shipping oil, motor fuel and aviation required for Operation Overlord took many months to organise, as consumption increased by 250,000 tons a month.[26] The oil terminals were being pushed to their limits, as imports increased by 60 per cent, but domestic use fell by 50,000 tons a month, as thousands more cars were taken off the road.

## The Invasion of Europe[27]

The Petroleum Warfare Department considered how to transport oil across the English Channel to support the invasion force under the codename Pluto. They planned to transfer 5,000 tons a day by tanker while another 5,000 tons would be piped along the sea floor, through a hollow armoured cable codenamed Hais and a welded steel pipe codenamed Hamel. A route linking Sandown Bay on the Isle of Wight to Port-en-Bessin in Normandy was codenamed Bambi. Another route codenamed Dumbo would connect Dungeness in Kent to a point near Calais in October, once the Allies had advanced across France.

The links for the pipes and cables were ready by March 1944, while small tankers were put on standby in case the plan failed. Temporary oil terminals codenamed Tombolas were also prepared, while vessels codenamed Chants were loaded with small fuel containers. However, the Pluto plan disappointed because the pipes took too long to install and they were easy to damage. Instead, the Tombola pipelines were used to transfer oil from ship to shore, so it could be pumped along pipelines to inland storage tanks.

The advance across France soon increased the demand for oil products from 1.4 million to 2.1 million tons per month. The demand for motor fuel also quadrupled. The amounts required for Operation Anvil in the south of France and for the Pacific campaign also increased.

The increasing commitments to the military operations resulted in British domestic reserves being reduced to dangerously levels.[28] However, the liberation of France reduced the threats from German U-boats and aircraft, allowing several restrictions to be lifted. Tankers were allowed to sail south of Ireland once again, after four years of having to divert around the north coast. Around sixty trains carrying oil left the west coast ports every day, while nine tankers permanently shuttled oil between Britain's ports. Greyhound tankers were also allowed to pass through the Channel in September 1944, providing London with direct supplies of oil once again.

## The End of the War[29]

Plans to reopen the French ports, so oil could be delivered directly had to be revised because the German troops wrecked Cherbourg and Brest. The Germans holding St Nazaire and Lorient would refuse to surrender until the end of the war. A lot of oil would be shipped to Le Harve, after it was captured in September work on tanker facilities in Cherbourg started around the same time. Ostend could only handle small vessels and while Antwerp was captured early, it would take until November to clear the Scheldt Estuary.

Arguments over oil deliveries intensified when it became clear that the Air Ministry had overestimated the amount of 100-octane spirit the RAF needed. The US Chiefs of Staff then challenged the calculations made by British Army and the Royal Navy before cutting their reserve limits. It left them all with minimum amounts, which Mr Harold Wilkinson, head of the British Petroleum Mission in Washington DC, referred to as 'military madness'.[30] At the same time, the allocations to the US troops fighting across the Pacific Ocean were being increased.

Discussions with the Army-Navy Petroleum Board Mission soon restored British military supplies to a safe level. However, first the Combined Chiefs of Staff and then the Munitions Assignments Committee decided how much oil Britain could have in future. While Britain struggled to distribute its dwindling stocks over the winter of 1944–1945, the US Chiefs of Staff were planning the upcoming invasion of Okinawa, off the south coast of Japan. Britain eventually had to reduce its demands and it took further negotiations at the Yalta Conference in February 1945 to smooth over the differences.

The United Nations Oil and Tanker Programme was reviewed in March 1945 but the situation remained unchanged until Germany surrendered and tankers could move freely in the Western Hemisphere. Over 5 million tons of oil products had been delivered to the Allied forces in Europe by the end of the war.

Some American politicians and economists thought Britain was stockpiling American aid to improve its post-war position. They were concerned that American oil reserves were being depleted while British ones in the Middle East left alone. They also thought that the Lend-Lease equipment was being used to improve refineries across the British Empire. Some were concerned that the amount of oil being sent to Britain could influence the presidential elections in November 1944. So, America decided to take control of the oil being delivered to Britain for the US armed forces, to prevent it being stockpiled for use after the war.

Altogether, 86 million tons of oil were delivered to Britain for domestic or military use. Nearly $1.5 billion (over $53 billion today) was provided through the Lend-Lease programme, while more was delivered for the US armed forces stationed in Britain and fighting across the Mediterranean and European theatres.

## Aviation Fuel

The Air Ministry had to source aviation fuel for the RAF's aircraft. Shell set up a plant next to its refinery in Stanlow on the River Mersey before the war and bought the iso-octanes it needed to make enough.[31] However, the quantity of aviation fuel and engine lubricants doubled when Scheme L increased the size of the RAF in 1938. The high-speed aircraft engines being designed also required a higher grade of petrol, so the Fuel Research Board started blending iso-octane and high octane to make an improved 100-octane spirit. ICI and Shell also built a new refinery in Heysham in Lancashire and two more in Trinidad.

A shortage of 100-octane spirit loomed in the autumn of 1941. The Air Ministry wanted an extra 20,000 tons a month for the planned bomber offensive and the RAF's training programmes. However, the USAAF doubled its requirements after the Japanese attack on Pearl Harbor in December 1941; far more than it would require. In the meantime, the Combined Munitions Assignments Board relied on the Aviation Petroleum Products Allocation Committee, to decide how much the RAF and the USAAF received.

The US Army and Navy increased their demands for 100-octane spirit from 140,000 tons a month in 1942 to 200,000 tons in 1943. Meanwhile, the RAF wanted an improved 100/130 octane mix, which had to be imported from America or the Persian Gulf.[32] So, Britain built a pilot plant to make it at Billingham on the River Tees before building a full-scale one at Heysham in Lancashire. America also built a plant that started making 100/130 octane mix in the autumn of 1943, securing enough stocks for the RAF. Tankers started delivering it to Thames Haven and it was then piped to the Air Ministry's inland depots. It meant that plans for a second plant at Stanlow on the River Mersey could be shelved.

Demand for aviation fuel soon outstripped supply, as the number of RAF and USAAF squadrons increased. It would end up being seven times the amount envisaged at the beginning of the war. The Joint Aeronautical Board asked for its fair share of aviation fuel but the Combined Chiefs of Staff gave the battles in the Mediterranean a higher priority. Britain was sure that too much was being set aside for the USAAF training programme, so the RAF and USAAF met in July 1943 to decide what their minimum stocks needed to be.

Arguments over aviation fuel resumed because the USAAF insisted on asking for more to train air crews, while the RAF needed extra for the bomber offensive. However, the Air Ministry had to reduce its order after it was discovered that it had overestimated the RAF's needs; but it demands were still not being met.

Imports rose again, as the demand for aviation spirit doubled ahead of D-Day. The plants in Billingham, Stanlow and Heysham then started making a 150-octane mix to power the fast aircraft used to chase the V-1 rockets aimed at London.

Greyhound tankers were once again allowed to pass through the Channel in September 1944. It meant that aviation spirit only had to be piped a short distance to the USAAF's airfields across southeast England. From then on, the supply of aviation spirit for the RAF was secure.

*Chapter 5*

# The Metal Industries

## The Iron Ore Industry

Britain imported iron ore from Sweden, France and Spain in the 1930s. It continued to do so throughout the first winter of the war, but there were often shortages, so furnaces had to dampened down (allowed to cool) until more arrived.[1] The invasion of Norway and Denmark in April 1940 stopped the import of high-quality Swedish imports through the Baltic Sea while the Fall of France a month later further cut supplies. Shipping routes from Spain and North Africa were also threatened by U-boats.[2]

Britain had lost over 75 per cent of its iron ore imports by June 1940, so the amounts shipped from North America had to increase by a similar amount over the summer. High quality ores were imported from Canada and standard ores came from America but the shipping available reduced over the winter of 1940–1941, due to bad weather and U-boat activity. So, finished steel was imported rather than iron ore because it took up less cargo space. A campaign to reduce the amount of steel used for domestic building across Britain also helped to replenish stocks by the end of 1941.

American ore and steel prices continued to rise, so the British buying agents tried to buy as much as possible from Canada. Meanwhile, the cost of shipping insurances went up as the U-boat danger increased. Fortunately, the Lend-Lease scheme started covering the costs after March 1941 and reasonably priced iron ore could be obtained over the summer. However, American iron ore supplies became scarce when the US military demanded huge amounts of steel to rearm after the attack against Pearl Harbor in December 1941.

One alternative considered by the British government, was to mine iron ore in Cumberland. However, poor working conditions, low wages and the isolated location made it difficult to recruit labour. The ore was also poor quality[3] and furnaces had to be upgraded so it could be used. It produced lower grade steel which was sold for building work.

Investment in excavation machinery helped to increase the amount of British iron ore available. Recruitment increased after checking registers for experienced men and offering them incentives. Irish workers and prisoners of war of war were also put to work in the quarries and mines. Working in the iron ore mining was even offered as an option to military service after the autumn of 1942 and it increased the iron ore workforce to 160,000. While the quantity of iron ore extracted was increased by 40 per cent, transporting it to the foundries put an added strain on the busy rail network.[4]

## The Steel Industry

### Manufacturing Steel Before the Wars[5]

There was a depression around the world in the steel industry following the First World War. An International Steel Agreement started securing ore sources, setting prices and agreeing how steel was distributed in 1926. However, individual companies continued to struggle and the English Steel Corporation Limited merged the interests of Vickers, Vickers-Armstrongs and Cammell Laird's in Sheffield. However, Britain's industry still faced stiff competition from America and Germany, while the Agreement was terminated after a second economic depression followed the Wall Street Crash in October 1929.

The British Iron and Steel Federation was set up in 1935. Stewarts & Lloyds had just completed its new steelworks at Corby in Northamptonshire, while Richard Thomas & Co. Limited had modernised its works at Scunthorpe and bought the Ebbw Vale Steel, Iron & Coal Company in South Wales. British (Guest Keen, Baldwins) Iron and Steel Co. Limited was improving its works at Port Talbot, while Colvilles Limited was making 25,000 tons a week at Ravenscraig near Glasgow. However, the British Iron and Steel Federation recommended that more steel works were built, but it would take time to build them.

Other major companies making steel, were the Consett Iron Company Limited near Durham and Dorman Long & Co. Limited at Middlesbrough.

The Lancashire Steel Corporation Limited was at Irlam near Manchester and the Park Gate Iron and Steel Company was at Rotherham. Firth-Vickers Stainless Steels Limited was also formed when the stainless steel concerns of the English Steel Corporation Limited, Thomas Firth & Sons Limited, and John Brown & Company merged in Sheffield.

However, the main problem was that the British Iron and Steel Federation and the Board of Trade could not agree about the quantity of steel the armed forces would need if the country went to war. Time was also running out by the time Britain and France started discussing their respective steel industries in 1938. The German occupation of the Sudetenland in October 1938 stopped the steel imports from Czechoslovakia and while it was a warning, it was too late to build up stocks of iron ore to make steel or bauxite to make aluminium. While the export of essential materials was banned, it was impossible to move foundries from areas likely to be bombed.

## Britain on its Own, 1939–1941[6]

There was a huge demand for steel from the armaments factories during the early months of the war. While the foundries could make enough, the railways struggled to move enough coal from the mines to the foundries and enough steel to the factories. A Materials Committee tried to make sure that all three supply departments received enough steel, distributing it according to priorities. Unfortunately, the engineering factories placed too much emphasis on making the basic parts which resulted in a shortage of specialist parts. This led to bottlenecks in the assembly factories and took time to redress the balance.

Each supply department used a different method to calculate how much steel they needed, making it difficult for the foundries to get the quantities right. It later became clear that all three supply departments were demanding more steel than they needed, so they could build up stockpiles.

Churchill's government discovered that only 60 per cent of new steel was being used for armaments when it took over in May 1940. So, a new licensing system made sure the armaments industry received more, while domestic supplies were cut. Another problem was that the steel foundries were struggling to produce enough parts which required special heat treatments, such as the prop shafts in aircraft engines. It resulted in a new Drop Forgings

Subcommittee coordinating the demands of the three supply departments, by making them estimate their long-term orders.

As we have seen, the industry faced a serious shortage of iron ore in the spring of 1940. The Germans had cut off the supplies from Scandinavia and France, while they were threatening the shipping routes from Spain and North Africa.[7] Meanwhile, the British Army needed to rearm all its units after abandoning its equipment in Dunkirk, while the RAF needed as many fighter planes as it could get.

The government wanted steel production to triple to 650,000 tons a month. However, it was too expensive to build new foundries and they would take too long to build. They would also have specialist labour and would it be impossible to recruit any unskilled labour to train up, because other industries paid better wages. Steel companies tried to stop their key men being enlisted but they were still having to prove how many they needed to run their foundries.[8] The government helped by taking a tight control of the steel industry, telling told the foundries exactly what they had to make, rather than them just churning out steel.

As we have seen above, the government took steps to import more iron ore from America, to make up for the deficit. It was also anxious to secure large quantities of finished steel because it took up much less shipping space than iron ore, however, the British Purchasing Commission had been arguing with the Iron and Steel Control over who should buy it. An Anglo-French Purchasing Board resolved the argument just before France's surrender caused the problem to resurface.

The change from European iron ore to American steel increased the monthly import costs from £1 million to over £8 million (£39 million to £315 million today) and Britain was soon running out of money. While the Lend-Lease programme ended financial worries in March 1941, it would cost Britain dearly after the war.

America wanted long-term programmes detailing exactly what Britain was going to use its steel for, now that it was financing the trade. It meant the Ministry of Production had to keep a tight rein on the supply departments, making sure they ordered the right amounts to keep them above the minimum stock levels.

The Ministry of Labour introduced a Works Order in the spring of 1941, to stop men leaving their job without permission, as well as stopping companies dismissing anyone without permission. The steel industry was then ring fenced in August, to stop men being transferred to other industries. The foundries needed skilled men but they also required strong unskilled men to do their heavy work, the sort being targeted by the armed forces. The scheme gave the foundries preferential calls on labour until another 200,000 had been found. Eventually, 430,000 men and 95,000 women would work in the steel industry.

## An Allied Effort, 1942–1945[9]

As seen above, the US War and Naval Departments wanted huge amounts of steel to rearm after the attack on Pearl Harbor in December 1941. Their demands pushed British steel orders to the back of the queue. American steel production would increase by 60 per cent in 1942, while demands for alloy steel increased by 230 per cent. Britain only wanted 4.75 million tons of steel a month but problems on the American rail network delayed a lot from reaching the ports. There were then issues arranging enough shipping as the U-boat attacks against the Atlantic convoys increased.

At times, there could be 500,000 tons stacked at the ports waiting to be shipped, causing British exports to fall by 10 per cent. It meant that British furnaces often had to be dampened down while engineering factories stood idle waiting for the next batch of steel. It left the British armed forces short of everything, even though they were fighting across North Africa. Tensions would grow when it became known that the US military was getting everything it wanted, while domestic building continued unabated across America.

A lot of the steel imported to Britain was required to build the airfields required by the USAAF aircraft squadrons being shipped over for the bomber offensive. Even more steel would be required to build the bases required by the tens of thousands of US soldiers heading to Britain, ready to take part in the invasion of Normandy.

Operation Torch, the large-scale amphibious landing in North Africa in November 1942 required a huge amount of shipping to support it, which caused shortages of all kinds of supplies, particularly steel. But a suggestion to form a Combined Steel Committee of the American, Canadian and British steel industries was rejected. It left the British Purchasing Commission having to negotiate with five departments:

- Office of Lend-Lease Administration
- American Requirements Committee
- Combined Production and Resources Board
- Production Board
- US Treasury

An Anglo-American Steel Committee started checking British steel requirements in 1943 but different management styles made it difficult to organise anything.[10] British requests were studied in detail and some were rejected, while lavish amounts of steel were made available for the US armed forces and building projects across America. Meanwhile, Britain had managed to reduce its domestic consumption down to just 15 per cent, making sure as much steel as possible was used for armaments. The financier Bernard Baruch would later state that the US War and Navel Departments' lavish approach to waging war had cost American an extra $100 million ($3.5 billion today).

## Summary of the Steel Industry[11]

Government control of the raw material industries had been haphazard at the start of the First World War but lessons were learned as the months passed. Controls were renewed at the start of the Second World War and many industrialists applied the same principles which had been successful twenty-five years earlier. Winston Churchill had been the Minister of Munitions during the final months of the First World War, at a time when the munitions industry was stretched to the limit. So, he was aware of the problems posed by the imports of raw materials, steel shortages and industrial unrest.

Key workers had remained at their jobs, while the government took control of the buying and distribution of what iron ore and steel was required to make armaments. The British Iron and Steel Federation helped set up Iron and Steel Control and its directorates mirrored how industry was organised.

The quantity of steel used by the armed forces increased from around 60 per cent of what the country needed in 1940 to over 80 per cent by 1943. However, the three supply departments always required different quantities because they had unique demands. The Admiralty needed a lot to keep enough warships and merchant ships afloat. It had increased its demand for steel to maintain and repair warships and merchant ships from 83,000 to 130,000 tons a month by 1943. The Ministry of Aircraft Production (MAP) used around 100,000 tons of steel a month but a lot of it was required for building new aircraft factories. Meanwhile, its demand for lightweight alloys doubled to 44,000 tons a month, as the demand for aircraft increased. The Ministry of Supply had more than doubled its demand for steel from 230,000 to 470,000 tons a month by 1942, to make tanks, equipment, weapons and ammunition for the British Army.

The quantity of steel made in Britain may have tripled during the war but its increase in production was small compared to its Allies. Canadian production had increased seven-fold. However, American steel production increased a massive twenty-fold to 32 million tons during the time it was at war.

## The Alloy Industry[12]

Large amounts of lightweight aluminium were required to build the modern cantilevered monoplanes required by the RAF. The loss of 25,000 tons of French imports a month in June 1940, followed by the loss of Greece in April 1941, meant Britain had to import aluminium from Canada. It, in turn, had to ship bauxite from British Guiana (now called Guyana) in South America.

Lord Beaverbrook wanted as much aluminium as possible when he was appointed the head of the Ministry of Aircraft Production in May 1940. However, he did not know how much of each alloy was required, nor when the deliveries would arrive. He got around the problem by announcing a scrap campaign in the summer of 1940, which involved a lot of sorting and testing what was collected, to make sure they were suitable alloys. Once the aircraft industry gained production experience, it was discovered that Beaverbrook had been asking for double the alloy the aircraft industry needed. However, the RAF had been supplied with enough fighters to defeat the *Luftwaffe* and end the threat of invasion.

The process of smelting bauxite into aluminium by the Bayer and Hall-Héroult processes required huge amounts of electricity, so new plants were built near hydro-electric power plants in mountainous areas such as Wales and Scotland. The British Aluminium Company Limited had smelters in Foyers, Kinlochleven and Lochaber in the Scottish Highlands; it also had one in Burntisland on the Firth of Forth. The company also had rolling mills in Milton in Cambridgeshire and Warrington in Cheshire.

There was a shortage of labour in these areas, so Irish labour and women who were willing to be relocated were drafted in. The smelting plants worked at full capacity because each worker could cast enough alloy ingots or sheets to create enough work for twenty-five others in the engineering workshops, rolling mills and assembly plants. Eventually, government investment in the smelting industry doubled home output of aluminium to 4,500 tons a month.

The fabricating factories were based around Birmingham and while labour and accommodation were in high demand, there was no spare labour to set up any other factories. Again, Irish workers were employed, while 5,000 labourers who had just finished building airfields were made available. Extensive mechanisation in the factories also allowed 32,000 women from the textile industry to be employed. By 1942, skilled workers had to be transferred from the iron and steel factories, as the demand for extra alloys increased. The iron, steel, and alloy industries eventually had to be considered as one and ring fenced, to make the best use of the limited labour available. Nearly 100,000 were eventually employed making alloy metal parts.

Britain started shipping bauxite direct from the Gold Coast on the west coast of Africa (now known as Ghana), when new smelting plants started work in 1942. It required four tons of bauxite to make one ton of aluminium and imports doubled as the MAP increased its demand to 44,000 tons of alloy metal a month.

A lot of aluminium was recycled from crashed aircraft and lorries would collect 12,500 tons of scrap every month, so it could be broken down and sorted at the MAP's two reclamation depots. It was around one third of what was required, reducing the amount of imported bauxite required by 60,000 tons a month.

Despite the increases in imports and home production, problems continue to interrupt production because the focus was on making the large parts. Shortages of smaller parts and sheet alloy would hold up the assembly lines from time to time, delaying the completion of aircraft. It took a lot of planning and organising to get the balance right, so that aircraft production could be maximised.

Improved aircraft designs resulted in faster speeds and that, in turn, caused problems. Higher quality aluminium was required make the increasingly complex parts for the new aircraft and engine designs.

# Chapter 6

# The Explosives Industry

## Making Explosives

Three types of Royal Ordnance Factories were involved in the making of shells and bombs:[1]

- Some Explosive ROFs produced the propellant, cordite; others produced the high explosives called TNT and RDX; the rest produced tetryl or ammonium nitrate.
- Engineering ROFs made the shell casings and fuse parts.
- Filling ROFs filled the shell casing with explosives.

Only a few of each type of factory had remained in business after the First World War and they were all in the areas vulnerable to bombing. So, large factories were built in safer areas, in the north and west of England, Wales and Scotland, during the rearmament period. However, most were not ready when war was declared on 3 September 1939. Fortunately, extra money and labour made sure the work was complete before the Germans attacked the BEF in the Low Countries and France in May 1940.

## Propellants

The Explosive ROFs made the two types of explosives required by shells. A propellant explodes in the breech of the gun, propelling the shell towards its target. The propellant was Cordite RDB (Research Department formula B), a mixture of 52 per cent collodion, 42 per cent nitroglycerin and 6 per cent petroleum jelly. The mix was moulded into spaghetti like sticks, so it was easier to insert into the cartridge, which was fixed to the shell base.

Before the war, most of the cordite was made by the Research Department at the Royal Arsenal, the Royal Gunpowder Factory in Waltham and the Royal

Naval Cordite Factory. Cordite SC (Solventless Cordite) used centralite instead of a solvent and it was mainly used by the Royal Navy. Towards the end of the war, nitroguanidine was used to make Cordite N or Cordite NQ. The improved formula reduced muzzle flash, making it harder for the enemy to spot a battery position. It also caused less damage, so barrels lasted longer before they needed relining.

The Royal Gunpowder Factory in Waltham, north London, could make 2,000 tons of propellants a month but it was vulnerable to air attack. The decision to increase the size of the British Army in 1937 resulted in the Holton Heath cordite factory reopening, even though Dorset was vulnerable. While work started on a large site in Bishopton, west of Glasgow, it took too long to finish. It then proved difficult to recruit and transport all the 17,000 workers. So, two smaller sites, which were easier to build and manage, were chosen in North Wales and Nottinghamshire.

- ROF Bishopton opened near Glasgow in June 1940.
- ROF Wrexham opened in North Wales in March 1941.
- ROF Ranskill opened in Nottinghamshire in March 1942.

## High Explosives

The high explosive detonates either when the shell hits the target or after a set time fixed by a fuse.

The Telecommunications Research Establishment started working on a proximity fuse during the early months of the war and Sir Henry Tizard shared the idea with the Americans in September 1940. A micro transmitter sent a continuous wave, which was received by the casing. The signal was interrupted when the shell approached the ground, creating a small electrical charge which triggered the fuse and detonated the explosive above the target. Air bursts were very effective against infantry and Pozit fuses were first used by American troops in December 1944 during the battle of the Bulge. Anti-aircraft guns used proximity fuses to explode shells near aircraft. They were also useful against V-1 flying bombs.

A mixture of Trinitrotoluene (TNT) and ammonium nitrate formed the part of the shell which exploded. The Billingham ammonium nitrate factory

Middlesbrough was thought to be vulnerable to air attack, so work started on alternative sites in safer areas.

The pre-war rearmament programmes for the expansion of the British Army meant that ICI was making most of the 1,750 tons of TNT a month by the time war broke out. Explosives factories had to operate a three-shift system to run the continuous process and while production increased steadily, explosives were still imported from North America as an insurance against emergencies.

Work started on two new TNT factories in 1936, so it could be made a safe, remote areas. Three more were added during the war years:

- ROF Irvine opened in Ayrshire in March 1939.
- ROF Pembrey opened in south Wales in November 1939.
- ROF Drigg opened in Cumberland (now Cumbria) in 1941.
- ROF Bridgwater opened in Somerset in August 1941.
- ROF Sellafield opened in Cumberland in March 1943.

A storage depot for explosives was built at Dunham-on-the-Hill in Cheshire.

A Director General of Explosives Production took over the manufacture of explosives in 1941, because the demand for the bombs required by RAF was about to increase. ROF Pembrey in south Wales also started making the ammonium nitrate required to mix with the TNT, removing the reliance on the vulnerable Billingham factory.

ROF Pembrey also made small amounts of tetryl, a booster explosive used to detonate the main charge in a shell or bomb. The Royal Arsenal also trialled small amounts of RDX (Research Department Explosive), which was 50 per cent more powerful than the standard mix of TNT and ammonium nitrate. New facilities in Bishopton near Glasgow and Bridgwater in Somerset, then started making it for the RAF's bombs, while extra supplies were imported from America.

Around 2,000 tons of cordite a month were being made in Britain in 1939 but the amount soon increased to over 5,000 tons. Around 1,750 tons a month of high explosive were being produced at the start of the war but the amount would peak at over 17,000 tons. By 1944, it was clear that too much ammunition had been made, so the Pembrey site started breaking up the surplus shells for recycling. Huge amounts of explosives would be dumped in Beaufort's Dyke, an area of deep water in the Irish Sea, between Belfast and Stranraer, after the war.

## The Royal Filling Factories[2]

The Royal Arsenal was the original filling factory but the War Office was given money to build new filling factories in 1935, because it was in a vulnerable area. No. 1 Chorley was built in Lancashire; No. 2 was built in Bridgend in South Wales, as was No. 3 in Glascoed. A second site in Bridgend was added to make shells for the Admiralty, which needed a different high explosive because excessive moisture made ammonium nitrate unstable.

It would take three years to complete the factories. Another seventeen small filling factories were authorised when the decision was taken to expand the British Army in 1939:

- No. 4 Hereford
- No. 5 Swynnerton, Staffordshire
- No. 6 Risley, Cheshire
- No. 7 Kirkby, Liverpool
- No. 8 Aycliffe, Durham
- No. 9 Thorp Arch, West Yorkshire
- No. 10 Queniborough, Leicester
- No. 11 Brackla, South Wales
- No. 12 Wootton Bassett (never built)
- No. 13 Macclesfield (never built and the number was reallocated)
- No. 14 Ruddington, Nottingham
- No. 15 Walsall
- No. 16 Elstow, Bedford
- No. 17 Featherstone
- No. 18 Burghfield, Reading
- No. 19 Tutbury (never built)
- No. 20 Northampton (never built and the number was reallocated)

The filling factories were ready by the time the Phoney War ended in May 1940 and a Deputy Director General was appointed to coordinate their work with that of the factories manufacturing the explosives. However, it was a challenge recruiting and transporting large numbers of workers to the factories. It was an even bigger challenge managing a new factory, because it involved inexperienced labour working on dangerous processes. Safety was paramount and the industry had to remember the lessons learnt from the accidental destruction of several filling factories during the First World War.[3] Air raids also caused problems and a large part of the Royal Arsenal's work was dispersed to other factories during the Blitz.

The two-shift system involved long working hours, which resulted in excessive fatigue and low morale. So, a three-shift system was introduced in the summer of 1941, to end the high turnover of workers. The number of workers employed by the filling factories peaked at 153,000 in 1942 and a few employed over 25,000, making them the largest factories during the war. However, the campaigns in the Mediterranean soon proved that the number of shells required was far less than estimated. It meant that production could slow down, while the workforce was reduced to 100,000 in 1943.

Four large and twenty-six small factories were also built to make bullets. These are the large ones:

- ROF No. 13 Radway Green in Cheshire (reallocated number)
- ROF No. 20 Blackpole in Worcestershire (reallocated number)
- ROF No. 21 Spennymoor in County Durham
- ROF No. 22 Steeton in West Yorkshire

Three ROFs were built to fill the bullets with propellants.

- ROF Summerfield in Birmingham
- ROF Hirwaun in South Wales
- ROF Southall in London

# Chapter 7

# North American Imports

## The Outbreak of War Until Lend-Lease[1]

The British government initially assumed that it would have to rely on its own industries if it went to war. America only had a small armaments industry and Britain could not afford to import huge amounts, even if it expanded. President Franklin D. Roosevelt had also a placed embargo on exporting military items when he passed a Neutrality Act in August 1935, to prevent America getting dragged into a European war.

Arthur Purvis set up a British Purchasing Commission in Washington DC when the revised Neutrality Act allowed Britain and France to start buying armaments in November 1939. A Coordinating Committee was set up to prevent competition between Britain and France and it told Roosevelt's liaison committee what the two countries wanted to buy.

American armaments companies were reluctant to expand their businesses because of the criticisms which had been levelled at them during the First World War. Those that did get involved either wanted advance payments for the orders or money to extend their factories. So, Britain struggled on making weapons, ammunition and equipment, while investing in American factories, in the hope they could help later.

Orders quickly increased to 5,800 tons of armaments and 400 planes a month but many were placed as an insurance, in case a British factory was bombed. Large amounts of steel and metal alloys were also bought from the United States Corporations and the Bethlehem Steel Corporation but steps were taken, to make sure British orders did not interfere with the American domestic market.

The US War Department also sent weapons and ammunition from its reserve to Britain. Obsolete weapons and ammunition rejected by the US Army were also offered. For example, large quantities of the M1917

Enfield Rifles, Lewis light machine guns and Browing M1917 machine guns were shipped to Britain to arm the Home Guard.

The deteriorating military situation across Europe reduced Britian's ability to make armaments. The invasions of Norway and Denmark in April 1940, followed attacks against the Low Countries and France in May, forced Britain to buy materials from other countries. It also had to find alternative shipping.[2]

The British supply departments wanted the American factories to use their designs and while the US armed forces thought some were better than theirs, American designs were easier to mass produce. The US War Department refused to adopt any British designs while the US government refused to make them, because they did not want to be left with stockpiles of British armaments if London capitulated.

Britain was not in a position to negotiate in the summer of 1940 because it had to reequip the tens of thousands of British soldiers who just been evacuated from France as quickly as possible. The RAF also had to expand to defend the nation from air attack, while the Royal Navy had to patrol Britain's coastal waters, as well as protect the convoys bringing vital raw material and goods.

So, Arthur Purvis accepted American weapons for the British armed forces, stating; 'that it is only if we agree promptly on common types of weapons, that we can hope to take advantage of the plan.'[3] It meant American factories could start on British orders. Meanwhile, London looked to Ottawa, to see if the Canadian armaments industry would work to British designs.

Spending on imports quickly increased to $750 million ($26 billion today) a month but Britain was soon running out of money. The Secretary of the American Treasury, Henry Morgenthau Jr, started covering Britain's expenses, so companies would continue to make armaments. He also suspended the Treasury's Income Tax demands against Britain's purchases and arranged to import more British goods, to counterbalance the debt.

America ended its neutrality policy in September 1940, when it agreed to supply Britain with fifty aging destroyers, to protect the Atlantic convoys. It also offered cargo space and the use of repair facilities in American shipyards. In return Britain issued ninety-nine-year leases for eight military bases in Newfoundland and the British West Indies.

The British Purchasing Commission was struggling to secure any more armaments suppliers until the US War Department stepped forward in

November 1940. Its agents helped with contracts, advice and supervision, as well as inspection, storage and transport. It meant over 2,000 tanks could be ordered, while 11,000 vehicles bought by the French were sent to Britain. Over 5,500 tons of explosives, 85 million rounds, and 500,000 shells were soon being shipped every month, as well as a wide range of items required to clear bottlenecks in the British factories.

Britain would spend $3.1 billion ($110 billion today) on armaments in 1940, more than the United States government's total defence budget. The President's deputy, Harry L. Hopkins, even visited Britain in January 1941, to ask Churchill's government why it was ordering so many armaments. President Roosevelt decided to start the Lend-Lease programme in March 1941, after hearing his assessment. He arranged for the government to buy the factories and shipyards which had been financed by British money, which restored Britain's dollar reserves and gave the American armaments industry a boost. He also set $13 billion ($460 billion today) aside, so tank and aircraft production could increase.

## Lend-Lease to Pearl Harbor[4]

Britain's financial struggles were eased after President Roosevelt signed the 'Act to Promote the Defence of the United States' on 11 March 1941. The Act stated that the American government would finance the making of armaments and then lend or lease them to Britain, so it could defend itself. The only proviso was that the US armed forces had priority over British requests. In future, the British Purchasing Commission would stop buying directly from the armaments factories and tell several American organisations what the British armed forces required instead:

- The US War and US Naval Departments organised armaments.
- The US Maritime Commission dealt with merchant shipping requests.
- The Department of Agriculture sourced food, cotton, and other raw materials.
- The US Treasury's Procurement Division bought everything else.

The Lend-Lease Act required President Roosevelt to get the US War and Naval Departments to approve the British requests before giving the Treasury permission to allocate the funds. The First Appropriation Act amounted to $7 billion ($275 billion today) but the money was soon spent. It was also a complicated and lengthy process getting orders to the delivery stage.

Washington DC had asked Britain for a shopping list following the Fall of France back in June 1940, but the British Supply Council had been unable to draw one up before the time the Lend-Lease programme was introduced in March 1941. So, a Defence Aid Division was set up to deal with Lend-Lease transactions while an Anglo-American Food Committee was set up.

Once the budget had been spent, the President had to prioritise American and British requests, so the War Production Board started drawing up a Controlled Materials Plan. It also decided that everyone's demands were too high, so it cut 25 per cent of items from both the United States and British requests. It meant that Lyttelton had to work with the US Army's Chief of Logistics, General Brehon B. Somervell, to decide the priorities. Their plan was to review the lists every six months, changing them if any strategic plans altered. The British also had to prove that its armed forces had run out of an item before it could ask for anymore.

General Archibald Wavell sent Brigadier John Whiteley to Washington DC in May, to tell the British Supply Council what the Middle East Command needed to defend the Suez Canal. However, Washington DC was still wary about making items only used by the British armed forces. So, items were split into three categories:

- Common warlike stores used by all the armed forces.
- Non-common warlike stores only used by the British or Soviets.
- Civilian supplies used by all nations.

Hopkins monitored Britain's demands, verified its requests and analysed what was being spent. He kept Congress informed, because its members wanted to know that the Lend-Lease money was being spent wisely and that Britain was not selling armaments to other nations. The many Republican members of the

Senate and House of Representatives who had voted against the Lend-Lease programme were particularly interested.[5]

Raw materials were ordered once a request had been approved but it took a different length of time to make each item. The Lend-Lease Administration Office then had to organise the rail transport and shipping and it could be weeks before an item crossed the Atlantic Ocean. Ships full of supplies could be randomly sunk by U-boats or mines and while storms would delay shipments for days, winter often reduced the amount shipped by a third.

The President and the Prime Minister agreed that requests would be made through the Supply Council at the Atlantic Conference in August 1941.[6] Roosevelt then signed off the final $300 million from the first appropriation before Edward R. Stettinius Jr was appointed head of the Lend-Lease Administration Office.

The British Supply Council had issued a comprehensive list of items before the second instalment of money (called the First Protocol) was agreed on 1 October 1941. The Admiralty and Air Ministry simply stated how many of each type of ship and aircraft they wanted. However, the Ministry of Supply had to list every weapon, type of ammunition and piece of equipment it needed, which took a long time to compile.

A Production Management Office dealt with America's industrial mobilisation for the first nine months of Lend-Lease and there was little urgency because the county was not at war. British demands did not fit well with the mass production methods preferred by American armaments companies either, so the orders were made low priority or even ignored. Firms also preferred to ship complete items rather than components, so only a fraction of the promised orders had reached Britain by the time a new production schedule called the Victory Programme was announced in October 1941. While the Defence Aid Division and the Anglo-American Food Committee worked towards compiling a list of items, Britain was never sure what it was going to receive. It made it difficult for the Admiralty, Air Ministry and the War Office to organise training or plan military operations.

Everything changed when Japan attacked Pearl Harbor on 7 December 1941 and the Philippines the following day; Germany and Italy then declared war on the United States on the 11th.[7] The recently agreed Victory Programme was abandoned just as a Second Appropriation Act was announced. It had set aside $5 billion ($200 billion today), which was enough for everything Britain wanted. Only this time the money had to be spent by a commitment date rather than a delivery date.

America was at war, so plans were put on hold while President Roosevelt and Prime Minister Churchill met in Washington DC over the New Year. The Arcadia Conference in December 1941 resulted in a new Munitions Assignments Board being set up to decide what Britain would receive.

The Admiralty, the Ministry of Aircraft Production and the Ministry of Supply were told to divide their demands into four categories:

- Urgent items required to keep British production going.
- Urgent items needed for the North African campaign.
- Items which could be made by British factories.
- Non-urgent items.

However, President Roosevelt stipulated that aircraft would only be delivered to Britain once there were no more American air crews available. So, only 4,000 out of 7,500 aircraft would be sent, leaving the RAF short during the North African and Burma campaigns.

Combined war production was supposed to follow the decision to attack Germany first, which had been decided at the Arcadia Conference. The Defence Aid Division may have been renamed the International Division but the US War Production Board had taken control of American industry. It interrupted armaments contracts to make sure the US War and Naval Departments could start ambitious rearmament programmes. Fortunately, for them, British investments had doubled the output of the American armaments industry over the past two years. American investment would double its output again over the next twelve months.

While 50 per cent of armaments had been exported to Britain for the past two years, its orders were now being reduced, delayed or cancelled. Some American officials even continued to object to the Lend-Lease scheme, causing further problems. Deliveries became increasingly random, which made British planning impossible. One example was the American decision to start mass producing its M4 Sherman tank, leaving the British tank factories short of the engines they had been promised.

The decision to attack Germany meant that hundreds of thousands of American servicemen would have to be shipped to Britain. There was a plan for British factories to supply them, while American factories sent their armaments directly to the British armed forces. However, it was rejected because both armed forces refused to adopt each other's weapons.

## A Combined Strategy[8]

The new Minister of Production, Oliver Lyttelton, visited Washington DC in June 1942 to tell the Combined Chiefs of Staff that British orders were not being fulfilled. So, five Combined Boards were formed in Washington DC, to coordinate the production programmes of the two nations:

- Combined Raw Materials Board
- Combined Munitions Assignments Board
- Combined Production and Resources Board
- Combined Food Board
- Combined Shipping Adjustment Board

It was down to the Ministry of Production to calculate what Britain's requirements were and relay the information to the Joint War Production Staff. The British Supply Council would continue to work with the Ambassador but the Joint Staff Mission had to overcome the challenges posed by Washington DC wanting to equip the US armed forces first.

The Combined Raw Materials Board worked out what raw materials were needed, so it could locate enough sources. It then looked at how America and Britain could reduce consumption. The Board also looked at how to stop the Axis nations buying up raw materials. America bought up anything useful across South America, while Britain scoured the Commonwealth and the Eastern Hemisphere. Canada worked with America and Britain but it did not join the Boards.

The Combined Raw Materials Board had to react to challenges around the world, to avoid bottlenecks at the start of the supply chain. Japan's capture of raw material sources in the Far East caused many shortages, while the U-boat campaign in the Atlantic Ocean caused long-term headaches. After 1943, the

Winston Churchill's newly appointed War Cabinet in May 1940.

Men and women assembling a Matilda II tank.

London Docks on fire following a bombing raid by the *Luftwaffe*.

An oil tanker sinks after being torpedoed by a U-boat off the east coast of America.

Sheffield's steel workers work through the night during the Blitz.

Propaganda poster encouraging men to work in their local shipyard.

Propaganda poster encouraging women to find work in the aircraft factories.

Bevin Boys on a training course with their instructor.

Convoys carried around 2.5 million tons of goods to Britain every month.

Hillington Aircraft factory, near Glasogow, where Merlin engines were made.

Bethlehem-Fairfield shipyards in Baltimore, Maryland, where many Liberty ships were built.

Merlin engines made by Packard Motor Car Company's factory in Detroit, ready for export.

C-47 Skytrain  aircraft made by Douglas in California, would be known as Dakotas by the RAF.

Detroit tank factory building Sherman tanks on assembly lines.

Artillery parked up ahead of the Normandy landings.

The Houses of Parliament lit up on VE night on 8 May 1945.

Board also had to consider how to exploit new sources in liberated areas such as North Africa, Italy and then France.

The Combined Raw Materials Board worked with the Combined Shipping Adjustment Board to ship raw materials to appropriate ports, so trains could be organised to take them to the factories. The Combined Food Board performed the same tasks for foodstuffs.

The Combined Munitions Assignments Boards organised the export of finished goods and items from several factories were often pooled so they could be shipped together. However, supplies sometimes had to be auctioned off, because they were no longer needed by the time they had been made. America's War Shipping Administration and Britain's Ministry of War Transport arranged the shipping with the Combined Shipping Adjustment Board. However, frequent changes made it difficult to plan efficiently until experience allowed accurate forecasts to be made.

The Combined Production and Resources Board had wanted to adjust the production programmes but there was little support from the American side, so the British and American armaments programmes remained separate. It would be the spring of 1943 before a full production programme was issued and while Britain was eventually allowed to say what its priority items were, most still went to the back of the queue. It was 1944 before the British and American economies were finally integrated.

Allied victories around the world, meant that restrictions on raw materials could be lifted as the war came to an end. However, the Combined Boards had to make sure that liberated areas were given their fair share, while the United Nations Relief and Rehabilitation Administration (UNRRA) needed supplies to help local industries restart. All the Combined Boards were shut down in September 1945 but discussions over regional shortages continued until the end of the year.

## Supplies from the United States[9]

America refused to supply small warships to the Admiralty at the start of the war, so it was down to Britain's shipbuilding industry to make them.[10] German U-boats started operating from French ports after France surrendered in June 1940, increasing the threat to the vital supply convoys. So, Britain asked again for small warships and this time it was offered fifty aging destroyers in exchange for leasing British possessions for US military bases. At the same time, Britain spent the last of its remaining dollars on fifty new tramp steamers, which would be vital for moving supplies across the Atlantic Ocean in 1942.

Britain was also short of aircraft carriers but they took a long time to complete. So, the Admiralty designed an auxiliary aircraft carrier which placed a flight deck on top of a merchant ship. They were quick to build and carried enough aircraft to provide air cover for convoys. So, the Admiralty asked America for six auxiliary carriers in the spring of 1941; its shipyards would eventually make thirty-eight for the Royal Navy.

The Admiralty again asked Washington DC for 100 convoy-escort ships after the Lend-Lease programme was approved in March 1941. However, the American shipbuilding industry turned to building ships for the Pacific Theatre, following Japan's attack against Pearl Harbor in December. It would be early 1943 before the first one convoy-escort was launched.

While American armaments production increased by 75 per cent during 1942, it was lower than the amount predicted, so the British Army only receive half of the items it had asked for. American output continued to increase until it was making 60 per cent of the armaments required by the British Army, mainly because US Army had overestimated its requirements. However, enough aircraft were sent to Britain, so the RAF could continue to expand.

American shipyards spent 1943 building auxiliary aircraft carriers, destroyer escorts and frigates to protect the Atlantic convoys. By the summer, they were building merchant ships faster than the US Merchant Marine could train crews, so dozens were transferred to the British Merchant Navy.[11] By the end of the war, American shipyards would have launched six times as many shipping tons for the Royal Navy and Merchant Navy as British ones.

The shipyards also started work on the many small vessels and landing craft needed for the amphibious operations planned in the Mediterranean and Normandy. They built all the Landing Ship Tanks (LSTs), required to deliver large amounts of equipment and stores to the beaches, because the British shipyards too busy to make them. British engineering factories would make hundreds of small landing craft while many more were transferred under the Lend-Lease programme.

When it came to importing aircraft, the Air Ministry had placed its first order for 450 American military aircraft as part of Scheme L before the war. British factories struggled to keep up with the RAF's demands, so the American aircraft industry continued to send light bombers and fighters. While it made all the RAF's transport planes and many aircraft for the Fleet Air Arm, it made very few heavy bombers.

Around 60 per cent of the warlike stores being sent to Britain by 1941 were aircraft. American industry would also export 35,000 aero engines, many of them Rolls-Royce designed Merlin engines built by the Packard Company in Detroit, Michigan. The number started to fall when Britain's aircraft factories increased production while the Ministry of Aircraft Production focused on making the items the American factories were reluctant to send.

American industry eventually made one in three of the British Army's 25,600 tanks and 50 per cent of its self-propelled artillery. It also shipped tens of thousands of wheeled vehicles, tank transporters, lorries, jeeps and amphibious transporters called DUKWs. Around 2,300 Shermans were armed with the British 17-pounder gun ahead of D-Day, ready to combat the *Wehrmacht*'s new heavy tanks.

By the spring of 1943, the American assembly lines were making enough tanks for the US Army, the British Army and the Soviet Union's Red Army. The British Army was eventually fully equipped by the end of the year, so it only wanted items for maintenance and repairs, as well as ammunition, in future.

The British armed forces would be left short of many items during the final months of the war because of two reasons. The US War Department had suggested that the British Army took more American tanks, so British engineering factories could switch to making something else instead. However, the London refused because it preferred British designs and because wanted to preserve its manufacturing base. So, the British Army was left short of tanks after American industry reduced its tank production.

The US government wanted to avoid large amounts of military surpluses being left over at the end of the war, as there had been at the end of the First World War. The American public was also demanding more consumer goods, believing that the war was nearly over. So, the Lend–Lease budget was cut by a quarter, based on the Chiefs of Staffs' assessment that the war in Europe would be over by the end of 1944. However, the Germans lasted longer than expected, so the British Army was suffering from widespread shortages by the time the war in Europe ended on 8 May 1945.[12]

Extension Acts had continued to set money aside for British armaments after the Lend-Lease Act expired in June 1943. Items totalling $31.4 billion ($1.2 trillion today) had been shipped by July 1945. The bill would take over sixty years to pay off, with Britain making its last payment in December 2006.[13]

## Supplies from Canada[14]

Canada's armed forces were in a poor state after years of recession and neglect between the wars. Attempts to increase the nation's military budget and rearm for self-defence were unpopular, while Britain was unsure if it could pay for everything it wanted. However, Canada expanded its armaments industry with British cash, following the Munich Crisis in September 1938. The National Steel Car Company of Hamilton, Ontario, started making shells and explosives. John Inglis and Company, also of Hamilton, made Bren guns, while the Marine Industries of Sorel, Quebec made 25-pounder field guns.

Prime Minister William Lyon Mackenzie King declared that Canada was at war with Germany in September 1939. It would also declare war on Italy, Japan, and the other Axis nations later in the war.

Britain's supply departments gave Canadian factories and shipyards many orders for armaments in 1940, as insurance in case of bomb damage to British factories. They were soon building Hurricane fighters, Hampden bombers and corvettes to patrol coastal waters. Canada also started to arm its own troops but Britain had to equip the 1st Canadian Division, when it arrived in England in December 1940.

Ottawa had less political opposition to overcome than Washington DC, when it came to supporting Britain and it was also willing to accept payments in pound Sterling. Canadian factories began making armaments before American ones, while the British Supply Board had more control over what they made. Two thirds of the items made in Canadian factories were exported to Britain. It meant that Canada armed more Britain troops than the United States during the critical early years of the war. The Canadian government was also happy for its armaments factories to work to British or American designs.

Canada's factories had started making a full range of weapons and ammunition for the Canadian Expeditionary Force in 1941. It was also making Ram training tanks and Bren gun carriers for Britain, as well as Valentine tanks for the Soviet Union. President Roosevelt and Prime Minister Mackenzie King agreed that American Lend-Lease contracts for Britain could be placed in Canada in April 1941. While it increased the output from Canada's factories, it also increased American influence over what they made.

The Canadian armaments industry peaked in the summer of 1942 because Britain had to cut back the number of divisions it could form. Many plants had only run at maximum output for a few months before they reduced output; some would resume production when new orders were issued.

The Canadian shipbuilding industry would build eighty-seven small warships and make 15 per cent of the supplies required by the Royal Navy. It was building as many merchant ships as Britain by 1943 and many sailed to Britain, where the Ministry of War Transport chartered them. Its dockyards also worked on Royal Navy ships earmarked for the Pacific Theatre Fleet Train during the final months of the war.

Canada ended up making 15 per cent of the supplies required by the British Army, including one third of its Bren machine guns and Boyes anti-tank rifles. It also made over 500 25-pounder artillery pieces, 600 anti-tank guns and 1,400 AA guns. Its car industry made 1,000 Valentine tanks for the Soviet Union, as well as 8,000 Bren carriers and thousands of unarmoured vehicles. It also made 110,000 rifles and 4 billion bullets.

While Canada's engineering factories made less than 5 per cent of the RAF's supplies, its aircraft factories did build 1,000 Hurricane fighters during the critical early phase of the war. They were followed by 2,000 Anson training aircraft, 200 Lancaster heavy bombers, 950 Mosquito light bombers and 770 Catalina flying boats. Eventually, Canada would make CAD $100 billion ($3.5 trillion today) of armaments for its allies.

# Chapter 8

# Merchant Shipping

## Pre-War Shipping Plans[1]

Britain's Merchant Navy shipped food, raw materials, troops and exports around the world but the depression between the wars had hit the shipping industry hard. Typically, over 3 million tons of shipping lay idle while less than 1 million tons were being built every year.[2] It meant that the Britain's share of the world's trade had reduced from 44 per cent down to just 28 per cent, while half of its goods were carried by ships chartered from other countries.

As the threat of war increased, the Committee of Imperial Defence (CID) had many problems to consider relating to merchant shipping. Would ships chartered from other countries continue to supply Britain in wartime? How badly would German U-boats, mines and warships interfere with the shipping routes? Could Britain be able to keep on paying the shipping companies?

Nearly a third of the country's imports were delivered to the Port of London and the CID knew it would be vulnerable to attacks both from the air and the sea. No one knew what damage would be inflicted on the docks, if the *Luftwaffe* chose to bomb them until Spanish ports were damaged during its Civil War (1936–1939).[3]

The port authorities reported that 75 per cent of imports could be directed to the west coast ports such as Glasgow, Liverpool and Bristol. The rest could be taken to other east coast ports such as Newcastle-upon-Tyne, Middlesbrough and Hull. But docks needed cranes to unload goods and railway links to take goods to their destination and there was no money to expand their facilities. While the CID estimated that there would be enough trains to move goods across country, it did not know how badly air raids would impact the network.

Following the Munich Crisis in September 1938, the Committee of Imperial Defence asked the Ministry of Shipping to check how imports had been dealt with during the First World War. While the port authorities objected to this second round of questioning, the Ministry concluded that the first report was 'complete nonsense' and neither the ports nor the railways would be able to cope with a switch to the west coast ports. While money was made available to resolve the issue in July 1939, it was far too late to make a difference.

The Ministry of Transport and the Ministry of Shipping merged their work following the outbreak of war in September 1939 and they set up a Diversion Room to monitor shipping movements. The Admiralty supplied daily lists of ships approaching the ports, while the Ministry of War Transport listed their cargoes. The Port Emergency Committees reported what they could offload, while the railway companies estimated how much they could move to the destinations given by the supply departments. The objective was to make sure goods made a smooth passage from the ships to where they were needed.

The shipping companies had asked successive governments for financial assistance between the wars but they had received none. However, the threat of war required the Board of Trade to find out how much had to be imported to feed the people and make armaments. It estimated that 2.67 million tons of raw materials and 1.25 million tons of food would be needed every month and the Mercantile Marine Department confirmed there was just enough shipping available. So, no merchant shipping reserve had been built up.

However, on the outbreak of war several economists reported that the country would need more food and raw materials, calling the Board of Trade's estimates absurd. While the Sea Transport Department was busy shipping the BEF to France, plans were being made to improve the import situation but it was a huge task. Ports had to be improved, railways had to be reorganised and storage facilities had to be expanded, if the country was going to stand a chance of feeding and arming itself.

## The Outbreak of War to the Fall of France[4]

The Ministry of Shipping was set up in October 1939 and it soon noted that imports were only half what they had been in peacetime. The reason was, companies had stopped making luxury items, unsure what was going to happen next. The *Luftwaffe* had not bombed Britain's ports yet but the

*Kriegsmarine*'s warships were laying mines and attacking merchant ships, making the east coast shipping lanes too dangerous to use.

Meanwhile, the government wanted to increase imports of bulk items like timber, wheat and iron ore, because stocks were running dangerously low. Food was simple to get but raw materials were more complicated to source. Armaments were particularly involved because many decisions had to be made before they were ordered.

The government also had to watch how it spent its money. While it was cheaper to import from the Commonwealth and Empire, the longer journeys from India and the Far East required more shipping.[5] Licenses were introduced to reduce unnecessary trade, while price fixing curbed profits on luxury goods. It meant that priorities had to be decided, cutbacks had to be made and ships had to be booked to move important goods. By January 1940, every merchant ship capable of carrying dry goods on deep sea routes was working on government contracts.

Matching the goods required to available shipping capacity was difficult, so the Ministry of Shipping started using block bookings to ease the problem. U-boats then started sinking neutral ships, putting shipping companies off transporting goods to Britain. Eventually the First Lord of the Admiralty, Winston Churchill, threatened to cancel insurances for foreign companies and ban their ships from British ports if they refused to bring supplies to Britain. A few companies accepted the risk but they demanded higher prices. Even so, there were shortages of imported goods and the Ministry of Supply often bore the brunt of them.

Germany invaded Norway and Denmark in April 1940, cutting Britain off from its Scandinavian supplies of iron ore and timber. It then invaded the Netherlands, Belgium and France a month later, ending the export of over 60,000 tons of coal a month to France.[6] All these countries had also been importing British goods to cover what they had been buying from Germany and Poland before the war.

A fleet of little ships started evacuating the BEF from Dunkirk at the end of May 1940 and nearly 340,000 British and French soldiers had escaped across the Channel by 4 June 1940. America offered to replace the huge amounts of armaments abandoned in Dunkirk, as long Britain paid for them in US dollars and provided the shipping to transport them across the Atlantic.

The *Luftwaffe* then started attacking Britain's ports and while the plan to offload all merchant ships on the west coast was implemented, it caused huge problems. Ships were directed to the wrong ports and there was a shortage of dockers to unload them. There was insufficient storage space at the docks, while the railways were unable to move goods quickly enough across the country. The plan ended after just two weeks and Churchill's new government had to consider the impact of the 'grave congestion', which had nearly caused a 'major national peril'.

## The Fall of France to Pearl Harbor[7]

The Fall of France in June 1940 resulted in Britain having a surplus of shipping due to the cut in exports, while the ships chartered by French companies were now free. Germany had captured 25 per cent of Belgian, Dutch, Norwegian and Danish ships and it commanded the owners of the rest not to carry goods for Britain. So, Churchill countered by launching a warrant scheme, preventing ships working for enemy countries from using British ports. The BBC also broadcast a welcome to foreign shipping companies, promising them insurance cover and cash payments if they headed to friendly harbours. Some did but a few pro-German owners sent their ships to America, to avoid getting involved.

Many Danish ships stayed in port and while Belgium handed over its small fleet, the Netherlands was reluctant to do the same because they needed shipping to move goods from its overseas possessions. Neutral Sweden promised 500,000 tons of shipping but Norway was wary of letting its ships carry British goods because they were one of its few remaining assets.

Eventually Churchill's government convinced half of the Norwegian and Dutch fleets to ship goods to Britain, after promising the captain's higher prices and the crew's higher wages. Greek and Yugoslavian ships added to the growing pool of ships, after Germany invaded their countries in April 1941. French ships captured in African ports would join them later.

By now, the War Cabinet estimated that Britain needed 1.25 million tons of food, 1.6 million tons of raw materials and 80,000 tons of armaments a month. However, the supply departments disagreed and they continued to order what they wanted rather than building up a reserve. The Ministry of Shipping estimated enough shipping was available but the Ministry of Transport did not think the ports and the rail network could handle everything.

Events outside the control of the War Cabinet and the Ministry of Shipping would prove them both wrong. The Mediterranean Sea shipping route was blocked when Italy entered the war in June 1940, requiring ships to sail around Africa. It increased the route from the Indian Ocean from around 3,000 miles (4,800 kilometres) to 9,000 miles (14,5000 kilometres), which required three times as much shipping and fuel to transport the same amount of goods.

The English Channel route was also blocked by German warships and U-boats, so ships had to sail around Scotland to reach the east coast ports. That doubled the journey from Ireland to London from 600 miles (960 kilometres) to 1,200 miles (1,930 kilometres). The longer routes meant that imports fell by 10 per cent down to just 2.63 million tons a month. However, both the ports and the railway companies continued to report that they could not handle any more goods.

The *Luftwaffe* started bombing the Port of London in earnest on 7 September 1940, putting 70,000 tons of shipping out of action over three nights. Meanwhile, *Kreigsmarine* patrols and mines blocked the approaches to the Thames Estuary; the coast of Kent would eventually be nicknamed Hell's Corner. Only small ships were allowed to sail to the remaining east coast ports, while trains moved coal from the northeast to London because the coastal waters were too dangerous for coaling ships.

The Blitz over the winter of 1940–1941 caused a host of other problems, as ports and inland cities were bombed. Ships had to wait to be unloaded and time was then lost moving goods across the damaged rail network. Altogether the delays caused by bomb damage reduced the amount of imports the country could handle by 250,000 tons a month, or another 10 per cent.

The Regional Port Directors organised labour to speed up the unloading at the docks in December 1940, while the Port Emergency Committees were given extra powers to sort out congestion. The Merchant Navy also tightened up the rules on the ships' crews because they were civilians who were employed for the duration of a voyage, resulting in a transient workforce.[8] One in three crew members working on merchant ships were non-British and they could jump ship anywhere. It made it difficult to assemble a crew at times, even more so as merchant ships losses increased.

Sailing on an unarmed ship was risky work and the U-boats gave no warning when they were about to strike. Heavily laden merchant ships sank quickly and there was a shortage of the protective kit and clothing that saved many lives during the later months of the war. To make matters worse, half of the merchant ships were old and poorly equipped, which made the long journeys unpleasant.

Only half of the merchant seamen could be forced to register under the National Service Acts, so many of them found jobs onshore, while out-of-date rules made it difficult to discipline unruly sailors. So, an Essential Work Order was issued in May 1941, which made all crewmen register and prevented them from leaving the Merchant Navy until the war ended.

The docks along the River Clyde, the River Mersey and the Bristol Channel were working much better by the time the *Luftwaffe* turned their attentions to them in March 1941. The plan was to interrupt the flow of supplies to the Soviet Union ahead of the German invasion codenamed Operation Barbarossa, planned to start on 22 June.

The heavy raids sank ships, damaged quaysides, blocked railways and demoralised the workforce. Hundreds of civilians were killed or injured, while thousands of houses were damaged. Liverpool was just one example and it endured heavy raids eight nights in a row, resulting in 90 per cent of the port's berths being put out of action. There were also 8,000 casualties while 200,000 houses were damaged.

Despite the air raids, the delays to unloading shipping were negligible because the berths could be repaired quickly. The bombers would have caused more problems if they had hit the railway links connecting the ports to the network instead. Even so, each port sent daily damage assessments to the Diversion Room, to check how many ships could be unloaded.

The Blitz had also hit many dockyards around the country, resulting in damage to one in five ships or 2.8 million tons by the spring of 1941. Owners did not want to send their merchant ships to the east coast yards because they were dangerous to get to, so many were directed to an American shipyards, to be repaired under the Lend-Lease programme. The easiest problems were repaired first, so more ships could be put back out to sea quicker. While the number of ships waiting for repairs was halved over the summer, it crept back up again during the winter months, due to the bad weather.

## The United States Goes to War[9]

The Neutrality Act prevented American owned ships from entering the war zone during the first two years of the war. However, the President excluded the Red Sea, which meant that armaments could be shipped close to where the British troops were fighting in the Middle East. The Act also banned American owned ships from carrying war material, so the US government paid foreign owned ships that were taking refuge in American ports to take armaments to Britain.

On 31 March 1941, the Prime Minister announced that Britain needed to import enough food and fuel to maintain the nation's morale, even if it took longer to build up the armed forces. He said, 'nothing must interfere with the supplies necessary to maintain the stamina and the resolution of the people.'[10]

The Merchant Shipping Mission asked America to build 12 million tons to replace losses and increase the size of the British fleet and President Roosevelt agreed to include them in the recently launched Lend-Lease scheme. While the largest ship owning nation and the largest productive nation started working together, many Americans were against the idea. Some thought Britain was going to be defeated, while others were convinced that Churchill was asking for too much.

The Ministries of Shipping and Transport were merged into the Ministry of War Transport in May 1941. Frederick Leathers, Viscount Leathers, was given instructions to close the gap between what Britian needed and what the Merchant Navy could carry, which was currently around 200,000 tons a month. The Ministry of War Transport covered all forms of transport but twelve of its divisions worked with merchant shipping:[11]

- The Ship Management Division chartered ships.
- The Shipping Operations Control Division allocated British, American and Allied shipping.
- The Sea Transport Division dealt with shipping for the armed forces.
- The Ship Management Division looked after privately owned ships.
- The Liner Division requisitioned liners.
- The General (Shipping) Division looked at general matters and tonnage replacement.

- The Allocation of Tonnage Division decided which ships moved which goods.
- The Tanker Division organised the shipping of fuel and other oils.
- The Coasting and Short Sea Shipping Division controlled ships in home waters.
- The Foreign Shipping Relations Division dealt with ships owned by other countries.
- The War Risks Insurance Office dealt with insurance and claims.

Germany attacked the Soviet Union on 22 June 1941 and the rapid advance east dislocated its industry. America and Britain agreed to send it supplies and the first convoy set off in August 1941. America signed a Lend-Lease agreement with the Soviet Union in October 1941, and while it was anxious to provide as much help as possible, it found it difficult to deal with Moscow. Britain had to fit out its best ships to cope with the cold weather and then send them around Iceland and German occupied Norway. The Arctic convoys were unloaded at the ports of Arkhangelsk and Murmansk, when the weather allowed.

The Japanese attacked Pearl Harbor and the Philippines in December 1941, followed by Germany and Italy declaring war against the United States.[12] The changing situation caused many new shipping problems. The requirements of the US War and Naval Departments were put first, meaning that Britain did not always get what it asked for. Meanwhile, Japanese troops overran a large part of Southeast Asia, capturing Singapore, Hong Kong, threatening the Indian Ocean and closing Calcutta (now Kolkata) to shipping. Axis troops even reached the Egyptian border in July 1942, within striking distance of Alexandria.

With Port Said and the Suez Canal threatened, temporary docks had to be opened in the Red Sea, presenting many new issues. The port authorities learnt to check they had the right machinery to offload goods, the quaysides had enough storage space and the railway links were functioning. The problems kept increasing and so did the number of merchant ships that were being sunk. The Prime Minister would later say, 'shipping was at once the stranglehold and sole foundation of our [Britain's] war strategy.'[13]

Pearl Harbor had changed America's focus at a time when Britain needed more help. Roosevelt and Churchill had given priority to the war in Europe at the Arcadia Conference at the end of 1941. However, American shipyards were instructed to build ships for the Pacific campaign, rather than for the Atlantic convoys. Unfortunately, the inexperienced US War and Naval Departments overestimated how much shipping and supplies they needed, leaving the British armed forces short of many items. Sir Arthur Salter, Parliamentary Secretary to the Ministry of Shipping, said 'the competition was no longer between British war needs and American peace needs, but between two sets of war needs.'[14]

The US Chiefs of Staff made it clear that they did not want any advice from their British counterparts, even though they had two years relevant experience. All Britain could do was to rely on American promises and see what arrived, knowing there was nothing to replace anything that was missing. A Shipping Committee had to start overseeing the shipping situation and forecasting what was needed to maintain reserves. But it was a complicated task balancing what was available in America against what was needed in Britain.

Many problems had to be overcome ahead of Operation Torch, the amphibious operation against northwest Africa planned for November 1942. Britain had to provide most of the shipping because America was deploying most of its ships to the Pacific Theatre.[15] The Shipping Committee sourced enough cargo ships for the landings, only to discover that the Chiefs of Staff had seriously underestimated how many were needed and how long for.

The impact of the landings on British imports was dramatic, so the Minister of Production, Oliver Lyttelton, visited Washington DC to explain what Britain needed. While the President promised to make enough shipping available, he did so without checking with the US Services and the War Shipping Administration first. So, they refused to help, again leaving Britain short of military and domestic supplies.

## Invading Europe[16]

The Prime Minister and the President met in Casablanca in North Africa in January 1943, to decide future strategy with the Combined Chiefs of Staff. The plan was to invade Sicily, codenamed Operation Husky, once North Africa had been cleared. They also discussed Operation Bolero, a plan to invade Europe if the *Wehrmacht* abandoned France. However, they concluded there was insufficient shipping to support a plan clear the Burma Road, codenamed Operation Anakim.

The shipping shortage was made worse by the fact that the Chiefs of Staff had forgotten to include the shipping required to move non-military supplies around the world as well. It was a serious oversight because the Allies needed accurate long-term shipping plans if they were going to sustain the offensive against Nazi-occupied Europe.

Britain did not have enough ships for Operation Husky, while the North Africa ports needed improving before they could be used. America did not have enough troopships either if Operation Bolero was triggered, while Britain's southern ports also needed a lot of work. To make matters worse, both Britain and America thought that each other was misusing their merchant shipping allocation.

The Chiefs of Staff answer was to switch merchant ships to the North African campaign, so it could be concluded as quickly as possible. They were taken from the Atlantic route and all Churchill could do to keep Britain fed, was to transfer shipping from the India Ocean to replace them. In doing so, he cut the rice imports being shipped to India. He had taken a gamble which failed because the country was left desperately short of food when the autumn harvest failed. Between 800,000 and 3.8 million people would die from starvation, malnutrition and malaria during the famine that struck Bengal over the winter of 1943–1944.[17]

The Allies' problems increased in line with their growing military presence in the Mediterranean Theatre during the spring of 1943. It meant the Chiefs of Staff needed to plan their shipping requirements carefully, a difficult task because the Americans and British faced different challenges. Armaments for the US armed forces were made in America and the completed items were shipped directly to North Africa. Meanwhile, London had to import raw materials from around the world, to make the armaments in the British factories, before shipping the finished goods to the Mediterranean battle zone.

Churchill eventually had to send his Foreign Secretary, The Right Honourable Anthony Eden MP, to Washington DC, where the President assured him that 7 million tons of American ships would be made available to ship what Britain required. Even so, the US War and Naval Departments refused to draw up budgets for their Chiefs of Staff ahead of the Trident

Conference in Washington DC in May 1943. The British Chiefs of Staff then learnt that the American Chiefs of Staff objected to the President's promise. Shipping budgets were eventually agreed at the conference and they forecast surpluses, providing the American armed forces were prudent.

The conference concluded that it was impossible to ship everything that everyone wanted at the same time because the German U-boats were sinking too many merchant ships.[18] So, the decision was taken to again postpone Operation Anakim in Burma. It was also decided that either Operation Husky or Operation Bolero could be launched but they would be insufficient ships to supply both operations at the same time.

During the conference it became clear that the US armed forces had been anything but prudent. US troops were being supplied double the amount of goods British troops were given, which accounted for most of the worldwide shipping shortage. It meant that future military operations were in danger of being cancelled because of American extravagance. So, the British Chiefs of Staff decided to write off the arms deficits it was waiting for and convinced their American counterparts to do the same. The move freed up extra shipping and the two sets of Chiefs of Staff decided to combine their estimates for future operations.

The President also agreed to hand over new merchant ships being build (known as SAM ships), because Britain had a surplus of seaman while America had a shortage. On average they only took four weeks to complete and the shipyards were working flat out to make as many as possible. Unfortunately, inexperienced labour, new welding techniques and prefabrication meant there were teething troubles with them.[19]

The Quadrant Conference in August 1943 reported hardly any deficits but the Sextant Conference in November 1943 again predicted shortages of shipping, landing ships and landing craft. The Americans were still reluctant to reduce their allocations and they were beginning to think that the British were looking for a shipping advantage after the war.[20]

The next problem was how to supply the D-Day landings. The operation would need 7,000 vessels, as well as temporary harbours to get supplies over the beaches until a deep water port was opened. Operation Overlord would have first claim on everything until a French port could be opened, which meant cutting imports to Britain again. In the meantime, there was a lot of planning to work out how to load the ships in British ports and then unload them onto the beaches at the mercy of the tides.

Britain ended up providing all the coastal ships, most of the troopships and many of the merchant ships. British dockers taught their American counterparts[21] how to load their ships efficiently and most deliveries went ahead smoothly, resulting in 3.4 million tons of goods being delivered during the first month of the Normandy campaign.

Budgets became irrelevant as the Allied forces advanced across Europe and the United States' armed forces made the most of it.[22] The Octagon Conference in September 1944 discovered that as much as possible had been shipped to the Pacific, to support the drive towards Japan. It had created 'unmanageable deficits' for the British armed forces, as its monthly supply of armaments fell from 350,000 tons a month to 290,00 tons; a 20 per cent drop. It meant Britain had to rely on sufficient liberty ships being handed over, to avert a crisis.[23]

The US Chiefs of Staff wanted to cut British domestic supplies, because they thought the London's demands were exaggerated. They again wanted to reduce food deliveries to India, where there were fears that another famine could kill hundreds of thousands more if the harvest failed again. There were also concerns about supplying the millions of people living in the recently freed areas across Europe, such as France and Italy. However, the US Chiefs of Staff were totally focused on ending the war as quickly as possible, because their primary objective was to save American lives. The only good news was that the British Shipping Mission and the US War Shipping Administration, were finally working together to try to solve the problems.

The President eventually had to tell the US Theatre commanders to stop being so wasteful with shipping in December 1944. However, only a month later, the US Chiefs of Staff disagreed with the British military and both civil authorities at the Argonaut Conference. While the Ministry of Transport said that the Chiefs of Staff should not be deciding shipping priorities, they were allowed to remain in control, so the conference could agree on its strategic aims. However, the British Chiefs of Staff insisted on no more cuts to the civil programme because Britain had run out of reserves.

The Argonaut meeting left Britain with a huge shipping deficit which had to be split between its military requirements and its civil needs.[24] When it turned out the US Chiefs of Staff had held back extra shipping for a military crisis in the Pacific which had failed to materialise, many ships could be transferred to the British. Unfortunately, there were no armaments waiting for them to carry, so the British armed forces had to rely on what scant reserves of equipment and ammunition they had until some could be made.

At the same time, America had cut back food production and ended rationing, because it thought the war would be over by Christmas 1944. While concerns about another Indian famine had fortunately not occurred over the winter, France and Italy were left short of essential items as their people tried to rebuild their lives.

The war in Europe ended on 8 May 1945 and merchant shipping could once again sail freely around large parts of the world. American and British shipyards spent the next ten weeks converting and repairing ships ready for the invasion of Japan. However, Emperor Hirohito surrendered on 15 August 1945, following the detonation of two atomic bombs on Hiroshima and Nagasaki. The war was over. For a second time in thirty years, both Allied nations had learnt an important lesson: 'though the organisation that controls merchant ships can do nothing directly to win a war, it can very easily cause one to be lost.'[25]

*Chapter 9*

# The Factories

## General Programming Challenges[1]

The armaments industry had to meet many challenges during the war and the three supply departments had to programme their requirements differently. The Admiralty had to balance the needs of the Royal Navy and the Merchant Navy, as well as decide whether to build, modify or repair ships. The Air Ministry had to build a set number of a few models of aircraft by a certain date. However, the Ministry of Supply had to make the many types of weapons and equipment demanded by the British Army. The War Office estimated long-term targets based on which part of the world the General Staff thought it would have to fight in. The Director General of Army Requirements had to compile information about the Army's expansion, what was needed for air defence and the requirements of Commonwealth units. Only then could the Ministry of Supply organise its factories.

The armaments industry faced new challenges in the summer of 1940 because it had to build as many aircraft and AA guns as possible. It also had to rearm the BEF, following its evacuation from Dunkirk, and equip the Local Defence Volunteers (later known as the Home Guard), in case Britain was invaded.

A Priority of Production Direction Committee made aircraft and AA guns Priority 1A, while items to rearm the BEF was classified Priority 1B. However, Lord Beaverbrook encouraged companies and skilled workers to build aircraft until the Prime Minister stopped the practice.

Once the threat of invasion subsided, many more AA weapons were required to protect the nation from air attacks. Repairing bomb damaged factories were then given top priority as the Blitz intensified, followed by improvements to the radar warning system. An allocation system was set up to distribute labour, plant and materials fairly between the three supply departments at the end of 1940.

Changes in what was imported were also made, to economise on shipping space. The government also took control of materials and launched a propaganda campaign called 'Waste Not Want Not', to improve recycling. Imported raw materials were reduced by 40 per cent while the number of completed items were trebled. It had, however, increased the cost of imports.

The Chiefs of Staff initially told the Prime Minister that it would take until 1942 to build the armed forces up to strength, only to push the date back to 1943. The unknown in the equation was, to what extent would America help Britain fight Germany? Prime Minister Churchill even went as far as to make the following plea to President Roosevelt on 9 February 1941:

> We shall not fail or falter; we shall not weaken nor tire. Neither the sudden shock of battle, nor the long-drawn trials of vigilance and exertion, will wear us down. Give us the tools, and we will finish the job.

British industry was soon busy making huge numbers of tanks, anti–tank guns and transport for the North African campaign. The Royal Navy also needed help to keep its warships seaworthy, so it could protect the convoys taking supplies to the Soviet Union, after the summer of 1941.

Everything changed when the Japanese attack against Pearl Harbor on 7 December 1941; Germany and Italy declared war against the United States four days later. President Roosevelt and Prime Minister Churchill met in Washington DC three weeks later, agreeing on a new strategy the War Cabinet would work towards. It had four objectives:

- Keep the Atlantic sea lanes open for the supply convoys.
- Send supplies to the Soviet Union.
- Build up a US bomber force in Britian, to attack German industry.
- Land US troops in North Africa, to engage Axis troops as early as possible.

British industry also had to come to terms with a different export policy, because the US War and Naval Departments took priority. It would leave Britain short of materials.

American troops landed in North Africa in November 1942 and the plan for 1943 was to clear North Africa before invading Sicily and then Italy.

Roosevelt, Churchill and Premier Josef Stalin met at the Eureka Conference in Tehran in November 1943, where they decided there would be a double pronged invasion of France; one in the north and one in the south in the spring of 1944. There would also be a large Red Army attack in the east. Each nation's industry had to react to every strategic plan, resulting in continual reassessments to meet the needs of their respective armed forces.

In the autumn of 1944, all three supply departments were asked to make two production estimates for the end of the war in Europe. The first assumed that Germany would be defeated by December 1944 and the second pushed it back to the spring of 1945. The situation was reassessed in December, based on the war ending in the summer. A third assessment published in April stated what was required to finish in Europe and what was needed for the Far East. The final revision in June extended production plans into 1946, however, the surrender of Japan following the detonation of two atomic bombs in August 1945, ended the war much sooner than expected.

## The Dockyards and Shipyards

### Programming Shipbuilding[2]

The Admiralty was used to planning construction years ahead to small budgets, while the depression between the wars had left the Royal Navy with a shrinking fleet of aging ships. The threat of war resulted in repair and conversion work backing up, as shipyards became busy. So, each region was given a Warship Production Superintendent who had to acquire enough steel, determine labour requirements and programme work. Many yacht and boat building firms started building small vessels for coastal protection, while engineering works made everything from gun mountings to engines; they also did repairs. Meanwhile, Engineer Overseers liaised between the firms making the parts and the shipyards.

The industry had to focus on what type of shipping was required and the strategy kept changing during the war. Sometimes large warships were urgent; at other times small ones were the priority. Merchant shipping took precedence when the nation's supplies were in danger. However, the changes made it difficult to coordinate the supply of steel to the shipyards.

The original plan was to reduce the work on warships, so more could be done on merchant ships. However, the Fall of France in June 1940 meant that the nation's coastal waters had to be protected. There was no time to build new shipyards, so a lot of work was given to inland engineering firms. There was no time to build large warships either, so shipyards focused on building convoy escorts and arming merchant ships. Heavy winter seas and inexperienced crews also caused a lot of repair work.

The Admiralty found it difficult to track progress because the shipyard owners made optimistic promises to get more work and then struggled to meet the deadlines. The expansion of the workforce from 200,000 to 260,000 involved employing a lot of unskilled workers, which complicated the situation. A survey also found that many shipyards had poor layouts and were using outdated production methods; many were short of cranes and machine tools.

Churchill suspended the construction of battleships[3] and cruisers in 1941 because he wanted the dockyards and shipyards to focus on building smaller warships instead:

- Destroyers for protecting fleets and amphibious forces.
- Frigates for escorting convoys and anti-submarine work in deep waters.
- Corvettes for patrols and anti-submarine work in coastal waters.

However, the Admiralty wanted two new battleships to redress the balance of naval power after several capital ships were sunk in 1941.[4] It also wanted more aircraft carriers but waited to find out why HMS *Ark Royal* had been lost in November 1941. Once a lack of backup power and a shortage of bulkheads had been identified, the Illustrious and Implacable class aircraft carriers could be redesigned.

Fortunately, the delay gave the Admiralty the opportunity to see what air power could achieve, when US Navy planes sank four Japanese aircraft carriers in Midway in the Pacific Ocean in June 1942. While the Admiralty wanted more aircraft carriers, fleet carriers took too long to build. So, sixteen auxiliary escort carriers, which involved fitting decks on top of American merchant ships, were ordered. They would still take until 1944 to complete.

The completion of the battleships HMS *Anson* and HMS *Howe* were followed by the scuttling of the French fleet in Toulon in November 1942, which gave the Royal Navy the advantage over the *Kreigsmarine* once more. It meant that the shipyards could again focus on building convoy escorts and anti-submarine ships, to reduce merchant shipping losses. While America had promised help, its shipyards were busy making escort ships to protect its own supply lines across the Pacific Ocean.

In 1943, the Admiralty grouped together experienced and inexperienced engineering firms, so they could share ideas. Shipyard Development Committees assessed each shipyard's needs and sourced new equipment. It also encouraged them to use welders because they were quicker to train than riveters; women could also be employed to weld. Inland factories started prefabricating components, which allowed the shipyards to catch up with their work. The improvements increased the quantity of tonnage being launched each month by 25 per cent.

In 1943, the Admiralty asked for extra labour ahead of the invasion of France but there were few men available to do shipyard work. While engineering and aircraft factories paid better wages, shipyard work was heavy and unpleasant. Fortunately, the U-boat threat diminished in May, so production could switch from merchant ships to escort ships, improving convoy security. Ship production focused on the invasion of France in 1944, with shipyards working on orders for frigates, destroyers and tank landing craft. Shipyards switched to repairing the damage caused during after the landings.

A new task relating to Far East operations, where the Royal Navy was fighting the Imperial Japanese Navy, emerged in 1945. Merchant ships were converted into supply ships, creating a Fleet Train to supply the warships, allowing them to remain at sea for weeks on end. Finally, as the war came to an end, the shipyards were kept busy converting merchant ships back to their peace time functions. Britain's shipbuilding industry had risen to the challenge posed by the war, after years in decline. Firms had done so by reorganising their shipyards, taking on extra labour and accepting new manufacturing techniques.

## Royal Dockyards[5]

The Royal Dockyards worked as a group but each one had a Dockyard Director who programmed the work. A Civil Assistant ordered the materials, maintained the plant and organised the labour. The facilities had been run down because work on warships dried up between the wars, but recruitment during the rearmament era had brought the workforce back up to 40,000 men.

Portsmouth, Devonport, Chatham and Sheerness had heavy lifting equipment, so they built submarines, destroyers and larger ships. They also dealt with complex repairs and conversions. An Emergency Repair Organisation helped the private shipyards with difficult tasks. It also deployed teams around the coast to repair damaged ships, so they could get back to their home port. The small dockyards worked on a range of ship classes up to corvette and frigate size.

Chatham Royal Dockyard made submarine hulls while Scotts Shipbuilding and Engineering Company Limited near Glasgow, Vickers-Armstrongs Limited in Barrow-in-Furness, and Cammell Laird & Co. Limited in Birkenhead, built their diesel engines. Davey, Paxman & Co. Limited of Colchester also made diesel-electric engines. While the Ministry of Supply took control of submarine construction during the early days of the war, a shortage of skilled labour resulted in a lot of engines and auxiliary machinery being imported from America.

Overseas shipyards played a large part in keeping the Royal Navy and Merchant Navy afloat. Many larger ships were repaired in American dockyards after March 1941, where there was no danger from air raids. However, the Royal Navy lost three large repair facilities when the Japanese captured Hong Kong, Singapore and the Dutch East Indies over the winter of 1941–1942. It meant the Admiralty had to send 9,000 skilled men from Britain to help set up new repair facilities in Gibraltar, South Africa, Ceylon (now Sri Lanka) and Australia.

## Conversion and Repair Programmes[6]

The Admiralty wanted to programme its construction and repair work but frequent changes in naval strategy made it difficult to plan. On the outbreak of war, many ships had to be converted and while passenger liners were turned into troop ships, small merchant ships were converted into armed patrol vessels.[7]

Many ships also had to be fitted with degaussing equipment that stopped magnetic mines being attracted to the concentrated magnetic field caused by a large steel ship. Expensive electromagnetic coils were used until it was discovered that dragging a cable powered by an electrical pulse in the water was just as effective. Over 400 small ships had to be fitted with degaussing equipment in just a few days, to keep them safe during the evacuation from Dunkirk.[8]

Shipping work became a low priority following Dunkirk, as armour plate was switched to the tank programme. But over 100 ships a month still needed to be refitted or repaired and while a small job only took a few weeks to complete, a large one could take many months. The amount of work steadily increased as dozens of ships needed repairing following the Norway, Dunkirk and Mediterranean campaigns. Shipyards also had to refit seized French ships, as well as fifty aging American destroyers, which were handed over in exchange for military bases in September 1940.

There was plenty of work to do on escorts required to protect the troop convoys heading to North Africa over the winter of 1940–1941 but frequent bombing raids against the shipyards causing delays. Fortunately, American yards started building and converting many ships during the summer, helping their British counterparts catch up.

Sailing on the high seas required regular refits, while enemy action and winter weather dramatically increased repairs. The Royal Dockyards had fifty dry docks (known as graving docks) and five floating docks but few were large enough to deal with the largest warships. While the dockyards were well-equipped and had a lot of experienced labour, they all suffered heavy damage during bombing raids. So, the Admiralty looked for new facilities in safer waters. New dockyards were added in Lyness on the Orkney Islands, Fort William and Oban on the west coast of Scotland, in Rosyth on the Firth of Forth, and at Pembroke Dock in South Wales.

The Admiralty leased Gourock Pier and the Great Harbour on the west coast of Scotland, as well as Yorkhill and the Dalmuir Basins on the River Clyde. It also used Jarrow Dry Dock on the River Tyne, as well as the Prince's Dock and Queen's Dock on the River Mersey in Liverpool. Two floating docks and a floating crane were also moved north to the River Clyde.

Private shipyards ended up doing two thirds of the repair, refit and conversion work required by the Royal Navy and the Merchant Navy. The Royal Dockyards also equipped derelict docks in Liverpool, Cardiff and Newport to help them out. The extra facilities meant that the number of workers employed on ship repairs was able to increase from 200,000 in 1940 to 280,000 in 1944.

## Merchant Shipping[9]

A Shipbuilding Consultative Committee had been appointed in 1937, to work out how to improve Britain's shipyards. A new Ministry of Shipping took over when war broke out and it worked out to coordinate warship building with merchant ship building. While the Royal Navy suggested converting merchant ships and trawlers into escort vessels and minesweepers, the War Cabinet wanted the tonnage of merchant ships to double.

A Merchant Shipbuilding and Repair Division checked that companies had enough labour and materials to fulfil their contracts. However, repair work often took longer than estimated, so the backlog of work soon increased, resulting in a shortage of merchant shipping. The Prime Minister even reduced the amount of new ship construction so that 10,000 men could be transferred to repair work, but the Merchant Shipbuilding Programmes Committee still struggled to find enough labour.

The Ministry of Labour put the Admiralty in charge of all shipyard labour and it had soon recruited enough men to clear the backlog of repairs, ahead extra work expected during the winter months. However, finding enough specialist tradesmen was always a challenge. Inland engineering works were eventually used to make prefabricated steel sections, so that shipwrights could assemble them into escort vessels. It meant that space could be freed up in the shipyards.

The large shipyards had marine engineering works which made turbine engines for large and specialised ships. Smaller shipyards had relied on engineering factories to make their engines but many had closed between the wars. Those still working had spluttered back into life during the rearmament period but there was still a shortage of engines for small ships. Firms that supported the fishing industry made piston engines for frigates and corvettes. Meanwhile, vehicle workshops made engines for minesweepers, motor patrol boats and landing craft.

Hundreds of other firms were contracted to build a wide variety of unconventional vessels. Boat building firms assembled over 3,000 wooden landing craft, while inland engineering firms built smaller boats. The Admiralty even took over the Surrey firm Fairmile Marine, when it got into financial trouble in 1940, so it could continue to make armed patrol boats.

## Shipbuilding Output

The number of shipbuilding workers fell in 1943 but output remained at 100,000 tons a month because they had better equipment and more experience. A big push on shipping work was made ahead of the invasion of Normandy in June 1944, so output could be reduced to 83,000 tons a month afterwards. It remained at that level for the rest of the war, as the shipyards focused on shipping for the Far East before switching to post-war projects.

Shipyards built the following number of vessels during the war:

- Large naval yards built 674 vessels or 1.4 million tons.
- Small naval yards built 590 vessels or 470,000 tons.
- Large merchant yards built 44 vessels or 60,000 tons.
- Smaller merchant yards built 36 vessels or 26,000 tons.

# The Aircraft Factories

## Programming Aircraft Construction

The Ministry of Aircraft Production (MAP) took over the building of military aircraft in May 1940. The need for fighter aircraft during the Battle of Britain delayed bomber production until the Germans cancelled their invasion plans in September 1940.[10] 'Output at all costs' had been the motto during the Battle of Britain. However, quality then took precedence over quantity, because the air crews needed confidence in their aircraft. So, production grew steadily and was even slowed down at times, to allow for improvements.

Aircraft firms were advised to stop working overtime in the autumn of 1940 because there was a shortage of raw materials and components. But the workforce faced a difficult winter, as the *Luftwaffe* stepped up its attacks against the aircraft factories. Bomb damage was sometimes severe, with engine, propeller and magneto production being hit the hardest. Many companies had to disperse, dividing their workforce between several sites. While it reduced the risk from air raids, the disruption caused delays and temporarily reduced production by 20 per cent.

Estimating aircraft production was difficult to begin with, with the forecasts varying up to 30 per cent from actual output. It meant that there were regular shortages of labour, materials, machine tools and components, which led to delays on the assembly lines. There were also problems when new engine designs proved to be unreliable or unsuitable. For example, the Griffon, Peregrine and Vulture made by Rolls-Royce, the Hercules VI and Centaurus made by Bristol Aeroplane Company and the Sabre made by D. Napier & Son Limited.

A new programme that called for 2,800 bombers by the end of 1941 was reduced to a realistic figure once output had settled down.[11] The Prime Minister then asked for a 30 per cent increase in the number of aircraft in September 1941 but the MAP could only promise an extra 10 per cent. The good news was that American aircraft were being delivered, with 600 being sent directly to the Middle East. Unfortunately, Washington DC switched to equipping its own Air Force following America's entry into the war in December 1941.

The plan for 1942 was to focus on making bombers, to attack German industry. The increase in aircraft production gave the MAP priority on labour but its initial demand for 60,000 workers per month was eventually cut to 10,000. Churchill's time as Minister of Munitions during the First World War meant he recognised the manpower balance between the armed forces and industry. So, he reduced the RAF's demands for manpower, to make more men available for the aircraft factories.

Experience made it easier to estimate output and the MAP produced its first realistic bomber programme in January 1943.[12] It prompted Minister Sir Stafford Cripps to say that it was 'the most accurate forecast of what we shall in fact get produced.' While the reduction from 890 aircraft a month down to 720 shocked the War Cabinet, aircraft firms finally had achievable targets. It also meant the MAP's labour allocation could be cut to a realistic figure, while the RAF could plan operations with confidence.

Thereafter, the MAP would give priority to the firms working on the Lancaster, Halifax, Spitfire, Tempest and Mosquito. Work on old designs, poor designs and those behind on development stopped, as would the manufacture of trainer aircraft. The MAP also set up a Production Efficiency Board to offer advice and share ideas between the factories. The improvements worked and the aircraft industry reached peak production and maximum efficiency in 1943. Cripps summed up the importance of having the best aircraft possible in September 1943:

> We have throughout applied one cardinal principle: that quality is more important than mere quantity. Nothing but the best and most up to date is good enough for our magnificent airmen. Whatever the complications or drawbacks arising from the rapid introduction of improvements or changes, we must introduce these at the earliest practicable moment.[13]

## Aircraft Delays, Spares and Repairs[14]

Changes in specification often resulted in lengthy postponements. For example, when the Air Ministry wanted new bombers that could carry heavier bomb loads and fly longer distances. Producing the Stirling, Halifax and Manchester bombers all took a year longer than estimated because of engine problems, resulting in a new four-engined Halifax and the redesigned four-engined Lancaster. Problems with D. Napier & Son Limited's Sabre engine delayed work on the Tornado and Typhoon fighters and they turned out to be slower than promised. Both the Warwick and Windsor bombers also took much longer than expected to get right and they played little part in the war.

The Admiralty also faced delays with its aircraft, because it insisted on two-seater models,[15] which fitted into the aircraft carrier hangars. It resulted in the obsolete Fairey Swordfish biplane remaining in service until 1943. The Fleet Air Arm eventually flew single-seater fighters, including American designs, such as the Martlet (later known as the Wildcat), Corsair and Hellcat.

Aircraft needed spares to keep them airworthy but the Air Ministry initially thought it would be too difficult or expensive to keep repairing damaged aircraft. However, experience proved that it was more economical to repair damaged aircraft than it was to build new ones. At the height of the battle of Britain, 40 per cent of the RAF's fighters had been repaired. The number of repaired bombers flying over Europe would increase to a similar number by 1944.

Aircraft requiring replacement parts were sent to an Aircraft Storage Unit (ASU).[16] The RAF's 41 Group were managing twenty-four Aircraft Storage

Units when the MAP took them over in May 1940. Aircraft were stored in hangars called purgatories until repair work was complete. They were then moved to dispersal points, ready to be flown to their squadron.

Morris Motors Limited initially organised repairs and it sent items requiring major repair work back to the factory where they had been built. Minor repairs were outsourced to small companies. The MAP took over in 1943 and it set up workshops on the airfields, so fewer aircraft had to be sent to the ASUs. It also set up a Spares Committee and it had soon halved the number of aircraft waiting for repairs and servicing. Even so, 41 Group was always looking after hundreds of planes at any one time.

## Numbers of Aircraft Built[17]

Vickers Supermarine started producing Spitfire fighter aircraft at its Weybridge factory in Surrey in 1938. It was making 130 a month when the *Luftwaffe* bombed it in June 1940. Production then switched to the shadow factory in Castle Bromwich in the West Midlands and it soon peaked at 320 a month; the Westland Aircraft made another thirty a month.

Hawker Aircraft Limited started making the Hurricane fighter aircraft at the end of 1937. The Gloster Aircraft Company Limited also started making them in October 1939, while the Austin Motor Company Limited followed in 1941. Production of the Hurricane peaked at 277 a month in 1942, but it stopped at the end of 1944.

The Bristol Aeroplane Company started producing the Beaufighter in 1940, followed by the Fairey Aviation Company Limited in 1941 and Rootes Limited in 1943. They increased the number to around 140 a month.

Gloster started making Typhoon fighter aircraft in 1941 and Hawker began building them the following year. Hawker improved the Typhoon II and it was renamed the Tempest at the end of 1943. Gloster's factory also started making the Meteor, the first British jet-engined fighter aircraft, early in 1944.

The Bristol Aeroplane Company started making the Blenheim light bomber in 1937 and shadow factories were opened in 1938. Rootes added another shadow factory in 1941, increasing monthly production to nearly 150.

Production of the Blenheim ended in the summer of 1943, when it was replaced by the Mosquito light bomber, which was privately designed by de Havilland. Different subcontractors started making the wooden framed aircraft and while most were made at de Havilland's factories, Standard Motor Company Limited, Airspeed Limited and the Percival Aircraft Company also made them. Production soon reached 150 a month and the number continued to rise as the aircraft was given more roles.

The Whitley, Hampden and Wellington medium bombers were already in production when war broke out. Armstrong Whitworth Aircraft Limited made the Whitley, while Handley Page made the Hampden with the help of a shadow factory run by the English Electric Company. The Halifax heavy bomber would replace the Hampden in 1942. Vickers built the Wellington and output peaked at eighty aircraft a month before the company switched to making Lancasters.

The Stirling was the first heavy bomber flown by the RAF in the spring of 1940 and they were made by the Short Brothers, and Short and Harland, while Austin Motor Company Limited ran a shadow factory. Production had to be dispersed to Swindon and Belfast after the Rochester factory was bombed in the summer of 1940, reducing output to only eighty aircraft a month.

The Halifax started flying operations in October 1940 and they were made by Handley Page or at English Electric Company's shadow factory. The London Aircraft Production Group and the Fairey Aviation Company Limited started making them in 1942, while Rootes shadow factory increased the output to over 200 aircraft a month.

Avro had to abandon its work on the two-engined Manchester due to problems with Rolls-Royce's Vulture engine. Less than 200 had been made by the time it was taken off operations in June 1942. A redesign with four Rolls-Royce's Merlin engines resulted in the Lancaster heavy bomber and it became operational in October 1941. It soon became the backbone of the RAF's bomber offensive as output increased to 260 aircraft a month by 1944.

The Bristol Aeroplane Company made the Beaufort reconnaissance aircraft, while Short Brothers, Short and Harlands, and Blackburn Aircraft Limited built the Sunderland flying boat. Both the Stirling and new Warwick aircraft were used as transport planes.

Twelve companies were making old-style wood and canvas trainer aircraft a month when war broke out. The Standard Motor Company of Coventry, Morris Motors of Birmingham and Abingdon, and Brush Coachwork of Loughborough started managing shadow factories and they had increased output to 600 aircraft a month by 1941.

## The Aircraft Factories[18]

The original aircraft factories dated back to the First World War and they had large assembly sheds and an airfield for flight testing. The components and sub-assemblies were made in several factories, often in different towns. Extensions were added to the existing factories while specialist factories were built where labour was available. However, fourteen out of the seventeen original factories were in areas considered likely to be bombed and many new ones had to be built in safe areas in the north and west of England. Some of the new factories were huge structures. For example:

- Castle Bromwich factory built over 12,000 Spitfires.
- Vickers' shadow factory in Broughton near Chester completed nearly 5,800 bombers.
- Avro's factory in Yeadon near Bradford built 700 Lancasters and 4,500 Ansons.
- Avro's factories in Chadderton and Woodford near Manchester made 3,000 Lancasters.

Aircraft firms had only employed a few hundred men back in the 1930s but wartime demands resulted in the workforce increasing many times in size. Vickers-Armstrongs Limited brought Vickers Aviation and Supermarine under direct management and its workforce eventually peaked at 53,000 employees, split evenly between them. Hawker Siddeley eventually employed 65,000 working in several factories, including Avro which had 35,000 employees. Rootes and the English Electric Company employed over 13,000, while the Austin Motor Company, Metropolitan-Vickers and the London Aircraft Production Group employed nearly 10,000 each.

Air raids resulted in the dispersal of work to smaller factories over the winter of 1940–1941. While it reduced the danger from bombing, it had also reduced production of aircraft down to 1,200 a month by the New Year. When possible, existing buildings were used, because new ones took too long to build. However, purpose built structures were still required to accommodate the aircraft's final assembly.

Aircraft were made from thousands of parts of all shapes and sizes. For example, the Lancaster bomber had 55,000 parts. Dozens of subcontractors had been contracted to make them during the rearmament period before the war, allowing the aircraft companies to focus on the final assembly. The firms had been organised into groups, so complete aircraft kits could be made. However, the number of firms involved had to be increased when the work had to be dispersed. Eventually hundreds of firms were involved, from car factories and textile machinery manufacturers to railway locomotive and carriage shops.

An assessment of the aircraft industry was made when dispersal was completed and the number of aircraft rolling off the assembly lines had increased to 2,000 a month by the end of 1941. The MAP considered introducing a second shift to build more Lancasters in October 1941 but there were insufficient supervisors and skilled workers available. However, most factories employed a night shift which prepare sub-assemblies for the day shift. Experience reduced the number of hours needed to build an aircraft, sometimes as much as 75 per cent.

The aircraft industry's workforce eventually increased to over 1.7 million, making it the largest sector of Britain's armaments industry. By the spring of 1944, 24 aircraft firms were making 2,500 aircraft a month and each firm managed several factories. It had taken two years longer than planned to meet the initial targets set, because building an aircraft industry had turned out to be far more complicated than anyone imagined. However, setting up a shadow industry and making use of hundreds of subcontractors had proved to be successful policies.

## The Manufacturers[19]

Companies were soon managing several factories at several locations but each one focused on making one model, once the Air Ministry had accepted the prototype. These are the companies that made each model and the main factories where they made them:

### Fighter Aircraft

- Vickers Supermarine built Spitfires near Weybridge in Surrey.
- Vickers-Armstrongs built Spitfires in Castle Bromwich.
- Westland built Spitfires and Whirlwinds in Yeovil, Somerset.
- Hawker built Hurricanes at Kingston-upon-Thames in London and Langley near Slough.

- Gloster built Hurricanes in Hucclecote near Gloucester.
- Austins ran a shadow factory making Hurricanes in Cofton Hackett, Worcestershire.
- Boulton & Paul built Defiants in Pendeford near Wolverhampton.
- Bristol built Blenheims in Filton near Bristol and at its Weston-Super-Mare shadow factory.
- Fairey built Beaufighters in Stockport and Ringway near Manchester.
- Bristol made Beaufighters in Weston-super-Mare.
- Rootes built Beaufighters at their Speke factory near Liverpool.
- Rootes ran a shadow factory in Blythe Bridge, Staffordshire.
- Hawker built Typhoon and Tempests in Langley near Slough.
- Gloster built Typhoons and Meteors in Hucclecote near Gloucester.

## Light and Medium Bombers

These are the main firms which built light and medium bombers:

- Vickers-Armstrongs built Wellingtons in Blackpool, Chester and Weybridge.
- Handley Page built Hampdens in Radlett, north of London.
- English Electric Company ran a shadow factory making Hampdens in Preston.
- Armstrong Whitworth built Whitley bombers at Whitley near Coventry before moving production to Lancaster.
- Bristol Aeroplane Company built Blenheims in Filton near Bristol.
- Avro managed a Blenheim shadow factory in Chadderton near Manchester
- Rootes ran a Blenheim shadow factory in Ryton-on-Dunsmore near Coventry.
- De Havilland built Mosquitos in Hatfield and Watford, north of London.
- Standard Motor Company ran a Mosquito shadow factory at Ansty near Coventry.
- Percival Aircraft Company made Mosquitos in Luton.
- Airspeed built Mosquitos at York and Oxford trainers near Portsmouth.

## Heavy Bombers

The following firms built heavy bombers, supported by companies running shadow factories:

- Handley Page built Halifax bombers in Cricklewood, north of London.
- Fairey built Halifax bombers in Stockport and Ringway near Manchester.
- English Electric Company ran a Halifax shadow factory near Preston in Lancashire.
- The London Aircraft Production Group coordinated the work of many factories that made parts for Halifax bombers in Preston, Speke and Stockport, as well as across London.
- Rootes assembled Halifax bombers at Speke near Liverpool and Blythe Bridge in Staffordshire.
- Short Brothers built Stirling bombers at Rochester, in Kent, dispersing to Swindon after the factory was bombed in the summer of 1940.
- Short and Harland built Stirlings in Belfast in Northern Ireland.
- Austin Motor Company ran a shadow factory building Stirling bombers in Cofton Hackett in Worcestershire.
- Rootes built Stirlings at its shadow factory in Stoke-on-Trent.
- Avro built Lancaster bombers in Chadderton near Manchester and Yeadon near Bradford.
- Armstrong Whitworth built Lancasters near Coventry.
- Vickers-Armstrongs built Lancasters at Broughton near Chester and Castle Bromwich.
- Metropolitan-Vickers ran a Lancaster shadow factory at Trafford Park near Manchester.
- Austin's built Lancasters at their Longbridge shadow factory in Birmingham.
- Austin's assembled Lancasters at its shadow factory at Cofton Hackett in Worcestershire.
- Short and Harland built Warwicks in Belfast.
- Vickers-Armstrongs made Warwicks at its shadow factory in Weybridge.

The number of firms involved in making each type of aircraft were:

- Thirteen firms made heavy and medium bombers.
- Fourteen firms made light bombers and fighters.
- Seven firms made reconnaissance aircraft.
- Ten firms made naval aircraft.
- Nine firms made transport aircraft.
- Fifteen firms made trainer aircraft.

## The Fleet Air Arm

The Admiralty took over responsibility for the Fleet Air Arm in 1939. It opened a repair yard at Fleetlands in Hampshire and another at Donibristle in Fife, to support the fleet based in Scapa; private aircraft companies also did a lot of repair work. Early models needed folding wings, so they could be stored in hangars, which increased their weight and slowed them down. Problems with the Albacore biplane and the Barracuda monoplane meant that the Swordfish biplane stayed in use until 1943. They carried out successful operations against the Italian fleet in Taranto in November 1940 and against the German battleship Bismarck in May 1941. Eventually, the Fleet Air Arm used eight types of aircraft but only the Swordfish and the Seafire lasted for some time. Production peaked at 280 aircraft a month in 1944:

- Fairey built Swordfish and Albacore biplanes in Hayes, Middlesex.
- Fairey made the Fulmar and Barracuda in Stockport and the Firefly in Hayes.
- Saunders-Roe Limited built the Walrus and then the Sea Otter on the Isle of Wight.
- Blackburn made Swordfish, Barracudas and Firebrands in Brough and Dumbarton.
- Boulton & Paul built Barracudas in Wolverhampton.
- General Aircraft built Fireflies in Hanworth, West London, but they were never used.
- Supermarine, Westland, Castle Bromwich, and Cunliffe-Owen Aircraft of Hampshire all made Seafires.

## The Engineering Factories

### Programming the Ministry of Supply's Output[20]

The Director General of Munitions Production was transferred to the new Ministry of Supply in August 1939. A Central Statistics Branch collected data, so The Right Honourable Leslie Burgin MP could monitor output and deal with problems. He also used the Production Secretariat's forecasts to create short- and long-term estimates. They enabled the War Office to plan its strategies and helped it decide what to order from American factories.

Prime Minister Winston Churchill appointed The Right Honourable Herbert Morrison MP his Minster for Supply in May 1940. He also appointed Sir Walter Layton as the Director General of Programmes and gave him the task of linking military strategy to industrial output. He collected information on the labour, machine tools, materials, buildings and shipping capacity required to make what the armed forces required. He then drew up long-term programmes and resolved any potential issues.

The BEF left all its equipment behind at Dunkirk in June 1940, so the British Army had to compile a 'deficiency list' to replace it, as well as an 'insurance programme' to build up a reserve. Meanwhile, Churchill and his Chiefs of Staff agreed on a strategy which gave the British Army's demands a low priority. The Royal Navy needed help to defend the country and the Merchant Navy needed resources to supply it. Meanwhile, the RAF had to be expanded, so it could attack Germany's industry, while the Civil Defence Service needed 490,000 staff, to counter air raids.

The British Army's plans and commitments soon increased, starting with extra armoured units required for the North African campaign, as well as commando and airborne units. So, while the RAF and the Royal Navy were getting the lion's share of what industry could offer, the Ministry of Supply sourced what it could.

Morrison arranged imports though the British Purchasing Commission in America and the British Supply Board in Canada. His plan was to create an 'insurance programme' of North American imports, in air raids interfered with production. He also started dealing with South Africa, India, Australia and New Zealand, forming them into the Eastern Supply Group.

A Victory Conference between Britain and America in September 1941 issued plans to equip the British Army. However, everything changed when Japan went to war in December 1941. The War Office had to consider how to defend Malaya, Burma (now Myanmar) and India, while supporting the Dominion, Colonial and Allied troops who also faced Japan. Meanwhile, the US War and Naval Departments wanted its units equipping first.

The Ministry of Supply worked hard to meet the War Office's demands for 10,450 tanks and 14,650 armoured carriers. It also wanted 10,200 anti-tank guns, as well as 22,650 field and AA guns. Huge amounts of ammunition were also required, including 8 million shells and 277 million bullets.[21] Churchill was suspicious of the numbers and an investigation soon reduced the quantities.

While the British armaments industry worked flat out to meet the targets, news from North Africa at the end of 1942 suggested that ammunition expenditure had been less than estimated. It meant that many factories could cut production soon after they reached their maximum output. The reductions were carefully planned, so that the workforce could be redistributed but many were made redundant, because there was no alterative work.

## Expanding the Royal Ordnance Factory Organisation[22]

Expansion of the ROF organisation resulted in three new types of factories being built with government funding. The first involved giving a grant to a company to extend their premises. The second involved giving a company a grant to build an agency factory on a different site. In the early days, ICI built most of the agency factories to make explosives. Later examples made bullets and AA guns. In both the above cases, the management company paid the employees. The third example was the shadow factory and they were built and run by private companies with the help of an experienced contractor.

Many new factories were built in the safe areas of Scotland, Wales and northwest England and while some of them employed as many as 25,000 workers, others had a workforce of less than 1,000. Factories were run by a Superintendent and they found it to be a challenge to safely organise inexperienced labour who were involved in dangerous processes.

There were twenty-five ROFs employing a total of 110,000 workers by the end of 1940, increasing to forty-three factories employing 294,000 by 1942:

- Nine explosives factories employed 41,000.
- Twenty-four weapons and ammunition factories employed 100,000.
- Ten filling factories employed 153,000.

Another 650,000 workers were employed by subcontractors working for the ROFs.

## The Engineering Factories[23]

The Royal Arsenal Factory in Woolwich employed 14,000 while the Royal Small Arms Factory (RSAF) in Enfield employed 6,000 at the start of the war. Managers from the two factories set up engineering ROFs across the North over the winter of 1939–1940 and around 60 per cent of the workforce were women. The gun and shell factories never employed more than 7,000, however, some of the small arms factories had nearly 10,000 workers while the largest bullet factory required over 14,000 for its labour intensive work.

Many of the private armament companies were in the danger zones, along the River Thames and the River Tyne. Others were in the unsafe zone, between Birmingham, the Midlands and Manchester. While no large extensions were built around London, other companies built extensions close to their parent factory, so skilled managers and workers were on hand. These are some of the engineering ROFs:

- ROF Dalmuir in Scotland made 25-pounder guns and AA guns.
- ROF Birtley in County Durham made cartridge cases.
- ROF Blackburn in Lancashire made fuses.
- ROF Beech Hill in Wigan made shells.
- ROF Patricroft in Manchester made AA guns.
- ROF Leeds in West Yorkshire made 25-pounder guns.
- ROF Nottingham in Nottinghamshire made field guns.
- ROF Cardiff in South Wales made field guns and tanks.
- ROF Newport in South Wales made anti-tank guns and AA guns.
- ROF Brackla and ROF Waterton in South Wales both filled fuses.
- ROF Hirwaun in South Wales made bullets.
- ROF Theale in Berkshire made Sten guns.

- ROF Poole in Dorset made AA guns.
- A factory at Melmerby in North Yorkshire inspected armaments.

## The Tank Factories[24]

Over 1,000 tanks had been delivered by the time the Ministry of Supply took over tank production in August 1939. The Royal Arsenal dealt with experimental tanks, while the Tanks and Transport Directorate focused on production. Locomotive and vehicle manufacturers made the parts while Vickers-Armstrongs assembled the tanks. The War Office also worked with Morris Motors Limited, resulting in the company setting up Nuffield Organization in Birmingham.

Production of tanks began in earnest in the autumn of 1939 and output had increased to seventy-five a month by the spring of 1940. The campaign in France proved that heavier tanks were needed and more firms were contracted to make them after the evacuation of Dunkirk in June 1940. While priority was given to the aircraft factories throughout the battle of Britain, output had still doubled to 150 tanks a month by the end of the year. However, it would take a long time to equip the nine armoured divisions and six tank brigades planned by the War Office.

The foundries made the steel, while engineering firms did the heat treatment and machining. However, the Tank Parliament was quick to point out that the industry was short of everything, so the Production Executive had to give tank production a higher priority.

Design and production problems were eventually ironed out and more companies were contracted to make Matilda, Valentine and Crusader tanks. Some built the subassemblies and transmission units, while others made specialised items like the engines, guns and radios. The parts were sent to the factories making the hulls, so the tanks could be assembled.

American factories never built British designed tanks but the US Ordnance Department took note of the British Army's experiences on the battlefield. They changed the sponson mounted 75-millimetre gun on the M3 (General Lee) to a turret mounted gun on the M3 (General Grant). The US Armored Force Boards' design of the M4 (Sherman) was also influenced. A US Tank Mission visited Britain in the summer of 1942, to coordinate

American manufacturing ideas with the newly appointed Armoured Fighting Vehicles Division. They both listened to the feedback from North Africa and noted that lower silhouettes and thicker armour improved a tank's defensive capabilities.

The percentage of cruiser tanks required by the British Army was increased from 50 to 75 per cent, while the crews reported that their top priorities were reliability and speed. Thicker armour was also requested but that required more powerful engines and improved suspensions. Crews also wanted a better designed fighting compartment, as well as more powerful guns, so the 6-pounder gun was introduced. The General Staff wanted a gun which could fire high explosive, because tanks often faced infantry or anti-tank guns. So, the American 75-millimetre gun was introduced, because it could fire both armour piercing and high explosive shells.

The number of companies involved in building tanks eventually increased to twenty-eight and production peaked at 750 tanks a month. By the end of the war, British factories had delivered 19,055 tanks.

## Building Cruiser Tanks

Vickers-Armstrongs Limited of Newcastle-upon-Tyne and Sheffield had started manufacturing the A9 Cruiser Mark I tank in 1936. It was armed with the 2-pounder Quick Fire gun but they proved to be unreliable in France, so only 125 were built. Vickers-Armstrongs had also started making the A10 Cruiser Mark II tank in 1938. It had thicker armour and was armed with a 2-pounder anti-tank gun and the purpose made Besa machine guns made by the Birmingham Small Arms Company Limited. However, only 175 were made.

The faster A13 Cruiser Mark III tank was equipped with the Liberty V12 engine and the Christie chassis. Nuffield Mechanizations and Aero Limited of Birmingham had only built sixty-five when they switched to making the A13 Cruiser Mark IV tank, which had thicker armour. The majority of the 955 tanks they made were deployed to North Africa.

The Cruiser Mark V Covenanter tank was built by London, Midland and Scottish Railway, as well as Leyland Motors and the English Electric Company, both from the Preston area. Problems with overheating only became apparent after it had gone into production, so all 1,700 tanks were used for training and auxiliary duties in Britain.

There was more success with the Cruiser Mark VI Crusader I tank manufactured by Nuffield Organization and the first ones reached North Africa in May 1941. It stayed in production much longer than expected because it took time to design something better and around 5,300 were made. It was eventually replaced by the American M3 Grant followed by the M4 Sherman.

The Cavalier Cruiser Mark VII was also built by Nuffield Organization but only 500 were used for training and auxiliary tasks because the Centaur and Cromwell were preferred. However, the A27L Centaur Mark VIII suffered from breakdowns while the 410 horsepower Liberty engine was underpowered. So, Leyland Motors, the English Electric Company, Harland & Wolff, London, Midland and Scottish Railway, Morris Motors, John Fowler & Co. Limited and Ruston-Bucyrus Limited of Lincoln built 950 Centaurs for training purposes. Nuffield Organization also started making them when it finished building Cavaliers.

The A27M Cromwell Cruiser Mark VIII was the same design as the Centaur but its 600 horsepower Meteor engine was more powerful and reliable, so they were deployed to Normandy in June 1944. Over 3,000 were built by English Electric Company Limited and the Metropolitan-Cammell Carriage and Wagon Company.

The Challenger A30 Cruiser Mark VIII was armed with the dual purpose 17-pounder gun. However, it needed a high profile turret which made it a conspicuous target. Factory space was limited so the Birmingham Railway Carriage and Wagon Company had only built 200 before it was decided to arm American built Shermans with the 17-pounder gun instead. They were called Sherman Fireflies.

The Comet A34 Cruiser Tank had a smaller profile and it was armed with the 77-millimetre high velocity gun. They were manufactured by Leyland Motors, English Electric Company, John Fowler's and the Metropolitan-Cammell Carriage and Wagon Company. The first ones were deployed in January 1945 and 1,200 were made.

## Building Infantry Tanks

The A11 Infantry Tank Mark I was only armed with a machine gun, it had a cramped compartment and was slow. Vickers-Armstrongs only built 140 and many were lost during the French campaign. The A12 Infantry Tank Mark II was a different design and it became known as the Matilda II. It was armed with a 2-pounder anti-tank gun and while it had thick armour, the Associated Equipment Company (AEC) engine was slow and the coil spring suspension was uncomfortable. While those deployed to France were abandoned around Dunkirk, many were sent to fight in the North African campaign. The Matilda proved its worth in the North African campaign and nearly 3,000 were made by six factories:

- North British Locomotive Company Limited in Glasgow.
- Harland & Wolff in Belfast.
- London, Midland and Scottish Railway Horwich works in Lancashire.
- Vulcan Foundry Limited on Merseyside.
- John Fowler & Co. of Leeds.
- Rushton and Hornsby in Lincoln.

Over 400 Mark II Matildas were shipped to Australia for use in the Pacific as late as 1943. The Mark III Matilda was powered by an engine that was produced by Leyland Motors, while the Mark IV was armed with a 3-inch howitzer.

The Valentine Infantry Tank Mark III was a successful design and while early marks were powered by an Associated Equipment Company (AEC) engine, later ones were fitted with imported engines made by General Motors. It had a Horstmann suspension, which gave a smoother ride on triple sets of wheels mounted on bogies. Vickers-Armstrongs, the Birmingham Railway Carriage and Wagon Company and the Metropolitan-Cammell Carriage and Wagon Company in Birmingham and Wednesbury built 6,855 of them. Another 1,420 were made by CPR Angus Ships in Montreal, Canada. There were nine Marks and they were in use from 1940 to 1945. More Valentines were built than any other tank and nearly 2,400 were shipped to the Soviet Union.

Charles Roberts & Company Limited of Wakefield and Dennis Brothers Limited of Guildford made the hulls and turrets of the A22 Churchill Infantry Tank Mark IV for Vauxhall Motors to assemble in Luton. Other parts were also made by many companies, including Whessoe Foundry and Engineering of Darlington, Babcock & Wilcox of Renfrew near Glasgow and the Metropolitan-Cammell Carriage and Wagon Company of Birmingham. Gloucester Railway Carriage and Wagon Company and Newton, Chambers and Co. Limited in Chapeltown, north of Sheffield, assembled many of Churchills.[25]

The first Churchill tanks took part in the Dieppe Raid in August 1942 but eleven different marks had been deployed by the end of the war. Early models were armed with the 2-pounder but later ones were equipped with the 6-pounder and 17-pounder; some were armed with the 75- or 95-millimetre howitzer.

## Building Other Armoured Vehicles

Attempts to make a self-propelled tank destroyer by fitting a 3-inch gun to a Churchill failed. So, the Archer self-propelled tank destroyer was built by placing a box structure on top of a Valentine hull. It was armed with a fixed 17-pounder gun mounted back to front, so the crew could fire from an ambush position before driving away. Vickers-Armstrongs built 655 and the first ones were deployed in October 1944.

The Universal Carrier or Bren Carrier was an Armoured Personnel Carrier and 57,000 had been built by the end of the war. Many factories were involved, including Vickers Armstrong, Aveling-Barford, Bedford Vehicles, Ford of Britain,[26] Morris Motors, Wolseley Motors, Sentinel Waggon Works and John Thornycroft.

## Tank Guns, Armour, Engines and Suspension[27]

The Director of Artillery did hardly any work on tank and anti-tank guns between the wars but the 2-pounder (40-millimetre calibre) gun had been adopted by January 1935. The A9 Cruiser tank and the Matilda II were the first tanks armed with the gun in 1937, while Vickers-Armstrongs designed a three-legged carriage so it could be used as an anti-tank gun. Although the gun could penetrate 25-millimetre armour plate at a range of 1,000 yards, tanks were soon being built with thicker armour.

The Germans were soon working on a 50-millimetre gun but the War Office hesitated to order the 6-pounder (57-millimetre calibre) in case it interrupted production of the 2-pounder. The North African campaign proved that the 6-pounder was needed, so the Ministry of Supply started making them in November 1941. The British Army eventually adopted the gun in April 1942 and then wanted them as quickly as possible, so 1,500 a month were soon being made.

Over fifty companies were involved in making tanks and anti-tank guns, when the General Staff declared it wanted a 75-millimetre tank gun which could fire both armour piercing and high explosive shells in September 1942. Eventually 50 per cent of tanks were armed with the 6- or 17-pounder gun, while 30 per cent of tanks were equipped with the dual purpose 75-millimetre gun. The remaining 20 per cent were equipped with the 95-millimetre howitzer, which could fire smoke, high explosive, or High-Explosive Anti-Tank (HEAT) rounds.

The 17-pounder (76.2-millimetre calibre) gun appeared in April 1943 and 2,200 had been made by the end of the war. While it could knock out most German tanks, it was so heavy it needed a large tractor to move the anti-tank gun version. Another 2,300 17-pounders were mounted on Shermans and while 200 were fitted onto the new Challenger tank, the combination was unsuccessful. A British made medium velocity 75-millimetre gun was fitted to Churchills and Cromwells for the invasion of Normandy, while the Vickers high velocity 75-millimetre gun (called a 77-millimetre) was mounted in the Comet.

Piercing caps improved the penetration capabilities of shells, while ballistic caps increased their range. Longer barrels, tapered bores, larger propellant charges and heavier shot weights also improved their effectiveness. Meanwhile, muzzle brakes were added to gun barrels, after finding one on a captured German anti-tank gun, because they reduced the recoil from a shot.

The Armaments Design Department produced a composite-rigid shot shell which had a tungsten core and improved ballistics. The Research Department then developed the Discarding Sabot shell, which lost its alloy body during flight, exposing the ballistic core. A high-explosive round that could be fired from a tank gun was also developed by 1944, inspired by the American dual purpose 75-millimetre gun.

Tank designers looked at which type of armour gave the best defence. Homogeneous plate had the same toughness right through and gave the best defence against capped projectiles. Meanwhile, face-hardened plate was better at stopping plain projectiles. Both were considered before the war but no one knew what shells the German guns would fire, so homogeneous plate was used because it was easier to make.

As the months passed, there was a need for thicker armour and that required better quality steel. There were also limitations on which parts could be cast. It was easier to weld during the assembly process but a lack of facilities meant that most parts were rivetted.

Increased armour resulted in heavier tanks and they required more powerful engines. Pre-war models were equipped with 150 or 190 horsepower engines, while they were 350 horsepower by the middle of the war and 600 horsepower at the end. The problem was how to fit a suitable engine into a low profile tank without overheating the crew compartment. Early models were based on commercial vehicle engines but later ones were based on lighter aircraft models which had a higher power to weight ratio. Here are some of the tank engines used:

- An AEC 150 horsepower petrol engine for the A9 Mark I Cruiser tank.
- The Meadows DAV Flat-12 340 horsepower petrol engine for the Covenanter tank.
- The Nuffield Organization's Liberty V12 340 horsepower petrol engine for the Crusader tank.
- An AEC 135 horsepower petrol or diesel engines, then the GMC 210 horsepower diesel engine for the Valentine tank.
- Two AEC or two Leyland Motors 190 brake horsepower engines for the Matilda II tank.
- A Vauxhall Motors (Bedford) 12-cylinder 350 horsepower petrol engine for Churchill tanks.
- A Rolls-Royce Meteor V12 600 horsepower petrol engine for A27M Cromwell and Challenger tanks.

Many engines were imported from the United States.

The original tanks rode on leaf spring or coil suspension systems. However, they were primitive and gave a rough ride, limiting the tank's top speed. The Christie suspension allowed wheels to be pushed up individually, while springs pushed them back down to their starting position. The system gave a smoother ride over rough terrain, which allowed the crew to drive at faster speeds.

Tracks were made from Hadfields Limited's manganese steel, a tough, hard wearing alloy. The Christie chassis needed a slacker track to cope with the higher speeds and greater movement, so they had to be made wider to stop them coming off the wheels.

## Artillery and Anti-Aircraft Guns[28]

A mixture of new ROFs, agency factories and private firms made all types of guns and their carriages. Vickers-Armstrongs Limited expanded production at its huge Newcastle-upon-Tyne factory, while William Beardmore and Company Limited built two agency factories and took over the ROF in Dalmuir near Glasgow. G. & J. Weir Limited assembled 25-pounder gun carriages made by a group of firms at their Glasgow factory. The addition of new factories allowed gun and carriage production to reach its peak by the start of 1942.

The British Army was still using the same AA guns it had used during the First World War in the mid-1930s, even though the German aircraft were flying much faster and higher.[29] The *Luftwaffe* was also increasing the number of aircraft it had, so the War Office wanted to double the number of AA weapons it had. While there were plans to disperse industry and prepare civilians for air raids, the Civil Defence Service wanted as many AA guns as possible to protect factories and urban areas.

The Swedish designed Bofors 40-millimetre and the Vickers-Armstrongs Limited 3.7-inch were chosen because they were mobile. The Nuffield Organization and ROF Nottingham made the guns while engineering companies made the mountings. Meanwhile, the Research Department worked on flashless propellants to keep the guns hidden and tracer compounds to help aiming, while looking at how to reduce barrel wear. It also designed 3-inch AA rockets but they proved to be inaccurate.

Many lessons were learned about AA guns during the battle for France and the battle of Britain. The 3.7-inch AA gun was too cumbersome but the 4.5-inch AA gun had proved its worth. Meanwhile, the 3-inch AA gun could shoot to a high ceiling while the 40-millimetre Bofors gun had a high rate of fire. A converted 3-pounder gun was also used until it was replaced by the lightweight 20-millimetre Oerlikon autocannon.

Engineers who had escaped Poland when Germany invaded, redesigned the 20-millimetre Oerlikon AA gun. They also designed the Polsten AA gun which was quicker and cheaper to make. Twenty firms made the parts while Sigmund Pumps of Gateshead and the Forgrove Machinery Company of Leeds assembled them. John Inglis of Toronto, Canada, also manufactured AA guns.

Initially specialist factories made 20-millimetre calibre shells but many other ammunition firms were soon making them. Motor car firms made 40-millimetre calibre shells while used shell casings were sent to Vickers-Armstrongs Limited's foundry, ICI and the ROFs to be recycled. Over 16 million AA shells would be made during the war.

Designs were modified to reduce the weight and speed up the production of all types of the guns. Professor Patrick Blackett worked with Lieutenant General Sir Frederick Pile at Anti-Aircraft Command to make further improvements to AA guns, including:

- Predictors to help the crew aim at a fast moving aircraft; a technique called leading the target.
- Radar devices to pinpoint approaching aircraft, particularly at night.
- Proximity fuses which detonated a shell close to an aircraft.
- Fuses which set automatically, according to the crew's assessment of the target's height.
- Automatic loaders which increased a gun's rate of fire.

The first V-1 rockets were aimed at London in June 1944 but they usually flew too high for the light AA guns and too low for the heavy AA guns. An improved target predictor device and a radio proximity fuze helped shoot them down, while Fighter Command worked with Anti-Aircraft Command to chase them down. Although nearly two thirds of the rockets were brought down, over 2,400 hit London causing over 24,000 casualties and damaging nearly 100,000 buildings. The V-1 threat ended when the final launch sites were captured in October, but another threat soon took its place.

The V-2 rocket travelled much faster and while they were inaccurate, they had a huge payload. The first ones were fired at London in September and plans to track the weapons, so they could be detonated by massed batteries of AA guns, were underway by the time the final one was aimed at the capital in March 1945. Over 1,350 had been fired at London and they had caused nearly 9,300 casualties. The Germans had started using the *Leitstrahl* (radio guide beam) system to guide them to their targets. However, false reports of them overshooting the capital convinced the operators to shorten the range. It meant that many landed in open countryside.

## Shell and Bullet Production[30]

A wide range of engineering firms made the parts for shells, however, filling them was a specialist task which needed purpose built factories. A First World War era factory near Hereford was reopened during the rearmament period, while work began on three large factories. Another five were added in 1940, to cope with the British Army's plan to form more divisions. A further expansion plan required four more factories but that included extra production, as an insurance against bomb damage. Sixteen other filling factories would be built for other ordnance, such as bombs and AA rockets.

Filling enough shells was a problem in the early days but the *Luftwaffe* caused less damage than anticipated. Filling also turned out to be faster than estimated; even more so when the organisation switched to a three-shift system at the beginning of 1941. A workforce of 150,000 were filling 2.3 million shells a month by the end of the year. Production increased so much, that plans for more filling factories were cancelled. Some were even shut down and their work concentrated into the remaining ones.

The Royal Arsenal, ICI, and Greenwood & Batley were making bullets at the start of the war. Eleven new factories were built and production reached its peak at 32 million a month in the summer of 1942.

## Equipping the Factories[31]

Every factory needed powered machine tools for trimming, drilling and milling steel and alloy parts. Britain was only making 1,650 machine tools a month in the 1930s and many were being exported around the world. There had been a shortage during the early months of the First World War, so a Supply Board was appointed to double the number made, when rearmament got underway. Motor car and engineering firms imported large numbers, in anticipation of an increase in business and a shortage of tools. The Supply Board checked what firms required, so machine tools would be sent where they were needed.

On the outbreak of war in September 1939, the machine tool industry employed 20,000 workers and while they were now making over 3,000 machine tools a month, another 700 had to be imported because they were better designs or did specialist tasks. A large number were still being exported, most of them across the Commonwealth. A big increase in armaments orders resulted in bottlenecks, backlogs and delays in the factories, so the Ministry of Supply appointed a Machine Tool Controller to sort out the problems. His staff worked out company requirements, reported shortages and distributed machine tools, so orders could be met. They also gave advice and making sure repairs were dealt with quickly, so firms could maintain their output.

The demand for machine tools doubled during the summer of 1940, with the MAP wanting to increase aircraft production, while the Ministry of Supply was trying to re-equip the British Army. An Inter-Service Machine Tools Committee eventually had to be set up, to get the best use out of the limited number of machine tools available. Long hours meant machine tools had to be replaced when they wore out or broke. Tools had to be recalibrated when a factory started making new components. So, an Emergency Machine Tool Utilisation Corps, helped factories train their labour to get the best use out of them.

The Priority of Production Direction Committee checked demands against the programmes and prioritised who needed what tools, so the Machine Tool Controller could distribute them. A licensing system was then put in place to stop unnecessary demands, while his staff made sure factories asked for the right model and then used them efficiently. The MAP had managed to import hundreds of machine tools during the summer of 1940 and while they had helped increased the output of aircraft during the Battle of Britain, many were hardly being used. The Machine Tool Controller had his staff redistribute them when he found out.[32]

The Soviet Union's entry into the war in June 1941 added an extra burden onto British industry, because the Arctic convoys had to take many machine tools to its northern ports. Britain made the standard designs, while large or unusual designs were shipped from America. British production eventually peaked at 8,000 a month in 1942, with another 3,000 being imported.

Over 600 firms employed 64,000 workers and more than 20 per cent were women. Every factory had what it needed by 1943 but the Machine Tool Controller was kept busy distributing replacements and dealing with repairs. Over time, armaments were designed so as many parts as possible could be made with standard tools, resulting in over 100 specialist tools being made obsolete. The Ministry of Supply alone eventually used 150,000 machine tools and nearly half were imported.

A wide variety of small tools were fitted onto machine tools to do the cutting, drilling and milling.[33] The Machine Tool Controller organised their manufacture but the emergency conditions during the summer of 1940 caused overordering and poor distribution. Production soon increased as did the number of carbide tipped tools being made, which economised on the use of hard-wearing high-speed and tool steel.[34] Eventually, 1,200 small tool firms employed 54,000 workers; 40 per cent of them women. They made hundreds of thousands of small tools; a similar number were imported from America.

The Industrial Electrical Equipment Directorate distributed electrical equipment, power tools, welding machines and cutting tools. It also sourced the jigs and fixtures required to hold larger parts in place, while they were being worked on. The Machine Tool Controller eventually took responsibility for testing and licensing all kinds of electrical equipment, including machine tools, cranes and welding equipment.

Inspectors needed gauges to check that every component was made correctly, so they fitted together well and worked correctly. They also needed to be precise, so that parts made by different factories were interchangeable. The British Standards Institute and the Machine Tool Controller issued specifications in 1940, as the demand for gauges increased to 7,500 a month. Private firms made them for the Ministry of Supply and Ministry of Aircraft Production but the Admiralty opened a factory to make its own gauges. The Electrical and Mechanical Equipment Inspectorate and the Fighting Vehicles Inspectorate also set up their own gauge workshops.

*Chapter 10*

# Expanding the Workforce

## Recruiting for the Factories

### Neville Chamberlain's Government[1]

The Ministry of Labour was renamed the Ministry of Labour and National Service on the outbreak of war, to reflect its role in recruitment for the armed forces. It had departments to deal with employment, industrial relations, training and unemployment; it also managed the Schedule of Reserved Occupations, which exempted workers from serving in the armed forces. The Military Recruiting Department dealt with conscription and the National Service Act required men of specified ages to register for a medical. Meanwhile, the National Service Department accepted volunteers for the Civil Defence Service.

Initially, the government's plan was to form fifty-five infantry divisions within twelve months. It also wanted industry to build 2,300 planes and 170,000 tons of shipping per month in the same period. That required a workforce of 2.2 million and the Military Recruiting Department aimed to train huge numbers of unemployed men and women to work in the armaments industry. While a study reported that these targets would be impossible to meet, the government kept them as something to aim for.

The expansion plans raised many issues over the winter of 1939–1940. Experienced firms found themselves overwhelmed with work, while inexperienced companies were ignored. Some firms reported that they were short of machine tools or raw materials. Many firms refused to release their skilled workers to help set up new factories, while the aircraft factories offered high wages to poach the best staff. Meanwhile, there were many reports of key workers being called up for the armed forces. Sorting out so many short-term problems meant there was no time to focus on the long-term problem of how to increase the workforce.

The Control of Employment Act meant that labour could be transferred to where they were needed but only with trade union agreement. The Customs Relaxation Agreement removed work demarcations, so workers could do different tasks, while unskilled workers could be trained to do jobs. However, many companies did not want to employ untrained labour, while the trade unions were anxious to protect their members' jobs.

Wages started to become an issue during the recruitment drive in the early months of the war. While workers and trade union leaders wanted to increase them, employers were concerned about poaching and industrial unrest. The government did not want them to rise either because it would increase inflation and the cost of living. So, it started subsidising the cost of food stuffs, to keep prices down. It also promoted an economy drive in April 1940, to reduce the amount of goods that had to be made or imported. Even so, wages rose steadily as companies struggled to find enough labour to meet their orders. Meanwhile, the supply departments refused to pressure their contractors to take on more skilled workers, in case it caused industrial unrest.

The lack of direction by the Ministry of Labour, Ernest Brown, had only increased labour in the armaments factories by 10 per cent by the spring of 1940. Unemployment was still high and very few women had been taken on either. There was also a shortage of labour for building the many new factories, military bases and home defence facilities required. First Lord of the Admiralty, Winston Churchill, eventually told the War Cabinet that he believed 'that the organisation of the manpower of the country for the production of munitions had hardly begun.'[2] He knew what it would take because he had been the Minister of Armaments during the final months of the First World War.

## The Churchill Government Takes Over[3]

Everything changed when Winston Churchill was appointed Prime Minister on 10 May 1940. He made Ernest Bevin his Minister of Labour and National Service. Bevin may have had no House of Commons experience but he had plenty of labour relations' knowledge, having served as General Secretary of the Transport and General Workers' Union for over twenty years.

Churchill learnt that the National Service Act had already directed 450,000 men into the armed forces, leaving the nation short of the skilled workers required to make armaments. So, Bevin drew up a scheme to mobilise the nation's workforce and hopefully resolve its labour demands. He also appointed a Production Council with instructions to make sure that the armaments factories made what the armed forces' required. A Manpower Statistics Branch resolve labour problems and it kept the War Cabinet up to date with the state of industry.

Bevin appointed a Labour Supply Inspectorate to improve the distribution of labour, as well as Regional Boards which had instructions to increase the number of training courses. A Factory Department and a Welfare Department also advised firms on how to improve welfare in their establishments. Meanwhile, a Women's Consultative Committee looked at how to help women into work.

Churchill's administration inspired a positive attitude across Britain's workforce, despite the disaster unfolding in Dunkirk. Bevin extended the Emergency Powers Act, to take control of the essential industries; it also imposed a 100 per cent excess profits tax on them. It gave the government control over civilian manpower, allowing it to direct anyone where they were needed. The Ministry's Employment Department then set about organising labour and while the Ministry of Supply cooperated, the Admiralty and the Ministry of Aircraft Production did not.

A Manpower Requirements Committee quickly concluded that 50 per cent more manpower would be needed to make enough armaments for the armed forces. Skilled labour would have to be distributed to the new factories being set up, to train the many unskilled workers needed to meet the numbers. However, the Manpower Requirements Committee discovered that it was impossible to identify labour shortages either by trade or by district. Instead, each supply department had to estimate how many workers they needed to meet demand. They, in turn, had to ask each of its contractors how many extra staff they would need to complete their orders.

The problem was that inexperienced firms asked for too many workers because they had no idea how many they would require. In some cases, they thought that asking more staff would result in more orders. Estimating the workforce required to make small items, like ammunition, was easy. However, it was impossible to guess how many would be needed to build large items, like aircraft, so companies asked for as many workers as they dare.

In the autumn of 1940, the Production Council discovered that the Ministry of Aircraft Production had used the Battle of Britain crisis to acquire skilled labour.[4] While its heavy-handed policies had increased aircraft production, it had also caused problems for the other armed forces. So, steps were put in place to make sure that labour was distributed fairly in future, to make sure all the supply departments could meet their targets.

Over time, all the companies learnt how long it took to fulfil their orders. They also learnt how many workers of each trade they needed. They soon identified bottlenecks on their assembly lines and removed them one by one. An accumulation of statistics also allowed the supply departments to predict when factories needed materials, tools, components and labour to meet their targets. The Manpower Requirements Committee also estimated that 118 workers would be required to make enough weapons, equipment and ammunition for every 100 men serving in the armed forces.[5]

The armed forces and the Civil Defence Service asked for 4.6 million men and 200,000 women at the end of 1940. The Manpower Requirements Committee also estimated that it would require 3.4 million men and 1.6 million women in the armaments industry. That meant another 580,000 men and 890,000 women were needed to make enough armaments. The problem was that there were only 500,000 men still unemployed and many of them were too ill or disabled to do armaments work.

The numbers may have been just estimates but it gave the Ministry of Labour something to work towards. The Manpower Requirements Committee's next concern was what would be the impact of the *Luftwaffe*'s air raids on industry over the coming year.

As all the relevant departments considered the information, the Army Council raised another problem. It pointed out that it had forgotten to include the large numbers of men required by its many support services. Bevin responded to the revised information by stating what changes to the law were needed to make the Ministry of Labour's work easier. The following regulations would be applied to companies:

- More factories would be put on national work.
- A Register of Protected Establishments would be drawn up.
- An Engagement Restriction Order would stop firms poaching staff.

- A Concentration of Industry Scheme would close non-essential factories, so labour could be distributed to essential factories.
- A Supplies Limitation Order would stop the unnecessary stockpiling of materials.

The following regulations would be applied to employees:

- Workers could not leave a job without a National Service Officer's permission.
- Workers could not be sacked without a National Service Officer's permission.
- Men and women had to use employment exchanges or recognised agencies to find a job.
- The importance of a man's job had to be considered before he was called up.

As the number of unemployed men continued to fall and the numbers of women in work increased, the Production Executive started checking everyone's National Insurance cards. It provided an accurate assessment of the nation's labour situation for the first time. There were 2.6 million working in the armaments industry and 500,000 were employed in building or distribution. Another 400,000 were doing other jobs.

The War Cabinet eventually revised the conscription ages for men to 18½ and 51, releasing another 300,000 for the armed forces. The age limits on National Service obligations for men and women were also altered, so anyone aged 18 to 60 was required to do their duty. It meant that virtually every working adult could be transferred onto essential war work.

## The Manpower Situation in 1941[6]

By the end of 1940, it was clear there was going to be a shortage of unskilled labour, because of the large numbers of young men being conscripted. It was estimated that over 1 million women would have to be recruited to replace them, if production targets were going to be met.

A Register of Protected Establishments, listing hundreds of firms engaged on armaments work, was issued in February 1941. It would eventually list thousands of companies doing all kinds of essential work; for example, making food, servicing utilities and providing transport. Listed firms were regularly inspected, to confirm that they met the Ministry of Labour's standards for safety, efficiency and welfare. They were not allowed to sack an employee without the permission of the local National Service Officer; an employee could not leave either. Essential Work Orders would have been issued to the 26,750 factories making armaments by the end of 1941. It gave the government control of a 4.5 million strong workforce.

Bevin had also appointed a Preference Committee early in 1941; to decide the priority of armaments' contracts and the labour they needed at a national level. It worked with Regional Preference Committees to decide which firms had priority in each area, while employment agencies dealt with local labour issues.

The need to increase the numbers required by the armed forces resulted in a Registration for Employment Order in March 1941. Everyone had to register according to their age. It allowed the Labour Coordinating Committee to identify how much labour was available in each area. However, the order only recruited 200,000 women, so another order was required to increase the numbers of them signing up for war work.

By the summer of 1941, 2.75 million men had joined the armed forces and an extra 500,000 men were working in the armaments industry. Attempts to transfer skilled labour from non-essential work to essential work often involved travelling and lodging costs, which workers objected to. Differences in regional wage rates and trade bonuses also had to be considered, to make sure industrial unrest was avoided.

Unemployment may have been reduced from 500,000 down to 150,000 but there were still pockets of unemployment where there was no war work available to replace the traditional industries that had closed. It was also proving difficult to recruit for the coal mines, steel foundries and shipyards, because the wages were low and the work was tough. Particularly, as there was plenty of better paid and easier work available in the engineering and aircraft factories. Welfare also had to be improved to stop the high turnover of staff.

Fulfilling the needs of the armed forces, the Civil Defence Force and the three supply departments from the diminishing numbers of available men and women was becoming a complex task. So, a Director General of

Manpower started looking at how to get more from them in August 1941. The employment exchanges found work for the unemployed, persuaded part-time workers to take on full-time work and asked full-time workers to transfer to other factories. The exchanges recruited another 500,000 women and companies trained them to do more jobs.

Steps were also taken to train school leavers and older men, to replace those who were going to be called up. Two call-up age limits were set and while the lower one applied to those doing non-essential work, the higher one applied to those engaged on essential war work. The age classes kept on increasing until the end of 1941, by which time every man who could be spared had been called up.

Despite all the steps being taken, some areas were still short of labour while others had too much. Men and women were pressured into taking jobs, while Local Appeals Boards dealt with anyone who refused to comply. The question was: could men and women be moved to where they were needed without causing unrest?

A Preference Committee started comparing the availability and demand for labour in each region in November 1941. The Statistics and Planning Directorate used the information to calculate that there were labour shortages in the Midlands and the northwest, which it labelled scarlet and red. Regions where the numbers were balanced were coded amber, while those areas with a labour surplus were marked green.

Companies were instructed to report how much spare labour they had in their factory or if they needed more. A Concentration of Industry Scheme was supposed to transfer labour to the firms doing essential work, while closing the ones doing non-essential work down. However, many managers refused to cooperate because they were worried that their factories would not reopen after the war. So, only 60 per cent of workers identified as being able to be moved had been transferred by the end of the year.

A Supplies Limitation Order was issued to reduce the amounts of non-essential consumer goods that could be made in each region. It resulted in many companies having to shut down and their workers were transferred to nearby factories doing essential work. The Ministry of Labour also made every unemployed man and woman register at their local labour exchange, so it could start placing them where they were needed.

Everything changed in December 1941. The Japanese attacked Pearl Harbor on the 7th and the Philippines the following day, starting a war with the United States. Germany and Italy declared war on the United States on the 11th. Churchill then visited Roosevelt, accompanied by Lord Beaverbrook, for three weeks of discussion. Thereafter, London and Washington DC would cooperate closely on deciding how to fight the war.

## The Manpower Situation in 1942[7]

The year was busy for the British armed forces. The British Army was fighting in North Africa, the Royal Navy was countering the U-boat threat and the RAF faced the *Luftwaffe*. A new Ministry of War Production was set up in February 1942 under Lord Beaverbrook. However, he left after a short time and Oliver Lyttelton renamed it the Ministry of Production, to reflect that it would cover non-war items as well. Meanwhile, a Joint War Production Staff started advising the government on materials and manpower shortages. While London welcomed America's support, the demands made by the US War and the US Naval Departments on their nation's industry would create difficulties for Britain.

The British armed forces had been given every man they asked for the first three years of the war, while industry was forced to work with who was left. By the start of 1942, the Ministry of Labour had worked out that the armed forces still needed another 1.6 million men and women while industry required another 1 million. However, there were only 1.6 million men and women available, so it was time for the Ministry of Labour and National Service to tell the armed forces and industry who would be placed where, not the other way round. Bevin started by prioritising where his staff would place labour: The armaments factories were classified as Group I and they were given first call. Other essential industries, such as transport, coal and agriculture were classified as Group II and they came next. Non-essential industries were Group III and they had to make do with who was left.

Everyone capable of taking on part-time work was registered and many were women with family commitments. The District Manpower Board helped companies find older workers, so their younger workers could be conscripted.

The fear of air attacks had subsided by early 1942, so the Civil Defence Service and National Fire Service were asked if they could release any of their 400,000 strong workforce. However, the *Luftwaffe* started dropping a new type of incendiary bomb that had the potential to cause widespread damage. So, the Civil Defence Service and the National Fire Service said they needed everyone they had to spot and deal with fires. The two services could only release 7,500 full-time workers. However, many part-time members were found part-time jobs in armaments factories or on military bases. A lot were put to work building the camps and airbases required by the 3 million American servicemen being shipped to Britain ahead of D-Day.

Many steps were undertaken to improve production in Britain's factories in 1942. Inspectors showed managers how to introduce dilution into their workshops. They helped them break down complicated tasks into several simpler ones, so teams of unskilled workers could be taught to do them. The inspectors also suggested how skilled workers could be used more effectively. Sometimes by supervising new part-time workers or transferring them to other factories. Women were trained, so that men could transfer onto heavier work or join the armed forces. Meanwhile, many workers were being recruited from Ireland, which would remain neutral throughout the war.

Registration for men had to end in September 1942, because everyone who could be moved had been moved. Young women were also included under the National Services Act, so they could replace men in the factories. They would continue to be registered and offered jobs until the end of the war.

## The Manpower Situation From 1943–1945[8]

The Allies spent 1943 pursuing an offensive strategy, as the British Army fought their way across Tunisia, Sicily and Italy. The Royal Navy escorted convoys across the Atlantic Ocean, while the RAF bombed targets across Europe.

Mobilisation had peaked and the armed forces had increased from 500,000 men to 3.8 million men and 450,000 women. The armaments industry had also employed an extra 1.25 million men and 2.5 million women. While the factories wanted more, there was there was no one left to give them. The armaments programmes would now have to match the size of the workforce rather than the other way round. All that could be done was to transfer workers from the engineering factories to the aircraft factories, where they were needed most. The registration age for women was also raised to fifty, so more could be employed.

Despite the shortage of manpower, the country had to be scoured again for skilled workers to work on secret projects ahead of D-Day. Harbours and roads had to be improved, while hard standings and railway links had to be built. Accommodation and storage parks also had to be prepared and camouflaged across the south of England.

One major project involved building temporary floating harbours, codenamed Mulberry, which would be required until the French ports had been captured and opened. The Ministry of Supply gathered 20,000 civil engineering workers to construct the concrete breakwaters, codenamed Phoenixes. It also employed 1,600 engineering workers to build the prefabricated pier heads and buffer pontoons, codenamed Whales. The Admiralty assembled 2,000 steel erectors in Southampton to make the deep water shelters codenamed Bombardons.

A lot of extra transport workers were rounded up to make sure that then tens of thousands of men and tens of thousands of tons of supplies reached the south coast on time. An extra 9,000 were put to work on operating the railways, while 13,500 more drivers were employed to move goods to the embarkation points. An extra 7,000 skilled dockers supervised many more unskilled men as they loaded the hundreds of ships and landing craft.

While D-Day was successful and the Allied forces started pushing inland, the Germans struck back against London. The first V-1 flying bomb hit the capital on 14 June 1944 and thousands of buildings a day were soon being damaged. As the last rocket site was captured in France in October 1944, V-2 rockets had started to explode across the capital. Men from across Britain, Northern Ireland and Ireland joined the 28,000 already clearing rubble, as did groups from the armed forces, the Civil Defence Service and the National Fire Service.

Workers were greeted at reception centres across London and stayed in temporary shelters because of the housing shortage. Eventually 135,000 were put to work clearing up rubble and repairing some of the 700,000 damaged houses. Meanwhile, a new Minister of Reconstruction was busy planning post-war reconstruction.

By the spring of 1945, the war with Germany was nearly over and it was time to plan the manpower allocations required to defeat Japan. The Chiefs of Staff had estimated that it would take three years and many thousands of casualties to end the war, based on the bitter experiences in Burma and across the Pacific Islands. So, the Ministry of Labour had to once again look at how many men it could take from industry and the Civil Defence Service to reinforce the armed forces.

Its first attempt was made obsolete by the end of the war against Germany in May 1945, while two atomic bombs shortened the war to a matter of weeks. On 15 August 1945, Emperor Hirohito announced Japan's surrender, formally signing confirming it on 2 September 1945. It brought the Second World War to an end.

## Dilution of the Labour Force

### Inadequate Policies[9]

The Ministry of Aircraft Production's workforce may have increased to nearly 800,000 as the Battle of Britain came to a climax but the rest of the armaments industry was still short of what it required to reach its targets. The Ministry of Labour did not know where everyone was working but it did know that widespread subcontracting, dilution and training was required if the workforce was to increase to 4 million workers by the summer of 1942.

The trade unions objected to any form of labour control but the experiences of the Ministry of Munitions during the First World War had proved that the armaments industry needed to be controlled by the government during wartime. While the Area Boards and trade unions tried to reduce unemployment, 750,000 men were still out of work by May 1940.

The First Sea Lord, the Secretary of State for Air and the Minister of Supply all asked the Ministry of Labour for help to increase production. However, a new government was formed a few days later and while the new Minister of Labour and National Service, Ernest Bevin, was against conscripting labour, he supported voluntary dilution and the redistribution of skilled labour.

### Training[10]

There was a shortage of skilled workers due to the high unemployment before the war. Dilution had proved to be successful during the First World War and Bevin wanted to use it again. It involved breaking complex jobs down into simple tasks, so workers required the minimum of training. The Ministry of

Labour encouraged large companies to carry out their own training, while smaller ones sent their workers to training centres.

Men had priority until the unemployment level fell to a low level in 1941 and women were then targeted. Initially, courses took sixteen weeks but they were cut down to six weeks, as the classes became more targeted to what the students needed to know. Courses for semi-skilled workers were also introduced in 1942, so they could cover for skilled men on certain jobs or during night shifts. Around 270,000 workers eventually completed a course.

A Training Within Industry Scheme taught 20,000 managers how to instruct workers, handle employees and improve their skills. Another 17,000 men and women attended specialist courses, such as using imported machine tools, shipyard welding, vehicle driving and canteen cooking. Meanwhile, coal mining centres trained 25,000 men and 21,000 Bevin Boys. The demand for industrial training declined after 1943 and training centres were then busy rehabilitating disabled and able-bodied servicemen.

## Redistributing Labour[11]

The Ministry of Labour saw to it that employers and trade unions made agreements in May 1940. However, firms objected to losing their skilled workers and having to train semi-skilled labour. But Bevin insisted because he was looking at the long-term situation and his inspectors checked that factories were making full use of their skilled workers. He also instructed companies to register, ready to give them government contracts.

The Production Council made armaments work a priority, but factories were sometimes left waiting for materials, leaving their labour idle. The Ministry of Aircraft Production also resisted attempts to take skilled labour from their factories, while it did not cooperate with the Ministry of Labour until the beginning of 1941.

The Ministry of Supply set up the Mobile Skilled Corps at the end of 1941, a group of skilled workers prepared to move anywhere to set a factory, in return for a high rate of pay. The eventual transferral of 200,000 skilled workers to the new factories worked so well, that there was a shortage of unskilled labour by the end of 1942.

Women had started working the factories in large numbers during the summer of 1940, particularly where there was a shortage of labour. The plan was to release men of military age for the armed forces. However, many were reluctant to pass on their skills before they left, worried that they would not have a job to return to. So, the women had to be registered as temporary employers for the duration of the war.

Women were paid the same wage as men, when they did jobs classed as men's work. However, they were paid according to the Women's Wages' Schedule if their work was classed as women's work. However, many jobs were new and it took time to decide which rate to use, causing disputes. The most serious one was at the Hillington aircraft engine factory, when 16,000 women stopped work for a month. Whatever rate they were paid, supervision and training fees were always deducted from a woman's pay.

## Other Sources of Labour[12]

Skilled British nationals living abroad were encouraged to sign up to the Overseas Volunteers Scheme in 1942. The Ministry of Labour paid their travel expenses and helped them find work and accommodation. Skilled men from the Dominions and the Colonies were also encouraged to move to Britain and work in the armaments industry.

Free movement from Northern Ireland and Ireland to Britain was stopped when France fell in June 1940; a ban that ended a year later. Even though the government of Ireland, based in Dublin, refused to actively recruit for British industry, men were encouraged to find work across the Irish Sea with assurances that they would not be conscripted. Individuals applied through agents but the complicated permit system limited the number who eventually found work. Men were typically employed on construction projects or in farming, while women worked in domestic service or hospitals. A pool of construction workers was set up in 1942, so labour could be sent to where it was needed most.

Travel restrictions were reintroduced in the weeks before D-Day, so the government of Ireland stopped sending men to work in Britain. The Ministry of Labour then streamlined the recruitment system and began matching applicants to the available work. Many men were eventually put to work on clearing bomb damage across London.

Nationals from other countries had to seek permission from the Home Office's Aliens War Service Department before moving to Britain. Some had come from Germany, Austria and Czechoslovakia before the war, while others came from Norway, Denmark, Belgium, the Netherlands and France after German troops invaded their countries. The Ministry of Labour's International Labour Branch found them work. Citizens of allied countries were registered for National Service in 1941 and those who did not join their own national armed forces, were liable to be called up into the British armed forces in 1943. French and American nationals were called up in August 1944.

Italian prisoners of war started arriving from North Africa in 1941 and they were put to work on labour intensive projects, such as drainage, quarrying, farming and forestry. Italy surrendered in September 1943 but many freed prisoners continued at their work. German prisoners started to arrive in large numbers in the summer of 1944 but they worked under armed guards and were banned from secure areas. By the end of the war, 132,000 Italian and 92,000 German prisoners of war had been sent to Britain.

## Recruiting for the Armed Forces

### Services Call Up[13]

The government wanted to control enlistment for the armed forces, to avoid the problems caused by the unrestricted volunteering encouraged at the beginning of the First World War. The Secretary of State for War, Herbert Kitchener, Earl Kitchener, had made the plea, 'Your Country Needs You' in August 1914. Anyone was allowed to join up, which left every industry short of skilled men, including those vital to making armaments, such as coal, steel and engineering industries.

The government wanted to make sure there was a measured and balanced approach to recruitment at the start of the Second World War. A National Service (Armed Forces) Act was issued on 3 September 1939, the day that war was declared, and it made every man between the age of 18 and 41 liability for service. The younger men started registering a month later and while those working in reserved occupations were sent back to work, the rest were forwarded to the armed forces. Around 730,000 were registered in 1939, followed by 4.1 million in 1940 and 2.2 million in 1941. It eventually brought the total to over 7 million.

All three armed forces were asking for more men by the spring of 1941, so Sir William Beveridge set up the Manpower Requirements Committee to find as many as possible for them. Its objective was to either get all fit men into the armed forces or to make sure they did the work that could not be done by older men or women. In some cases, it meant they were doing specialist work or they had certain skills. But some jobs needed men who could do heavy physical work, such as working down a coal mine, in a steel foundry or for a shipyard.

The Manpower Requirements Committee was concerned that tens of thousands of key workers were in danger of being called up if recruitment was too zealous. So, the Schedule of Reserved Occupations was updated to include the many jobs that were proving to be essential to the armaments industry. It also included vital infrastructure industries that it relied on, such as the mining industry or the railways. The Ministry of Labour eventually drew up a Register of Protected Establishments because it was easier to cover everyone working in a type of factory rather than creating a long list of trades.

The reservation age was increased three times over the summer, giving companies time to find older workers before their younger employees were called up. Many occupations were given two reservation ages and while the lower age limit applying to key operatives, a higher one applied to the rest of the workforce. The idea was to comb as many men out of industry as possible, while disrupting production as little as possible. Over 2.75 million men were in the services by the summer of 1941. All men up to the age of 40 had been registered, so the Manpower Requirements Committee started on 19 year olds.

Over 100,000 women had also joined the three Auxiliary Services where they did a variety of support roles for the armed forces, releasing men for combat duties. The Women's Royal Naval Service (WRNS) supported the Royal Navy, the Women's Auxiliary Air Force (WAAF) supported the RAF and the Auxiliary Territorial Service (ATS) supported the British Army.

The armed forces asked for skilled men to maintain and repair their equipment and vehicles in 1942. However, the Ministry of Labour discovered that they were not using the ones they had been given to the best of their abilities. So, it stopped sending any more until they were used properly.

All three armed forces also wanted more men to fight the Japanese in the Far East but the Civil Defence Service, the National Fire Service and the Land Army all wanted extra men or women as well. All the Manpower Requirements Committee could do was to report that there were insufficient men and women to go round unless the National Service obligations were changed. So, the Ministry of Labour altered the call up age limits. Men were called up as soon as they were 18 years old, while both men and women could be called up until they reached 60.

The Prime Minister was desperate to put all the younger men and women into the armed forces and all the older men and women into industry but it took time and effort to move everyone around. In the meantime, the armed forces had to cut their demands and adjust their strategic planning to suit.

## Reserved Occupations and Deferment[14]

The British Army was short of men after the evacuation from Dunkirk, so sixteen weekly call ups by age classes were made over the summer of 1940. The Schedule of Reserved Occupations stopped skilled men joining up by occupation and more jobs were added, as soon as their importance was recognised. The only exception to the exemption was anyone who wanted to enlist as a pilot or aerial observers because the RAF was short of them.

The National Service (No. 2) Act was implemented in December 1941 and it required every man and woman between 18 and 60 to perform some form of National Service. Recruiting Officers reported what the armed forces, auxiliary services and Civil Defence Service needed. Meanwhile, Labour Supply Officers reported what the firms' needed to meet their targets. The District Manpower Board made sure that everyone received their fair share, while Deferment Officers were on hand to deal with any objections and anyone with unusual personal circumstances.

Many professions required technical staff to keep society functioning, such as teaching, law and finance. Many industries needed manual workers to keep the nation functioning, such as the coal and steel industries, building work and agriculture. Everyone needed their cases considering, to see where they were needed the most. Students of key subjects, such as medical, science and engineering, often asked for their military service to be deferred, so they could finish their courses. In many cases, it was allowed but most courses were shortened, so they could be called up sooner.

The District Manpower Board eventually dealt with 4.7 million deferment claims from men and rejected 660,000. They also dealt with 620,000 claims from women and rejected 255,000. They always made sure companies had assistance and enough time to replace any worker destined for the forces.

## Labour for the Supply Departments

### Admiralty Labour[15]

Shipbuilding required the marine, engineering and electrical industries to work together. There was enough berth capacity when war broke out but many shipyards were short of workers, cramped and equipped with old tools. The Admiralty took over the Ministry of Shipping's production and it had two objectives: to secure the nation's coastal waters and protect the shipping lanes. Some shipyards were organised to build convoy escorts and anti-submarine vessels. Others were earmarked to convert merchant ships or degauss ships, to protect them against magnetic mines.

The Royal Dockyards employed 38,000 at the start of the war, while another 120,000 worked in the private shipyards. Double that number would eventually be required but other jobs paid more and were more appealing. Only some shipyard jobs were protected, so firms had to argue to stop their skilled workers being enlisted. However, they failed to stop many of their unskilled men being called up, even though they were needed for the heavy manual jobs.

Essential Work Orders had to be implemented to prevent from men leaving the shipyards for better wages and conditions. However, the *Luftwaffe* then targeted the dockyards and shipyards over the winter of 1940–1941 and again in the spring of 1941, which hindered recruitment. Those who were recruited often had to be trained, so they could work on ship conversions.

Labour became such a problem that the shipbuilding industry eventually had to be excluded from the Essential Work Order, which required workers to transfer jobs, to try and maintain morale and discipline across the workforce. It meant there were always skilled workers on standby to carry out urgent warship repairs. Meanwhile, the Ministry of Labour continued its search for unskilled labour to help the shipyards out.

The Admiralty started repairing merchant shipbuilding in the spring of 1941, as turnover topped 150,000 tons a month. It set up a Priority Branch to organise the complicated labour situation it had inherited. It faced labour shortages for different trades, in different regions at different times. So much of the work was specialist that around half the workforce had to be skilled tradesmen, even after dilution was introduced. It meant that dilution was mainly used for electrical work and welding work on smaller vessels; jobs that could be done by women.

Steps to introduce dilution were also rejected for some time because the men worked in gangs that were paid piece rates according to how fast they worked. They argued that splitting up their gang to make way for unskilled men would slow their work down and reduce their wages. Managers always objected to their best men being transferred to their competitors. So, the Admiralty had to appoint a Shipyard Development Committee to deal with skilled men and a Preference Committee to place the unskilled ones.

The loss of Singapore in February 1942, resulted in 5,000 repair specialists having to be sent to the Indian Ocean to set up new shipyards, which resulted in shortages across Britain. The Contract Labour Branch and the Admiralty Labour Branch then faced difficulties trying to balance labour. The problem was that employers did not want to lose their best men, while men preferred shipbuilding work over ship repair work because it was better paid. So, Regional Officers had to be appointed to coordinate recruitment with the Ministry of Supply, the Ministry of Aircraft Production and with the Ministry of Labour. They kept transfers between shipyards to a minimum because workers faced often prejudices, were usually paid different rates and always had to live in poor accommodation at their new shipyard.

By 1943, the five Royal Dockyards employed 48,000 in the south, while 52 large private firms employed another 175,000 workers across Scotland and the north of England. A lot of shipping work would be subcontracted to inland engineering firms, particularly prefabrication, components and marine engines. It eventually boosted the workforce working on all kinds of shipping to 835,000, which was four times as many as there had been at the start of the war.

By the end of the year, the Admiralty was recruiting workers from the Ireland because the aircraft factories once again had priority. However, the

Tyneside factories refused to employ any Irish workers, while there were security objections to them working on the south coast, during the months before D-Day. A lot of men were moved to the southern ports for invasion related work, leaving the northern shipyards having to take on over 10,000 women, mainly on electrical or welding work.

Tensions rose as the end of the war approached because there were concerns about a shipbuilding slump and job losses in the post-war environment. It meant that the trade unions successfully argued to restore the pre-war terms and conditions, leaving the women without jobs.

## Ministry of Aircraft Production Labour[16]

As we have seen, the Ministry of Aircraft Production had misused the Battle of Britain crisis to acquire skilled labour.[17] It continued to hoard the surplus and steps had to be put in place to distribute labour fairly, so all the supply departments could meet their targets.

The aircraft factories continued to have no trouble recruiting because the wages were good and a lot of the work was indoors. They were already employing 1.25 million men and women when Churchill said that he wanted Bomber Command expanding in September 1941. While the Ministry of Aircraft Production estimated it would require 2.1 million workers by the end of 1942, the Ministries of Labour and Minister of Production correctly guessed that firms were overstating their requirements. The number would eventually increase to 1.7 million.

## Ministry of Supply Labour[18]

Recruitment for the Royal Ordnance Factories peaked in 1941, as 40,000 men and women were taken on every month. Many of the factories the women had been working in had been closed, so they transferred en mass to their nearest ROF. For example, women from Lancashire's cotton industry worked at Chorley filling factory, while the women from Staffordshire's pottery industry worked at Swynnerton filling factory. Over 1.5 million women had been given work by 1942. However, many women preferred civilian work because it offered shorter hours and less travelling, so they were eventually compelled to register for war work.

Despite the push on recruitment, the factories working for the Ministry of Supply faced many issues by the end of 1942. There were labour shortages in London and across the Midlands, because many people had moved away during the Blitz. The new ROFs also faced shortages because they had been built in isolated areas to avoid the air raids. Shorter hours and better welfare facilities were also required, to improve the morale of the workforce.

Some of the filling factories were huge. For example, Chorley in Lancashire and Bridgend in South Wales employed around 29,000 each, working across three shifts. While they had a high labour priority, there was also a lot of absenteeism and a high turnover of staff, because of the unpleasant work and poor conditions.

The ROFs were employing over 930,000 by 1941 and while there was a demand for more workers over the winter, it was soon realised that the filling factories were making more shells than estimated. Productivity was much higher than anticipated due to mechanisation, training, experience and bonuses. It meant that output had to halved by the summer of 1943, while many workers were transferred to other jobs:

The following table lists the number of workers employed by each type of ROF:

|      | Filling | Explosives | Engineering | Woolwich | Total |
|------|---------|------------|-------------|----------|-------|
| 1939 | 10,000  | 5,000      | 14,000      | 25,000   | 54,000 |
| 1940 | 49,000  | 13,000     | 31,000      | 19,000   | 112,000 |
| 1941 | 144,000 | 40,000     | 72,000      | 20,000   | 276,000 |
| 1942 | 133,000 | 38,000     | 96,000      | 23,000   | 290,000 |
| 1943 | 106,000 | 26,000     | 88,000      | 22,000   | 242,000 |
| 1944 | 93,000  | 23,000     | 75,000      | 18,000   | 209,000 |
| 1945 | 77,000  | 20,000     | 58,000      | 16,000   | 171,000 |

## Professional and Scientific Staff[19]

It was recognised that a core of professional staff was required to run the country, while selected scientific staff was needed to invent and improve weapons and equipment. The Ministry of Labour had set up a central register of civil servants and scientists before the war but it proved difficult to assess what everyone's skills and qualifications could be used for. The threat of invasion in the summer of 1940 sharpened everyone's focus, and the following technically qualified persons were required to register:

- High-grade engineers and scientists.
- Lower-grade engineers and scientists.
- London-based professionals, executive and administrative staff.
- Nursing staff.

Churchill valued the scientists' view and he asked the Scientific Advisory Council for a list of war winners in September 1940. Meanwhile, the Royal Society, an organisation that promoted science and its benefits, had been recruiting members. It had also been improving contact between the scientists, the manufacturers and the armed forces.

The conflict was soon proving to be one in which science and invention were important. Britain's scientists found themselves engaged in a game of military chess, as they figured out how to help the armed forces beat their German counterparts on land, across the oceans and in the air.

More and more technical personnel were required as the months passed, ranging from the mechanical engineers required to maintain the RAF's aircraft, to the wireless specialist needed to operate the radar equipment. A Technical Personnel Committee began recruiting staff in August 1941, while an Appointments Department started placing scientists, professionals, executive and administrative staff in March 1942. Training schemes and apprenticeships which supported students with financial bursaries were also set up, to boost future numbers of technical staff.

## Women and Youngsters

### Women in Industry[20]

Only a few thousand women were employed in the armaments industry in the 1930s. Concerns over male unemployment, the distribution of skilled labour and the need to find unskilled men for heavy work, meant little was done to take on more during the first nine months of the war. Instead, thousands of women were put out of work when their factories stopped making non-essential goods, such as pottery, clothing and shoes. Employers were also reluctant to take them on because they thought engineering was man's work, while the trade unions were concerned it would undermine their members' position. It seems that they had both had forgotten that tens of thousands of women had kept the munitions industry going during the First World War.

Everyone was slow to realise the important role women could play in the Auxiliary Services, in the armaments factories and in other essential jobs. Only 300,000 had been taken on by the spring of 1940, but the new government understood that 2 million female workers would be needed to expand the armaments industry. Churchill had been the Minister of Munitions during the final year of the First World War and he recognised that they would have to be found essential work, the same as their mothers had.

A detailed assessment of the national labour situation had been mapped out by the beginning of 1941, so contracts could be placed to get the best use out of the available labour. Recruitment then started in earnest and firms were encouraged to set up training courses, improve welfare and modify shifts to entice more women into the armaments factories.

Thousands of women were registered at government training centres and then interviewed to identify their personal circumstances. The majority accepted the work offered to them, while Local Appeal Boards and Tribunals dealt with the few who objected. Initially, they were allowed to choose between industrial work or military service but they were soon directed to where they were needed the most. Eventually, those without family responsibilities were sent to where they were needed, often away from home.

A Women's Consultative Committee considered how women could help industries and services in March 1941. It suggested an expansion of the three Auxiliary Services, so women 300,000 could do support tasks and release soldiers for combat duties. So, New Defence Regulations made the three services part of the armed forces, making members subject to forces' discipline.

The Ministry of Labour also wanted to use women to reduce the labour shortages in the Midlands and the northwest. However, attempts to move young women to other areas often failed because of the poor welfare and accommodation. It would take time to address the problems and reduce the high turnover of staff.

While 500,000 women had been recruited for the armaments industry by the end of 1941, the Ministry of Labour was instructed to take over recruiting. A second National Service Act required all unmarried women and childless widows under the age of 30 to register. A Control of Engagement Order allocated them into the Auxiliary Services, the Civil Defence Service or the armaments factories; whichever had priority in their area.

While another 600,000 women had been signed up by the summer of 1942, 900,000 more were needed. So, registration and placement were accelerated, while the age limit was increased to 46. In September 1942, the decision was taken to recruit those with family commitments who could only work part time or were unable to move. It allowed many women who were willing to move to other factories to do so.

By the end of the year, the Ministry of Labour knew exactly which regions had surplus labour and which needed more. The transfer of thousands of women from London, the North and from Scotland to the aircraft factories in the Midlands increased bomber production. The Ministry of Labour started registering women up to the age of 51 in the autumn of 1943, so older ones could release younger ones for the Auxiliary Services. Over 900,000 women had been placed in part-time work by the end of the year.

The government also wanted more hospital and nursing staff ahead of the invasion of Europe, so all nurses and midwives had to register with the Nursing Appointments Offices in 1943. It was complicated deciding whether it was better to take people from of their jobs or leave them where they were, but 58,000 had still been placed ahead of D-Day.

## Employment for Boys and Girls[21]

Ernest Bevin initially did not want to force youngsters into jobs but Ministry of Labour issued an Essential Work Order requiring them to register in March 1941. Over 1.6 million adolescents had registered at their local Labour Office by the end of the war. They were given the same responsibilities as adults and they were interviewed by a National Service Officer and a Juvenile Employment Officer if they failed to do their job correctly.

By the summer of 1941, there was a shortage of coal miners and while the Mines Department wanted young workers, other jobs paid more and offered better working conditions. Bevin introduced a minimum wage for juveniles and he organised better training, to try and stimulate recruitment. Medical examinations, safety equipment, pithead baths and canteens were also brought in, but mining was still an unattractive option. Eventually a lottery had to be started, creating the Bevin Boys.[22]

Many other adolescents were employed building new military bases or clearing bomb damage. While they were paid high wages, there were no apprenticeships, just harsh working conditions and bad influences. By 1943, younger boys were banned from construction jobs and from working away from home. Older boys were also banned from working on London's bomb sites.

A Building Apprenticeship Training Council started training boys in 1944 and the government sponsored building projects that were run by building companies. An Apprentice Master Scheme made sure the boys were supervised and trained for the future on housing programmes and other rebuilding projects.

## Summary[23]

The War Cabinet had put a lot of thought into how to get enough manpower for the armed forces. However, Ernest Brown did not think enough about how much labour was required for the armaments factories over the first winter of the war. The Schedule of Reserved Occupations prevented the disastrous uncontrolled enlistment which happened at the start of the First World War. However, it took the Ministry of Labour too long to find out what labour was available and where it was needed the most. Ernest Bevin cooperated with the Joint Consultative Committee and the Women's Consultative Committee, when he took over as Minister of Labour in May 1940 and he worked hard to gain the confidence of the labour force.

The supply departments initially relied too much on the firms they knew well. They then expanded haphazardly, without what labour was available or required. They also failed to coordinate their orders with the other supply departments, resulting in bottlenecks and delays. The Lord President's Committee gave each supply department a labour allocation in 1942 but it still took time to find, train and place enough labour to match the orders.

Changes in production methods and training meant that dilution became possible but it had taken too long to remember that women had kept the munitions industry going during the First World War. The number of women employed in the armaments industries increased from a few thousand at the outbreak of war to 1.5 million by the end of 1943. Many others were in the armed forces' Auxiliary Services or doing essential work, replacing the men who had been enlisted.

Chapter 11

# Industrial Relations

## Working Hours and Wages

### Working Hours[1]

The Engineering Employers' Federation and the trade unions agreed what the working hours were in peacetime. While there was a basic forty-seven hour week and up to thirty hours overtime could be worked per month, the maximum working week was fifty-four hours and thirty minutes. A Factories Act introduced in 1937 limited the hours that women and young persons could work and they were not allowed to work night shifts.

A sense of urgency and loyalty during the early months of the war meant that men and women were prepared to work long hours, with some working as many as eighty hours a week. At the end of 1939, an Emergency Order was introduced to regulate what hours were being worked, because many people were struggling to do their job and fulfil their Civil Defence or Home Guard duties.

However, two crises shook the nation on 10 May 1940. The Germans launched *Blitzkrieg* attacks against France and the Low Countries, while Prime Minister Neville Chamberlain resigned. Three days after Winston Churchill was appointed as Prime Minister at the head of a coalition government, he told the House of Commons, 'I have nothing to offer but blood, toil, tears and sweat.' A week later he told the nation, 'The hours of labour are nothing compared with the struggle for life, honour and freedom.' The evacuation of the BEF from Dunkirk began soon afterwards

The Fall of France at the end of June 1940 resulted in all holidays being postponed. However, the Industrial Health Research Board reported that nine months of hard work long working hours were affecting output. Production may have increased but quality was falling. Morale was also falling, while absenteeism was rising. So, the Ministry of Labour issued an Emergency Order, which reduced the women's working week to sixty hours. Anyone aged 16 or less could only work forty-eight hours but a plan to end Sunday work was rejected.

The new Ministry of Labour Ernest Bevin tried to send more labour to the factories struggling to meet their targets. The Ministry of Supply again suggested one day off a week but the workforce wanted the money from the overtime. The recommendations of the Industrial Health Research Board were eventually accepted in November 1941 and companies had to ask for permission before they could ask workers to do more hours to meet a target.

A year later, a man's working week was limited to sixty hours a week, while a woman's was reduced to fifty-five. Checks by the Industrial Health Research Board discovered that the change increased output and improved quality. The Ministry of Labour took note and acted against companies that persisted in working longer hours.

The armaments industry eventually got on top of orders by the autumn of 1943 and overtime was reduced, workers raised concerns over the reduction in their wages. At the same time, basic hours were lowered to fifty-five hours for men and fifty hours for women, with similar cuts to youngsters' hours. However, the Ministry of Aircraft Production could make its women work extra hours, because the bomber campaign was reaching its climax. The working week was reduced to fifty hours for men during the final months of the war.

Holidays were staggered around D-Day, to keep enough trains free for troop movements to the south coast. Reduced requirements for weapons and equipment, as well as a desire to lower costs, reduced overtime even more over the winter of 1944–1945. The Ministry of Labour made sure that cuts were implemented slowly, to limit concern connected to a loss of earnings. While the engineering ROFs and then the private contractors were the first to cut back their hours, the filling factories maintained their high output, to meet the armed forces' demand for ammunition.

## Working Hours Exceptions[2]

The Royal Dockyards kept its working week at around fifty-six hours a week throughout the war and it never asked its workforce to do Sunday work. While a national agreement set shipyard hours at forty-seven hours per week, local agreements could increase it to eighty hours, when there was a backlog of repair work. Meanwhile, the private shipyards worked long hours, with seven day weeks becoming common in the winter months, to compensate for the short daylight hours. While few women were employed in the shipyards, many boys worked long hours alongside their fathers. The maximum number of hours was eventually set at sixty hours, with essential work being carried out on Sundays. Hours were reduced as the war ended and employers carefully asserted themselves, to avoid causing unrest.

Steel foundries, explosives factories and chemical works required around the clock shift working because they involved continuous processes. Meanwhile, the new Royal Ordnance Factories had been designed to accommodate two shifts, to get more use out of the machine tools and to reduce overtime. The War Cabinet wanted other factories to do the same but a shortage of supervisors meant extra shifts were only used to finish urgent orders. The Ministry of Aircraft Production considered implementing double shifts in 1942, to speed up the bomber programme, but it was stopped by the same issue. So, again extra shifts were only used to clear bottlenecks on key machines.

## Wages[3]

Trades had been setting minimum wages since the Trade Boards Act was introduced in 1919, to prevent employers running sweat shops. Basic wages were either set nationally or by districts, while firms agreed piece work rates and bonuses. Labour shortages during the first winter of the war resulted in companies offering skilled workers higher wages, a practice known as poaching. The trade unions refused to accept any controls, as did the Minister of Labour, Ernest Brown, fearing they could cause unrest.

Ernest Bevin was appointed Minister for Labour in May 1940 and he wanted new regulations to control the movement of labour. He had been General Secretary of the Transport and General Workers' Union, when the Road Haulage Act 1938 allowed different trade unions to address local issues. He used a similar approach with Order 1305 which relied on a Joint Consultative Committee of seven employers and seven trade unionists to discuss matters. Regional tribunals and wages boards dealt with most issues, with difficult cases being referred to the National Arbitration Tribunal.

Serious problems were referred to the Minister of Labour and he was allowed three weeks to conclude a settlement before workers could go on strike or owners could declare a lockout.

Bevin objected to limiting wage increases and firms objected to centralised wage control, resulting in inflation rising over the summer of 1940. So, Prime Minister Winston Churchill's government subsidised important items, such as foodstuffs and shipping. The policy successfully curbed inflation, reducing the demands for wage rises. Bevin then placed firms doing essential work on a schedule, putting them under government control. While employees were no longer allowed to switch jobs for better pay, the government guaranteed their jobs and their wages as compensation.

The Ministry of Labour introduced Essential Work Orders banning companies from making high wage offers in April 1941, to stop poaching altogether. It also forced companies to agree to certain working conditions and minimum welfare standards, to maintain morale and reduce absenteeism. Bevin was also allowed to become involved in any wage negotiations that concerned vital work. For example, he awarded an increase to the agriculture industry in the spring of 1942, to guarantee there were enough workers to collect the harvest. He also agreed wage increases to stimulate recruitment in the coal-mining industry in 1942 and 1944; albeit not always with success.

Men's wages stayed ahead of the cost of living, with the help of bonuses. Women's earnings in the armaments factories and other essential industries even faster. The Wages Council Act forced employers and trade unions to start using collective bargaining in March 1945 and the wage negotiations resumed their prewar position when the war ended.

## Industry Earnings[4]

The shipbuilding, aircraft and engineering industries had different experiences with wages and working hours during the war. Shipbuilding was hard work, especially in winter weather, but wages were low. There was unrest in the Clyde shipyards after miners and steel workers were given pay rises at the end of 1941, so the National Arbitration Tribunal awarded the shipbuilders similar increases, to calm the situation. Even so, poor wages continued to limit recruitment and while piece work rates were introduced to attract workers, they caused arguments between the trades. Skilled apprentices were eventually awarded a large pay rise because unskilled workers could earn more doing piece work.

Wages in the motor and aircraft industries across the Midlands had always been higher than other areas but they increased even more during the pre-war rearmament period. Poaching of workers over the winter of 1939–1940 resulted in them rising to over 50 per cent higher than other areas. The Restriction on Engagement Order, introduced in June 1940, forced firms to take labour from employment exchanges, to reduce the practice. An Essential Work Order restricted labour movement in March 1941 to end it altogether. Even so, wages kept rising across the Midlands because there was so much work around. It did make it difficult to transfer labour to other districts around the country because firms refused to pay the same inflated wages.

The Ministry of Aircraft Production asked the aircraft companies what they were paying in the summer of 1941 and while most refused to divulge the information, some were employees were getting huge bonuses. The Production Efficiency Board even blamed the high payments for the high rates of absenteeism and lazy working attitude across the Midlands. Eventually, bonuses were converted into the basic wages to try and limit the practices. Firms had to reduce what they paid their workers, when orders were cut during the final months of the war.

The Royal Ordnance Factories paid the district wage rates determined by the Fair Wages Resolution, which were supplemented by national and factory bonuses. A lot of skilled men were moved around the country on the outbreak of war, to set up the new agency and shadow factories. It allowed widespread recruitment to take place and 54,000 workers were working in ten huge ROFs by the end of 1939. The Ministry of Supply used bonuses called 'leads' to reward the unskilled workers running teams or doing complicated work. A schedule of rates for women and a National Wages Agreement for youths were also issued.

The Ministry of Labour introduced a national engineering rate, to make it easier to negotiate wage rates in the summer of 1940. Workers in London and South Wales received a higher rate, to cover the cost of living. Everyone was paid the same basic rates February 1941, to make wage negotiations simpler. The industry continued to grow and it peaked at forty ROFs employing around 300,000 workers.

Piece rates became more widespread as the months passed, because they encouraged everyone to work faster and more efficiently. Eventually, two out of three workers were paid according to their output. However, those doing dangerous jobs, like making explosives or filling shells, were excluded from piece-rate schemes because working fast caused accidents.

Skilled workers who supervised the work were not included in piece work either, and neither were the logistics workers and inspectors. The problem was they had to work faster to keep up with the piece workers, which resulted in the piece workers earning more than their supervisors. Unrest in March 1943 resulted in all the time workers and support workers being awarded a 25 per cent increase to bring their wages into line and calm the situation down.

## Women's Wages[5]

Women had been employed in huge numbers in the munitions industry during the First World War, only to be laid off following the Armistice. Attitudes to them working in traditionally male industries had also relaxed between the wars, so that 380,000 were working in them by July 1939; or 15 per cent of the workforce. Production lines and mechanical handling meant that more women could be employed in engineering during the Second World War. However, trade unions were once again anxious to protect their members' position, especially after the prolonged period of high unemployment between the wars.

Unemployment remained high during the early months of the war and there were concerns that women could be used as cheap labour. So, the Women's Relaxation Agreement made sure that women were paid the same as men, when they were doing jobs traditionally done by men. However, they were paid lower rates, when they were doing jobs traditionally done by women. The problem was there were many new jobs in the armaments industry and they all had to be classified before the appropriate wage scales could be set.

Women's rates were agreed with the relevant trade unions over the first winter of the war but many were still paid less that men. Bevin made sure more key jobs were classified as men's work over the summer of 1940, to encourage women to apply for them but filling shells remained at a lower rate of pay. Some factories offered their bonuses to stimulate recruitment but three quarters of women were paid around one third less than men.

The trade unions refused to let women be paid extra under the 'leads' system in the Royal Ordnance Factories, setting rates according to whether there were more men or women doing a task instead. This led to discussions and compromises, which occasionally resulted in unrest. Private factories were more likely to be engaged in specialised work and they often had to deal with several trade unions and many new wage rates, when they employed women.

As happened before, the women were laid off and the men returned from the armed forces, to reclaim their jobs when the Second World War was over. However, discussions over whether to pay men and women the same across the board, would continue for many years. The Equal Pay Act eventually came into law in 1970 but it was 2010 before the Equality Act offered men and women the same contractual terms and conditions.

## Industrial Unrest

### Industrial Relations[6]

Trade unions and employers had been cooperating at national level since the general strike in 1926. The Trades Union Congress (TUC) agreed there would be joint control of industry in wartime in the spring of 1939. Unfortunately, the agreement did not work well between the supply departments and the Ministry of Labour and National Service until Winston Churchill's government took over in May 1940. The National Production Advisory Council would eventually take over from the TUC in 1942.

A Joint Industrial Council started dealing with nationwide issues such as working hours, holidays and travel, in government owned factories after July 1941. An Industrial Committee dealt with wage negotiations, while the Ministry of Labour and the trade unions resolved major disputes. Company managers discussed wages with trade union representatives, while departmental Joint Councils dealt with other serious issues.

Trade unions were well established in the engineering factories and they relied on Works Committees to deal with minor disputes. However, many non-trade union women worked in the ROFs, so they referred their issues to consultation groups, called Whitely Committees.[7] Good cooperation was required but issues were often allowed to drag on, leading to disputes. It resulted in Joint Factory Committees being formed and they involved shop stewards.

Private firms initially used consultation to keep the peace on the shop floor. However, an unofficial shop stewards' movement opposed the trade union leadership. Yard Committees started dealing with issues in the shipyards after a series of stoppages along the Clyde over the winter of 1940–1941.

The Central Production Committee started reporting on production improvements in July 1941; Joint Production Committees would do the same the following spring. They took ideas from the Works Committees and Whitley Committees but success depended on the personalities involved and the trade unions' pre-war role in a factory. The Admiralty Industrial Council worked in a similar way with Yard, Departmental and Shop Committees. The supply department and company managements used the same framework to explain their problems and they often prevented disruption.

Discipline had been maintained by threats of redundancy or bonus deductions before the war. Wartime meant that there was plenty of work around, so employers had to incentivise their employees. The Minister of Aircraft Production, Lord Beaverbrook, used his media skills to start a propaganda campaign during the Battle of Britain; to make workers feel they were important to the war effort. The Public Relations Directorate started another campaign in the summer of 1941, sending trade union representatives and servicemen to speak in the factories. It also distributed posters and information films. Managers and workers cooperated to improve welfare, reduce absenteeism and counter rumours; they also produced their own propaganda.

## Order 1305[8]

There were only short, minor stoppages during the first eight months of the war, so Minister of Labour, Ernest Brown, was able to rely on the Conciliation Act 1896 and the Industrial Courts Act 1919 to secure amicable settlements. Ernest Bevin introduced the Conditions of Employment and National Arbitration Order, when he took over the Ministry of Labour in May 1940. Order 1305, as it was called, banned workers from striking and managers from using lockouts, unless the Ministry failed to act on an issue within twenty-one days.

Bevin used Order 1305 if he thought agitators were organising stoppages, either imposing fines or referring the matter to a Court of Inquiry. Around 2,200 cases were referred to an arbitrator and while 180 were investigate by an Industrial Court, 920 were referred to the National Arbitration Tribunal.

By the autumn of 1943, Bevin was concerned that political activists might encourage stoppages, to try and change government policy. He made it illegal to incite a stoppage following a widespread miners' stoppage in March 1944. He also made picketing illegal.

## Stoppages[9]

Order 1305 made arbitration compulsory and both the regional controllers and the industrial Conciliation Officers had to keep the dialogue open. In many cases, the Joint Production Committees dealt with disagreements before they escalated. Even so, there were over 1,500 stoppages per year. The fewest occurred during the Battle of Britain in the summer of 1940 and most occurred during in the final months of the war, when everyone became worried about their future.

Many stoppages were short, unofficial affairs and while 1,250 cases were referred to arbitration, 1,060 were passed to the National Arbitration Tribunal. There were over 100 cases of prosecution, involving 6,281 strikers, but the Ministry of Labour rarely fined offenders because their co-workers paid them. Even fewer activists were imprisoned because the government were wary of creating martyrs and did not want to escalate a dispute.

Altogether 1.9 million working days were lost due to industrial action, which was less than half the number lost during the First World War. Around half were in the coal-mining industry, with the largest taking place a few weeks before D-Day. The engineering and shipbuilding industries accounted for another quarter of the stoppages.

Many stoppages followed demands for an increase in basic wages or piece rates. Others were caused by long hours or poor transport links. However, some were due to a lack of cooperation between the managers, trade union leaders and shop stewards. The Joint Production Committees and personnel managers then had to step in to resolve them.

Wage issues were negotiated at the national level, to stop claims being made by other districts or trades. Other issues were initially discussed between the workers and the foreman, before they were referred to the shop stewards and then the factory manager. The employers' association and the relevant trade union then held a local conference before an issue was referred to a national conference. The process took time, but the workers were banned from stopping work until all consultation levels had been exhausted.

The fact that trade union officials worked with the government and employers left some workers believing they had been sold out. So, it was often left to the shop stewards to speak out, resulting in many issues being resolved on the factory floor.

## Examples of Stoppages[10]

What follows is a non-exhaustive list of stoppages during the war and how they were resolved. Around 12,000 apprentices across the country went on strike in March 1941 because unskilled workers being were paid more on piece rates to use machines that they were being paid on hourly rates to maintain them. The Ministry of Labour ended the stoppage by issuing call-up notices for medicals to all the apprentices.

The first major coal mining stoppage occurred at Betteshanger Colliery in Kent in January 1942. Miners went on a go slow after being refused a higher allowance for working in a more difficult seam. The trade union organisers were imprisoned, while over 1,000 underground workers refused to pay their fines. The Ministry of Labour back downed and release the organisers before the situation escalated around the country. While Bevin had prevented a nationwide stoppage, it proved that Order 1305 did not work.

Around 12,000 bus drivers and conductors stopped work over wage demands in May 1943, while 16,000 Merseyside dockers withdrew their labour in August after colleagues were suspended for refusing to work overtime. Around 7,000 stopped work over piece rates at the Vickers-Armstrongs' dockyard in Barrow-in-Furness a month later and 100,000 working days were lost.

The longest stoppage took place at Rolls-Royce's Hillington factory in Glasgow in November 1943. Over 16,000 women stopped work because they were paid less than men doing the same work on Merlin aircraft engines. Agnes McLean campaigned for equal pay for a month and over 730,000 hours were lost before Rolls-Royce agreed to pay workers according to their job rather than their gender. The Amalgamated Engineering Union took the opportunity to enrol many women, so it could act on their behalf. Other trade unions followed suit, increasing their membership.

The Ministry of Labour believed political activists were involved in a stoppage by shipbuilding and engineering apprentices in January 1944. It started after a young man selected to work in coal mining (one of the Bevin Boys) was prosecuted after failing to attend a Training Centre. The rest of the apprentices were threatened with military service but nearly 12,000 apprentices in other workplaces stopped work in solidarity. Trade unions condemned the stoppage and it ended after two weeks, with four members of the Trotskyist Movement being charged.

The introduction of a national minimum wage for coal miners, called the Porter Award, caused the biggest stoppage in March 1944.[11] The new rates had been decided without consulting the Miners' Federation of Great Britain and they had resulted in uneven wage increases across the workforce. It resulted in 250,000 miners across South Wales and Yorkshire stopping work when the review dragged on. The loss of coal production threatened to interfere with the preparations for the invasion of France, so a new offer was made and everyone was back at work after just a week.

There were two stoppages in August 1944. The first involved 2,000 Glaswegian engineering operatives downing tools for two months, after a colleague was dismissed. Boilermakers on the River Tyne also halted work after semi-skilled workers were put to work operating a new machine from America. Around 4,500 were fined and they were advised to pay up before they returned to work in January 1945.

## Improving Relations

### Personnel Management[12]

Personnel management was in its infancy in the 1930s and many factories did not have a personnel manager at the start of the war. The reason was, companies had relied on the fear of unemployment during the recession to maintain discipline. The first group of personnel managers were more likely to cause more problems than solve them, because they had been given no training and most just kept a company's records.

At the beginning of 1942, the Women's Consultative Committee suggested employing female personnel managers, to try and reduce the high turnover of women. It was another year before the Production Efficiency Board started training courses but it was some time before the first personnel managers were able influence the hire and fire regimes most firms relied on.

The Shipbuilding Employers' Federation objected to using personnel managers but the Admiralty, the Confederation of Shipbuilding and the Engineering Unions all wanted them. The Admiralty continued to transfer labour between the Royal Dockyards when it required. It also refused to rely on Yard Committees to deal with disputes. However, absenteeism remained low because workers were granted twelve days' unpaid leave a year, which seemed to maintain morale. The private shipyards disciplined workers through their wallet, either banning them from doing overtime or suspending them from work for short periods. Persistent offenders were sacked.

Area labour managers started working with the managers of the Royal Ordnance Factories over the summer of 1942. They wanted to improve cooperation with the workforce but there was little support from the shopfloor. Despite the difficulties, companies looked to the Personnel Management Advisory Service to help them organise redundancy programmes, as the demand for armaments fell over the winter of 1944–1945. Many women were anxious to quit their jobs during the final months of the war and they left as soon as it ended. Meanwhile, companies had to decide who they would make redundant and in what order they would leave. The Ministry of Labour was then kept busy helping tens of thousands workers find work.

## Improving Welfare[13]

Companies initially focused on recruiting as many workers as possible and managers ignored the difficulties their employees had finding accommodation, travelling to work or running a home. So, long hours and poor working conditions resulted in excessive absenteeism and a high turnover of staff until problems started to be addressed at the end of 1941. While some problems required disciplinary action, most just required attention to make the workers' lives easier.

Some of the worst instances occurred in the original Royal Ordnance Factories in Woolwich, Waltham and Enfield where employees were housed in cramped buildings with outdated facilities. While attempts were made to improve welfare, there were always high levels of absenteeism, particularly during the Blitz. It did not help that there were problems maintaining the blackout in the outdated buildings, picking the factories out as targets.

The buildings used by the Royal Dockyards were also cramped and out of date. The Workmen's Society did their best to organise welfare facilities but their efforts were ruined when the dockyards were bombed. The Treasury gave the Contract Labour Branch the authority to open hostels and canteens during the summer of 1942.

Improved working conditions, shorter shifts and listening to the workers' concerns usually reduced absenteeism. However, persistent offenders were invited to appear before a Factory Committee or a Yard Committee. The Ministry of Labour introduced an Essential Work Order in the spring of 1941, which gave National Service Officers the power to prosecute or dismiss an undisciplined worker. They also had the final say over whether a worker could change jobs. However, they also made sure that factories conformed to the safety and welfare standards demanded by the Ministry of Labour.

Good welfare made recruiting easier, reduced absenteeism and stopped workers looking for other work. But a factory needed to have suitable amenities, as well as a positive relationship between the workforce and the management. The Ministry of Labour insisted that companies complied with the Industrial Health Research Board's welfare and safety recommendations, while the Factory Inspectorate insisted that they were implemented before contracts were issued.

The Institute of Labour Management, the Industrial Welfare Society and several universities eventually set up courses to train welfare managers. Welfare officers were appointed in the summer of 1942, to make sure women's needs were addressed. A Production Efficiency Board investigated industry wide issues over the winter of 1942–1943, while an Industrial Panel identified problem firms and dealt with their management.

Over time, absenteeism levelled off but it was always higher amongst married women, because they struggled to run a home as well as work. The number of short strikes and go-slow movements increased as the war dragged on, due to fatigue. Absenteeism would also increase as the war came to an end.

## Welfare Inside the Factory[14]

The Ministry of Labour ran many safety campaigns, to instruct the tens of thousands of inexperienced workers working on new machines. Factory inspectors also helped managers make their premises healthier and safer to work in. Working hours were eventually reduced to improve the health and efficiency of the workers.

A Medical and Welfare Services Order required companies to employ medical, nursing, first aid and welfare staff after July 1940. A Committee on Industrial Health started advising companies on dangerous substances and factory hygiene in the spring of 1943.

Dockyards had always had canteens, but the Port Authority was instructed to improve them in February 1941. The long working hours and the shift systems meant that meals were often at unusual times for factory workers, so the Ministry of Labour made larger premises and construction sites open canteens. Nearly 12,000 factory canteens were eventually opened.

## Welfare Outside the Factory[15]

Many workers struggled to get to work during the first two winters of the war because air raids interrupted transport routes and forced factories to disperse their work. Public transport was often disrupted because drivers and conductors were being called up, while many buses were required by the emergency services.

Factories started organising reception committees to meet new employees, to ease them into their new jobs. Voluntary organisations often escorted young women on their journeys or welcomed them at railway stations, as many had never been away from home before. Eventually, over fifty reception hostels were set up to house workers and help them find lodgings.

An Assisted Travel Scheme covered the travelling costs of those who preferred to stay at home. But there were never enough local workers, so a Housing Committee started organising hostels in January 1940. However, private companies started overcharging guests, so many remained empty until the National Service Hostels Corporation started running them in May 1941. Initially, some were filled by families bombed out of their homes, but the Ministry of Health had to stop the practice when workers found it difficult to find lodgings. He also compelled householders to provide rooms at a reasonable price.

The National Service Hostels Corporation was soon running sixty-five hostels around the Royal Ordnance Factories and dispersal factories. Sleepless nights caused by air raids over the winter of 1940–1941 resulted in many workers being offered hostel spaces as respite accommodation. The Ministry of Agriculture also opened hostels for seasonal agricultural workers, while the Ministry of Fuel ran hostels for the Bevin Boys training to be coal miners. Dozens of camps set up next to construction projects brought the number of places to 73,000 beds. Unfortunately, most were poorly built and the staff were often overwhelmed by their unruly guests.

Many skilled men working away from home had been promised their families would join them. However, most local authorities refused to give permission for temporary houses and only 13,000 married quarters were built. It meant that many families remained separated.

The government organised several types of morale boosting events to entertain the workforce. It set up a National Council of Social Services and put on concerts and other entertainments. Meanwhile, a Central Consultative Council organised voluntary organisations to help societies and recreation facilities. The BBC started making 'Music While You Work' programmes to broadcast in the factories in the summer of 1940. The Entertainments National Service Association (ENSA) and the Council for the Encouragement of Music and the Arts (CEMA) put on shows, as did orchestras, military bands and mobile film units.

*Chapter 12*

# The Blitz

## The Bombing Raids

Many of the *Luftwaffe*'s bombing raids targeted British industry, starting with small daylight raids in the summer of 1940 and culminating in heavy nighttime raids over the winter that followed. This is a short account of what the raids targeted, how the factories were protected and how the damage inflicted affected industry and the workforce.

## The First Bombing Phase[1]

The first phase of the *Luftwaffe*'s bombing campaign started on 7 September 1940; it lasted for nearly two months. Operation London targeted the capital and while the rail network and docks were damaged, and there were heavy casualties, the British government did not capitulate. Meanwhile, Operation Sea Snake targeted shipping, sinking over 100,000 tons.[2] There were also bombing attacks against factories across the southeast but the RAF was winning the battle for the skies. Adolf Hitler indefinitely postponed the invasion of Britain, codenamed Operation Sea Lion, on 17 September 1940.[3]

Heavy aircraft losses resulted in the *Luftwaffe* switching to night attacks on 7 October 1940, making the work of the RAF's fighters and the Civil Defence Force's AA guns much harder. Bombing raids became heavier with industrial targets in London, Birmingham, Coventry, Liverpool, Hull and Glasgow being attacked. Meanwhile, German fighter bombers continued precision attacks against factories during the day.

Over 11,600 tons of high explosive and 1 million incendiaries were dropped on London alone in September and October, causing 33,000 casualties. Docks were damaged, barges were sunk, the Underground was disrupted and railway lines were cut but the factories continued production and life continued amongst the ruins. One of the biggest concerns was how to get coal from the North to London before the onset of winter.

## The Second Bombing Phase[4]

The *Luftwaffe* widened its bombing campaign in November 1940, looking to reduce the production of steel and aircraft, as well as the movement of coal. London and Birmingham were hit first on the night of 13–14 November. The following night, Coventry was targeted and the Nazi Propaganda Minister, Joseph Goebbels, invented the word '*Coventried*', to describe the destruction to the city. Over twenty aircraft factories were wrecked, while damage to public utilities stopped work at nine others. The raid caused a temporary 20 per cent reduction in aircraft production, illustrating how dangerous the *Luftwaffe* could be.

Around 200 bombers attacked every night over the next two months, weather permitting. Steel foundries, aircraft factories, docks and railway lines were bombed, time and again. Over 18,000 tons of bombs were dropped on London alone, causing 54,000 casualties and widespread damage. The following list shows the *Luftwaffe*'s main targets and the industries they wanted to destroy. In London's case they were also targeting the railways and docks, which brought coal and other goods to the capital.

| Target | Number of Raids | Bomb Tons | Main Industries |
| --- | --- | --- | --- |
| London | 781 | 18,291 | Engineering and Shipping |
| Liverpool | 8 | 1,957 | Shipping and Imports |
| Birmingham | 8 | 1,852 | Engineering and Aircraft |
| Plymouth | 8 | 1,228 | Shipping |
| Bristol | 6 | 919 | Shipping and Imports |
| Glasgow | 5 | 1,329 | Shipping |
| Southampton | 4 | 647 | Shipping |
| Portsmouth | 3 | 687 | Shipping |
| Hull | 3 | 593 | Shipping |
| Manchester | 3 | 578 | Engineering |
| Coventry | 2 | 818 | Aircraft |
| Belfast | 2 | 440 | Engineering and Shipping |
| Sheffield | 1 | 355 | Steel and Engineering |
| Newcastle-upon-Tyne | 1 | 152 | Shipping |
| Nottingham | 1 | 137 | Engineering and Shipping |
| Cardiff | 1 | 115 | Shipping |

The air war became more sophisticated as it intensified. The *Luftwaffe* used heavier bombs to cause more damage, incendiaries to start fires and destructive parachute mines, which detonated after impact. Meanwhile, British radar stations tracked the bombers, while electronic countermeasures interrupted the German radar. Initially, the Germans used the *Knickebein* (Crooked Leg) radar system, codenamed Headache, which guided bombers along one beam until they intersected a second one over the target. The British scientists had developed radar equipment codenamed Aspirin to jam it by November 1940.

The Germans then used the *X-Gerät* system (known as Ruffian by the British), which used several intercepting beams to warn the crews they were approaching their target. Equipment codenamed Bromide was developed to jam them. The Germans then used the *Y-Gerät* system, which measured the time it took to bounce a beam off an aircraft, to calculate the distance to its target. It was also quickly countered by the British scientists. Countermeasures codenamed Benjamin and Domino often deflected the beams of a third system called *Wotan* (known as Benito by the British), causing the German pilots to lose confidence in their navigational aids.

Bomber streams sometimes struggled to find targets due to industrial haze and smoke, so pathfinder aircraft marked them with incendiary bombs. The *Luftwaffe* was struggling to keep up the pressure by January 1941 because it was short of experienced air crews and serviceable aircraft. The winter weather also restricted when they could fly. However, the RAF and the radar scientists had learnt from the *Luftwaffe*'s techniques and the difficulties its crews faced. They would devise their own methods for finding and hitting targets when the Allied bomber force was ready.

### The Final Attacks[5]

Hitler's Directive 23 called for a renewal of bombing operations against British industry in February 1941. However, British radar countermeasures stopped the *Luftwaffe* making major inland raids on cloudy nights. Radar tracking equipment helped the British night fighters intercept them on moonlit nights, so they often hit coastal targets instead. Some raids targeted the docks on the west side of Britain where North American imports were being unloaded. Clydebank and Greenock near Glasgow, Newcastle-upon-Tyne, Sunderland,

Belfast, Hull, Cardiff, Portsmouth and Plymouth all suffered extensive damage and heavy casualties in March 1941, as did smaller ports. The raids against London also continued until mid-May 1941.

The number and size of raids reduced after the *Luftwaffe* redeployed large numbers of aircraft to Austria in April 1941, ahead of the invasions of Yugoslavia and Greece. However, Liverpool was still hit hard, leaving 75 per cent of the docks damaged beyond use, while 150,000 tons of shipping were lost. By the end of May, the bombing raids had all but ended, as the *Luftwaffe* moved even more aircraft east, ready to support the attack against the Soviet Union, which started on 22 June 1941.

Over 40,000 tons of bombs had been dropped during the Blitz, killing 41,000 and injuring another 139,000.[6] Meanwhile, the *Luftwaffe* had lost 2,265 aircraft and suffered over 8,000 casualties; many of them experienced air crew. Nine months of raids had damaged one million houses, sunk or damaged over 500,000 tons of shipping and forced armaments companies to disperse their factories. While the raids had reduced output from time to time, British production had continued to rise steadily.

## Later Raids[7]

The RAF carried out its first large bombing raid against the port of Lübeck in northern Germany on 28 March 1942. Fires caused substantial damage to the historic city centre, so the *Luftwaffe* planned retaliatory raids against targets with cultural or historical significance. It chose Exeter, Bath, York, Norwich and Canterbury from the *Baedeker* guidebooks. While the raids caused over 3,300 casualties and damaged 50,000 homes at the end of April and beginning of May 1942, they caused insignificant military or economic damage.

The *Luftwaffe*'s final attempts to bomb the London area were made between 21 January and 29 May 1944. They were carried out for propaganda purposes, as a counter to the RAF's bombing campaign against Berlin. While the Germans called the riads Operation Steinbock or Operation Capricorn, the British called them the Little Blitz or the Baby Blitz. British air defences and fighter tactics had improved so much that around 70 per cent of the German aircraft that flew over the capital were shot down.

It left the *Luftwaffe*'s unable to interfere with Allied shipping during Operation Overlord. Instead, it was down to the V–1 rockets and then the V–2 rockets to hit targets around London. They were called Vengeance weapons and that is all there were, because they were unguided missiles that were as likely to hit urban areas as they were to hit industrial ones.

## An Evaluation of the *Luftwaffe*'s Raids

The Air Ministry assessed the impact of the Blitz in August 1941, to see what lessons Bomber Command could learn. It concluded that it had to focus on one industrial target a night, to cause as much damage as possible. It noted that hitting urban areas caused distress to the workforce and disruption to the infrastructure, further reducing production. It also judged that incendiaries reduced production more than high explosives, if enough fires could be started to overwhelm the emergency services. The strategy that was decided on was for the USAAF to carry out precision raids against industry in daylight because its bombers carried a smaller payload. The RAF bombers would conduct area raids against infrastructure at night with their heavier payloads.[8] Between them, it was hoped they could severely damage German industry.

## Air Defences and Dispersal

### British Air Defences[9]

Britain had poor air defences to begin with. There were insufficient AA guns and many were obsolete and unable to hit the bombers. Only a few had tracking systems that warned the crews of approaching aircraft and they could not identify if they were friend or foe. Searchlights were underpowered and in short supply but lighting up the night sky for the guns was good for morale. Usually, all the Air Raid Precaution (ARP) members could do during a raid was to direct members of the Fire Service to where they were needed the most. Meanwhile, the RAF had no technology to find the bombers in the dark, so few fighter aircraft could operate at night.

Over time, the AA guns became more mobile, allowing them to be moved to where they were needed. New tracking devices alerted the crews, while improved fire-control systems allowed them to target enemy aircraft with the help of powerful searchlights. Eventually, the number of rounds required to shoot down each bomber was reduced from 20,000 down to just 3,000. Bit by bit, Britain's air defences were getting the better of the *Luftwaffe*.

Fake sites were built to divert the bombers away from key airfields and factories. While 'Drem K' sites were designed to attract the German air crews' attention during daylight hours, 'Drem Q' sites used lights to divert them from their target at night. Starfish sites used lights and fires to simulate pathfinder bombs, to trick the air crews into bombing the countryside rather than urban or industrial areas. However, the main threat from the *Luftwaffe* was over by the time they were ready.

## Dispersing the Factories[10]

The Air Ministry had outlined the part of England that it thought would be vulnerable to air attack as early as 1934. The danger area covered the south and east of England, which included London's many factories, as well as the aircraft factories and shipyards near the south coast. It thought the safe area was west of a line drawn from the Bristol Channel, northeast through the Cotswolds to Stow-on-the-Wold and then north through Stafford to Stockport, southeast of Manchester. It then ran north along the Pennines to the Scottish border before heading northwest to Falkirk, west of Edinburgh. While the Midlands were classified as unsafe, it included many of the aircraft and engineering factories around Birmingham and Coventry. These areas would be adjusted in October 1940, once the Blitz was under way.

Ten of the main aircraft factories were in the eastern danger area and four were in the central unsafe area; only three were in the western safe area. It would have been too expensive and caused too much disruption to relocate the factories, so they were extended instead. Many of the new agency and shadow factories were built in the safe areas to increase the security of the industry. They were also located where there was high unemployment, caused by the industries that employed women shutting down.

The Admiralty could not move its dockyards and shipyards but it was banned from using factories in vulnerable areas along the south and east coasts. The Air Ministry had to rely on private firms based around Bristol, Gloucester, Birmingham and Coventry, where there was skilled labour and experienced engineering works. However, the Ministry of Supply was able to build its new factories in safer areas.

Companies were urged to move out of London or away from the south coast when the *Luftwaffe* started targeting factories in October 1939. However, many had not moved from their vulnerable locations by the time the Blitz started in the autumn of 1940. All three supply departments were warned to disperse their work but Lord Beaverbrook argued that it would interfere with the Ministry of Aircraft Production's production. The Ministry of Labour pointed out where labour was available and 300 factories were discreetly taken over. Work was divided between them and production was often duplicated in case one was damaged. For example, production of the Hurricane production was eventually divided between forty-eight sites. While aircraft output dipped significantly over the winter of 1940–1941, it was soon back on track.

The Industrial Capacity Committee and the Area Boards monitored bomb damage to factories, so the Production Council could assess its impact on output. Birmingham Small Arms Company Limited was just one company that had to spread its manufacturing work across three counties, after its Birmingham factory was seriously damaged in April 1941. The company ended up employing 28,000 workers across many sites and they would make over half the small arms required by the armed forces.

Some companies set up production groups to make parts, spreading the manufacturing across a wide area to make it easier to find workers and to reduce the risk from bombing. For example, the London Aircraft Production Group dispersed its work across 700 factories and workshops around the capital; over half of its 50,000 employees were women. They made tens of thousands of parts, so Handley Page's factory near St Albans and de Havilland's factory near Watford could build 2,300 Halifax bombers.

The Supply Board considered building underground factories but decided not to in September 1940 because it would look like those working inside were being treated differently. Only four major schemes were tried and they were all slow and expensive to build. The also proved difficult to recruit for and were unpopular to work in:

- 8,000 workers made aircraft equipment in a London Underground tunnel.
- Browning guns were made in a cavern in the Midlands.
- Engines were manufactured in a tunnel after the air raid on Coventry.
- Bristol Aeroplane Company made engines and airframes in underground quarries.

*Chapter 13*

# The War Ends

## Planning for Peace[1]

There had been plans to wind the munitions industry down when the First World War ended but factories were shut down immediately after the Armistice on 11 November 1918. While it reduced the quantities of surplus weapons and ammunition left over, it resulted in problems for industries and mass unemployment. They were soon followed by a prolonged economic depression. So, British industry was told to prepare for a three-stage wind down of production during the final months of the Second World War, to try and avoid a similar situation:

- Stage I: a gradual reduction of armaments as the European campaign came to an end.
- Stage II: a buildup of armaments for the Far East campaign after Germany surrendered.
- Stage III: maintain the stocks required during the fight to defeat Japan.

The number of people employed by the armaments industry had peaked at 5.2 million in the summer of 1943, by which time the British armed forces were fully equipped and supplied. It had taken four years to achieve the goal set at the beginning of the war. It had also required huge amounts of help from America and Canada; both industrial and financial. British industry just had to make enough for spares and repairs, while maintaining the levels of ammunition. The point of equilibrium between supply and demand had been reached at just the right time because the country had run out of labour reserves.

As demand fell, the Royal Ordnance Factories started running out of orders, so they were closed one by one until only half were left open.

Several chemical firms, particularly ICI, took over some of the explosives factories but most would be closed and abandoned. On a positive side, the aircraft industry had been expanded and modernised during the war years. Britain's shipbuilding industry had been revived and many yards had been modernised and reequipped. The nation's coal and steel industries had also seen improvements both in mechanisation and industrial relations.

Preparations for Stage I of reducing production began after the landings in Normandy in June 1944. The British government was wary of telling industry to cut production too early, in case the Americans reduced the amounts shipped under the Lend-Lease programme, in favour of the Pacific campaign. However, the uncertain progress of the European campaign meant that the estimated date of Germany's surrender kept changing. It was originally set as June 1945, only to be brought forward to December 1944 after the *Wehrmacht*'s rapid withdrawal from France. It was then pushed back to February 1945 and finally to June 1945, as Germany fought to the bitter end. The actual date would be 8 May 1945.

It was expected that the British Army would require large numbers of tanks and huge amounts of ammunition to defeat the *Wehrmacht*. It would then need many troops to maintain control over the German population and make a show strength to the Red Army. Maintaining such a visible presence meant there would be a delay in the deployment of troops to the Far East.

The *Luftwaffe* had already been beaten, so the RAF needed fewer replacement aircraft. However, the Air Ministry muted talk of cutting back military aircraft production, so America did not think that the British aircraft industry was looking to switch to civilian aircraft. While the RAF could scale down its efforts, the Admiralty required more ships for naval operations against Japan. The plan was for the Royal Navy to join the US commands in the Pacific, so the British shipyards were busy preparing warships for service in the Far East.

On top of everything, the British government had to consider how to convert the armaments industry back to civilian work, without setting it up for the sort of economic misery experienced in the 1920s. It also had to work out how to cope with a population overjoyed about victory in Europe, while there was still hard fighting ahead in the Far East.

America stopped sending supplies to Britain as soon as Germany had been defeated and directed them to the Pacific Theatre. Stage II was going to be more difficult to plan for because no one knew what supplies would be needed to defeat Japan. The plan was for the British fleet to help the US Navy but that involved upgrading warships for service in the tropics. Many merchant ships also had to be converted into supply ships, to serve in what would be known as the Fleet Train. A lot of new small warships were also needed to counter the Imperial Japanese Navy. Meanwhile, the British troops who would have to drive the Japanese Army out of Burma and Malaya had to be supplied. The same applied to the RAF squadrons deployed in the Far East.

The US Navy turned down the Royal Navy's request for help, so it had to rely on British and Canadian shipyards to covert the support ships and make the landing craft it would need to recapture Burma (now Myanmar) and the Malayan Peninsula. However, the work was cancelled when Japan surrendered following the detonation of two atomic bombs on Hiroshima and Nagasaki at the beginning of August 1945.

## The End Arrives

### Closing the Factories[2]

The War Cabinet had started looking at how reconstruction would affect post-war Britain as early as 1941 and one issue it considered was how to shut down the armaments industry. The Board of Trade took control of organising the post-war economy, to make sure there were adequate supplies of all essential goods. It told armaments factories what to make and while some were put on urgent work relating to reconstruction, others started making items for export. It took factories several months to change their machinery around and it took some several years to return to their pre-war output.

The Royal Dockyards started repairing its tired warships and converting merchant ships for civilian use. The private shipyards focused on building and repairing merchant ships, so the shipping companies could resume moving imports and exports. The RAF had more than enough planes for peacetime conditions, so the Ministry of Aircraft Production cancelled many contracts and closed the agency and shadow factories, leaving tens of thousands of men and women out of work.

The Ministry of Supply ended contracts with its private contractors and halved its workforce when the war ended, again making thousands unemployed. It further reduced what it required over the months that followed, virtually ending production by the end of 1945. One by one factories closed or switched production and industry eventually reached the level of production required for domestic consumption and exports at the start of 1947. The combined reductions by the three supply departments reduced a workforce which had peaked at 5.2 million in the summer of 1943 down to 500,000 in just eighteen months.

A Ministerial Storage Committee was set up to dispose of the huge quantities of surplus components, finished items and ammunition left over when the war ended. It had to choose the dumping areas and organise the transportation to them. Around 3 million tons of munitions and toxic goods were dumped in a deep trough in the Irish Sea called Beaufort's Dyke; an area used after the First World War.

As the nation emerged from nearly six years of war, few would have taken the time to consider the advantages the conflict had left on industry. A huge amount of industrial capital had been built up and it could now be used to make items for the domestic market or for export. There had been a spread of engineering skills across the workforce, giving it back the confidence it had lost between the wars. There had also been a lot of constructive changes in production methods and positive advances in management attitudes and industrial relations. The question was: would the nation use these advantages wisely to rebuild itself?

## Laying Off the Workforce[3]

Another issue which the War Cabinet had been considering since 1941, was how to demobilise hundreds of thousands of men and women from the armed forces and armaments work. It decided to release those with the skills required to help the nation back on its feet early. The rest of the men would be released according to their age and length of service. But huge amounts of training had to be funded, while careful thought had to put into how to organise the masses of men and women looking for work. Meanwhile, the armed forces had to decide who they needed to retain, both to garrison a war-torn Europe and to end the fight against Japan.

Demobilisation started after the surrender of Germany and the armaments firms were instructed to release women with household responsibilities or those wishing to rejoin their husbands first. Men who were required for priority civilian work or who had worked away from home for over one year were also allowed to leave early. Several industrial agreements made with trade unions at the start of the war also had to be honoured, so their customs and practices were reinstated, bringing dilution to an end.

However, the whole process was thrown into chaos when the Japanese surrendered in August 1945. Everyone wanted to get home to their families and find employment as quickly as possible. So, the government kept registering young men and women for National Service, so they could replace those who had served and to help speed up the demobilisation process. They were either directed into the armed forces or into important civilian work, so the time-served men could go home.

The Ministry of Labour prepared the huge numbers of men leaving the services for civilian life by organising lectures, films and leaflets both at home and overseas. Resettlement Advice Service centres advised men about employment, training and housing while employment exchanges and appointment offices helped find them work. Between them, they were soon dealing with over 120,000 queries a month.

Many young men needed help to restart (or start) their career after they left the armed forces. Some returned to their university studies or their professional training, while others enrolled on business courses. Many attended trade or occupation classes at training centres or technical colleges; others trained while working part time. An Interrupted Apprenticeship Scheme helped those who needed to finish their training. They were all supported by a range of grants designed to get them back to work.

The Ministry of Labour had started talking to disabled ex-servicemen and their doctors as early as 1941, to help them find suitable training and employment. Their staff interviewed over 425,000 men and they were able to place 310,000, many of whom would work alongside the able bodied. The rest attended Emergency Training Centres, which helped them with their physical and mental rehabilitation. Eventually, many would find work in technical, executive and clerical roles, which suited their physical condition. Sheltered occupations also were established for the seriously disabled, to help them with their care and recovery.

## The Financial Cost[4]

As the Second World War came to an end, it was possible to add up the huge contributions made to Britain's armed forces by the British, American and Canadian factories between 1939 and 1945. Here are just a few of them:

|  | Britain | United States | Canada |
|---|---|---|---|
| Tanks | 3,600 | 24,800 | 25,600 |
| Artillery and Guns | 13,400 | 132,000 | 10,300 |
| Rifles and Machine Guns | 1.45 million | 7.6 million | 2.76 million |
| Vehicles | 582,000 | 683,000 | 265,000 |
| Aircraft | 5,400 | 96,100 | 23,000 |
| Landing Craft | Nil | 4,300 | 2,600 |
| Bullets | 4.5 billion | 11.1 billion | 7.5 billion |

British industry had made 69 per cent of the armaments required by its armed forces during the war. It had bought 4 per cent from America during the early months of the conflict. Another 17 per cent of its requirements had been supplied under the Lend-Lease Act. Canada had supplied 8 per cent of the required armaments while the Commonwealth had supplied the remaining 2 per cent.

In financial terms, the United States had spent 11 per cent of its war budget on the Lend Lease Act, while the British Commonwealth had contributed 9 per cent of its budget to the United States. America had supplied $31.4 billion ($1.2 trillion today) of armaments to Britain; it would take it until December 2006 to pay off the debt.

# Other Books by Author

## Battlefield Guides (Pen & Sword Books)

*Battleground Europe: Loos: Hohenzollern Redoubt* (2002)
*Battleground Europe: Loos: Hill 70* (2002)
*Walcheren: Operation Infatuate* (2003)
*Remagen: Crossing the Rhine* (2004)
*Festung Cherbourg: Normandy* (2004)
*Battleground Europe: 9th US Army Crosses the Rhine* (2005)
*In Pursuit of Hitler: A Battlefield Guide to Bavaria* (2007)
*The Peninsular War: A Battlefield Guide* (2009)
*Auschwitz: The Nazi Solution* (2015)
*Schindler's Krakow: The City Under the Nazis* (2015)
*Ancestor's Footsteps: The Somme 1916* (2020)

## Western Front Centenary Series (Pen & Sword Books)

*BEF – The 1914 Campaign* (2014)
*BEF – The 1915 Campaign* (2015)
*BEF – The Somme Campaign* (2016)
*BEF – The Arras Campaign: April and May 1917* (2017)
*BEF – The Passchendaele Campaign: July to November 1917* (2017)
*BEF – The Cambrai Campaign: November 1917* (2017)
*BEF – Lys Offensive: April 1918* (2018)
*BEF – Somme Offensive: March 1918* (2018)
*BEF – Advance to Victory: July to September 1918* (2018)
*BEF – The Final Advance: September to November 1918* (2018)
*Learning Process – The British Army's Art of War* (Helion & Company, 2019)

## Images of War Series (Pen & Sword Books)

*The Battle of the Bulge* (2005)
*Victory in Europe* (2005)
*Victory in the Pacific and the Far East* (2005)


## Military Handbooks (The History Press)

*British Army Handbook* (2006)
*Vietnam War Handbook* (2008)
*Rise of the Third Reich Handbook* (2010)


## Battle Stories (The History Press)

*Battle of the Bulge: 1944–5* (2011)
*Iwo Jima: 1945* (2012)
*Tet Offensive: 1968* (2013)


## Other Titles

*Baghdad Operators: Ex-Special Forces in Iraq* (Pen & Sword, 2012)
*Showcasing the Third Reich: The Nuremberg Rallies* (History Press, 2012)
*Eyes Only: Marshall's and Eisenhower's Top Secret Correspondence* (History Press, 2012)
*Organising Victory: The War Conferences* (History Press, 2013)
*A Clash of Thrones: European Royalty* (History Press, 2015)
*Treachery and Retribution: England's Dukes, Marquesses & Earls* (Pen & Sword, 2017)
*Poland's Struggle: Before, During and After the Second World War* (Pen & Sword, 2020)
*Balkan Struggles: Civil War, Invasion, Communism and Genocide* (Pen & Sword, 2021)
*Britain's Munitions Industry in the First World War: Doing Their Bit* (Pen & Sword, 2025)

# Bibliography


## History of the Second World War, United Kingdom Civil Series: War Production Series

Behrans, C. Betty A., *Merchant Shipping and the Demands of War* (HMSO, 1955)
Collier, Basil, *The Defence of the United Kingdom* (HMSO, 1957)
Court, W.H.B., *Coal* (HMSO, 1951)
Hall, D., Wrigley, C. and Scott, J.D., *Studies of Overseas Supply* (HMSO, 1956)
Hancock, W.K. and Gowing, M.M. *British War Economy* (HMSO, 1949)
Hornby, William, *Factories and Plant* (HMSO, 1958)
Hurstfield, J., *Control of Raw Materials* (HMSO, 1953)
Inman, P., *Labour in the Munitions Industry* (HMSO, 1957)
Parker, H.M.D., *Manpower* (HMSO, 1957)
Payton-Smith, D.J., *Oil* (HMSO, 1971)
Postan, M.M. *British War Production* (HMSO, 1952)
Postan, M.M., Hay, D. and Scott, J.D., *Design and Development of Weapons*, (HMSO, 1964)
Scott, J.D. and Hughes, Richard, *Administration of War Production* (HMSO, 1955)

## Other Books

Churchill, Winston, *The Second World War: Volume 2* (1949)
Clarke, Peter, *The Cripps Version* (Penguin Press, 2002)
Rawson, Andrew, *Britain's Munitions Industry in the First World War: Doing Their Bit* (Pen & Sword Books, Barnsley, 2024)
Thomas, Roger D. and Patterson, Brian, *Dreadnoughts: A Photographic History* (History Press, 2010)

## Websites

Grace Guides: https://www.gracesguide.co.uk
History of the Second World War, United Kingdom Civil Series: https://www.archive.org
Pen & Sword Books – Andrew Rawson: https://www.pen-and-sword.co.uk/search/author/Andrew+Rawson


## Illustrative Material

All images are sourced from American archives and are in the public domain.

# Notes

## Introduction

1. I refer to First World War industry as the 'munitions industry' and Second World War industry as the 'armaments industry'. They were the preferred words at the time but they are interchangeable.

## Chapter 1: Rearmament

1. *British War Production*, Postan, M.M., pp.9–14 and pp.34–41; *Design and Development of Weapons*, Postan, M.M., Hay, D. and Scott, J.D., pp.49–68; *Manpower*, Parker, H.M.D., pp.18–51; *Factories and Plant*, Hornby, William, pp.1–9 and 24–35.
2. It required 78 workers to support 100 servicemen during the First World War. The number would rise to 112 workers to every 100 servicemen during the Second World War.
3. *British War Production*, Postan, M.M., dockyards refer to government owned facilities and shipyards refers to privately owned facilities.
4. *British War Production*, Postan, M.M., pp.76–95; *Manpower*, Parker, H.M.D., pp.51–60.
5. *British War Production*, Postan, M.M., pp.53–8, pp.76-81 and pp.102–14.
6. *British War Production*, Postan, M.M., pp.95–102; *Manpower*, Parker, H.M.D., pp.212–25; *Labour in the Munitions Industry*, Inman, P., pp.20–35 and 428–38.
7. *British War Production*, Postan, M.M., pp.81–6; *Administration of War Production*, Scott, J.D. and Hughes, Richard, pp.310–9 and 332–7.
8. *British War Production*, Postan, M.M., pp.23–7, pp.47–52 and pp.58–66; *Administration of War Production*, Scott, J.D. and Hughes, Richard, pp.82–8; *Factories and Plant*, Hornby, William, pp.36–44.
9. For example, a battleship could be no larger than 35,000 tons and their largest gun could be a 16-inch calibre.
10. *British War Production*, Postan, M.M., pp.14–23, pp.34–41 and pp.66–9; *Administration of War Production*, Scott, J.D. and Hughes, Richard, pp.33–44; *Factories and Plant*, Hornby, William, pp.194–226; *Design and Development of Weapons*, Postan, M.M., Hay, D. and Scott, J.D., pp.83–95.
11. Both the *Luftwaffe* and the *Aviazione Legionaria* (Legionary Air Force) deployed their aircraft during the Spanish Civil War (1936–1939) and learnt many lessons.

12. Vickers had to take over the Castle Bromwich factory in May 1940, because there had been so many problems and delays. It would be making 70 per cent of Spitfires by 1943.
13. The shadow aircraft industry would make nearly half of the RAF's heavy bombers by the end of the war but it made only 10 per cent of other types.
14. *British War Production*, Postan, M.M., pp.27–76; *Administration of War Production*, Scott, J.D. and Hughes, Richard, pp.19–29.
15. *Administration of War Production*, Scott, J.D. and Hughes, Richard, pp.281–3; *Design and Development of Weapons*, Postan, M.M., Hay, D. and Scott, J.D., pp.304–21 and 353–72; *Factories and Plant*, Hornby, William, pp.77–91 and 183–94.
16. It was known as the Metropolitan-Cammell Carriage and Wagon Company at the time but later changed its name to Metro-Cammell Carriage and Wagon Company.

## Chapter 2: The Administration

1. *British War Production*, Postan, M.M., pp.86–95; *Administration of War Production*, Scott, J.D. and Hughes, Richard, pp.49–68 and pp.241–50; *Manpower*, Parker, H.M.D., pp.97–116.
2. See the Chapter 7 for a full account of imports from North America and the Lend-Lease programme.
3. *Administration of War Production*, Scott, J.D. and Hughes, Richard, pp.3–16.
4. Ibid, pp.33–48.
5. Lend-Lease would provide over 10 per cent of the Soviet Air Force's aircraft, including 1,200 Spitfires.
6. Clarke, Peter, *The Cripps* Version (Penguin Press, 2002), p.373.
7. *Administration of War Production*, Scott, J.D. and Hughes, Richard, pp.68–80.
8. Ibid, pp.213–9 and 233–41.
9. Large quantities of weapons and ammunition were provided from the US War Department's stores; however, a lot of it was obsolete.
10. *British War Production*, Postan, M.M., pp.248–74; *Administration of War Production*, Scott, J.D. and Hughes, Richard, pp.435–80.
11. *British War Economy*, Hancock, W.K. and Gowing, M.M., pp.268–79.
12. Great Western Railway (GWR), London, Midland and Scottish Railway (LMS), London and North Eastern Railway (LNER) and Southern Railway (SR) and been formed from many smaller companies in 1923.
13. *British War Economy*, Hancock, W.K. and Gowing, M.M., p.278

## Chapter 3: Research, Design and Development

1. *Administration of War Production*, Scott, J.D. and Hughes, Richard, pp.363–70; *Design and Development of Weapons*, Postan, M.M., Hay, D. and Scott, J.D., pp.440–59.
2. *Administration of War Production* Scott, J.D. and Hughes, Richard, pp.270–90; *Design and Development of Weapons*, Postan, M.M., Hay, D. and Scott, J.D., pp.472–9.

3. *Administration of War Production* Scott, J.D. and Hughes, Richard, pp.29–32 and 370–2; *Design and Development of Weapons*, Postan, M.M., Hay, D. and Scott, J.D., pp.459–72.

4. *Administration of War Production* Scott, J.D. and Hughes, Richard, pp.29–32; Design and Development, pp.433–9.

5. *Administration of War Production* Scott, J.D. and Hughes, Richard, pp.89–97; *Dreadnoughts: A Photographic History*, Thomas, Roger D. and Patterson, Brian, pp.26–97.

6. Merchant aircraft carriers.

7. *Factories and Plant*, Hornby, William, pp.58–63.

8. A tool used to shape steel.

9. *Administration of War Production*, Scott, J.D. and Hughes, Richard, pp.127–34.

10. Ibid, pp.105–108.

11. Initially, electrical coils were fitted to reduce the ship's magnetic field. A cheaper method involved dragging a large electric cable in the water to counter the magnetic properties of the ship, a technique known as wiping.

12. Anti-Submarine Detection Investigation Committee equipment.

13. *British War Production*, Postan, M.M., pp.284–6 and 292–4.

14. *Administration of War Production* Scott, J.D. and Hughes, Richard, pp.150–7.

15. *Administration of War Production*, Scott, J.D. and Hughes, Richard, pp.372–82; *Design and Development of Weapons*, Postan, M.M., Hay, D. and Scott, J.D., pp.479–87.

16. *Administration of War Production*, Scott, J.D. and Hughes, Richard, pp.338–47; *Design and Development of Weapons*, Postan, M.M., Hay, D. and Scott, J.D., pp.50–67.

17. *Design and Development of Weapons*, Postan, M.M., Hay, D. and Scott, J.D., pp.68–83.

18. Ibid, pp.83–95.

19. Ibid, pp.153–56.

20. Ibid, pp.1–24.

21. *British War Production*, Postan, M.M., pp.339–44; *Administration of War Production*, Scott, J.D. and Hughes, Richard, pp.347–9; *Design and Development of Weapons*, Postan, M.M., Hay, D. and Scott, J.D., pp.159–74.

22. *Design and Development of Weapons*, Postan, M.M., Hay, D. and Scott, J.D., pp.122–38.

23. *Administration of War Production*, Scott, J.D. and Hughes, Richard, pp.383–406.

24. *Design and Development of Weapons*, Postan, M.M., Hay, D. and Scott, J.D., pp.139–53.

25. *Administration of War Production*, Scott, J.D. and Hughes, Richard, pp.349–58.

26. *Factories and Plant*, Hornby, William, pp.279–84.

27. *Factories and Plant*, Hornby, William, pp.180–1 and 274–6; *Design and Development of Weapons*, Postan, M.M., Hay, D. and Scott, J.D., pp.107–21.

28. Aiming ahead of a fast moving target, so the bullets will intercept it.

29. *Factories and Plant*, Hornby, William, pp.271–4.

30. *Factories and Plant*, Hornby, William, pp.253–71; *Design and Development of Weapons*, Postan, M.M., Hay, D. and Scott, J.D., pp.96–107

31. Humber Limited was part of Rootes Securities Limited, which was renamed the Rootes Group in 1941.

32. *Design and Development of Weapons*, Postan, M.M., Hay, D. and Scott, J.D., pp.175–228.

33. The flow is parallel to the shaft.

34. *Administration of War Production*, Scott, J.D. and Hughes, Richard, pp.281–3; *Design and Development of Weapons*, Postan, M.M., Hay, D. and Scott, J.D.

35. The designer of the first tank which went into action in 1916.

36. Named after Major General Percy Hobart, the Commander-in-Chief of the 79th Armoured Division.

37. *Design and Development of Weapons*, Postan, M.M., Hay, D. and Scott, J.D., pp.274–8; *Factories and Plant*, Hornby, William, pp.183–94.

38. *British War Production*, Postan, M.M., pp.358–70; *Factories and Plant*, Hornby, William, pp.276–9.

39. *Design and Development of Weapons*, Postan, M.M., Hay, D. and Scott, J.D., pp.373–81 and pp.479–87; *Studies of Overseas Supply*, Hall, D., Wrigley, C. and Scott, J.D., pp.386–96.

40. *Design and Development of Weapons*, Postan, M.M., Hay, D. and Scott, J.D., pp.381–90 and 413–428.

41. Ibid, pp.393–9.

42. Ibid, M. Postan, D. Hay and J. Scott, pp.399–413.

43. Also known as the Cat and Mouse system.

44. *Design and Development of Weapons*, Postan, M.M., Hay, D. and Scott, J.D., pp.390–3.

45. *Studies of Overseas Supply*, Hall, D., Wrigley, C. and Scott, J.D., pp.396–413

46. Either an acronym of Military Application of Uranium Detonation or taken from an anagram, or just a random codeword.

47. Some immediately during the explosion, some days later from injuries received and some from weeks or months later due radiation poisoning.

48. Letter from Major General Leslie R. Groves, head of the Manhattan Project, to the US Army's Chief of Staff, General George C. Marshall. He made it clear it was 'not to be released on Japan without express authority from the President'.

## Chapter 4: The Fuel Industries

1. *British War Production*, Postan, M.M., pp.211–7.

2. From the draft of Winston Churchill's memoirs, *The Second World War: Volume 2* (1949), Book IV, Chapter XV, p.3.

3. *Coal*, Court, W.H.B., pp.3–52.

4. Ibid, pp.53–106 and 296–332.

5. The government had limited the production of luxury goods at the start of the First World War. Many factories had stopped ordering coal, so the mine owners

had laid many miners off. Around 200,000 out of 1.1 million miners had enlisted, leaving the country short of coal.

6. *Coal*, Court, W.H.B., pp.107–27.
7. Ibid, pp.163–77, 201–72 and 372–98.
8. Son of The Right Honourable David Lloyd George MP, the Minister of Munitions and then Prime Minister during the First World War.
9. *Manpower*, Parker, H.M.D., pp.252–5.
10. *Coal*, Court, W.H.B., pp.273–91.
11. *Oil*, Payton-Smith, D.J., pp.39–75.
12. The Anglo-Iranian Oil Company was known as the Anglo-Persian Oil Company before 1935. It would be renamed the British Petroleum Company in 1954.
13. The 1935 Neutrality Act placed a general embargo on trading arms and war materials with any country. Revisions would change the conditions in 1937 and 1939.
14. *Oil*, Payton-Smith, D.J., pp.77–112.
15. Ships which were able to run on coal or oil.
16. The period of relative inactivity from 12 September 1939 to 9 May 1940, when German troops waited along the country's western border. Known as *Sitzkrieg* (Sitting War) in Germany.
17. *Oil*, Payton-Smith, D.J., pp.127–94.
18. Many would also be camouflaged but the work took until 1943 to complete, by which time the *Luftwaffe* threat had virtually ended.
19. *Oil*, Payton-Smith, D.J., pp.195–217.
20. Canada, Australia and New Zealand implemented rationing.
21. *Oil*, Payton-Smith, D.J., pp.249–65.
22. Ibid, pp.283–325.
23. Ibid, p.319.
24. Ibid, pp.325–39.
25. Ibid, pp.363–89.
26. Ibid, pp.391–411.
27. Ibid, pp.413–49.
28. 30 million tons were delivered for the European campaign and 21 million tons for the Pacific campaign.
29. *Oil*, Payton-Smith, D.J., pp.467–79.
30. Ibid, p.425.
31. Ibid, pp.267–81.
32. The 100 number is the octane rating of the lean mixture and the 130 number is the Performance Number of the rich mixture.

## Chapter 5: The Metal Industries

1. *Control of Raw Materials*, Hurstfield, J., pp.189–206.
2. Ibid, pp.151–75.
3. It had a higher phosphorous and sulphur content, which lowered the toughness and increased the brittleness of the steel. It was suitable for building and manufacturing but not for shells and other armaments.

4. *Control of Raw Materials*, Hurstfield, J., pp.331–48; *Labour in the Munitions Industry*, Inman, P., pp.155–64.
5. *Control of Raw Materials*, Hurstfield, J., pp.8–32.
6. Ibid, pp.66–81, 107–14, 151–75, 189–206 and 253–83.
7. Ibid, pp.331–48.
8. *Control of Raw Materials*, Hurstfield, J., pp.309–31; *Labour in the Munitions Industry*, Inman, P., pp.155–64.
9. *Control of Raw Materials*, Hurstfield, J., pp.283–300.
10. Ibid, pp.300–309.
11. Ibid, pp.385–402.
12. *Control of Raw Materials*, Hurstfield, J., pp.331–48; *Labour in the Munitions Industry*, Inman, P., pp.155–64.

## Chapter 6: The Explosives Industry

1. *Factories and Plant*, Hornby, William, pp.107–21.
2. Ibid, pp.91–107, 134–46 and 154–166.
3. For example, there were over 380 casualties during an explosion at the Chilwell Filling Factory near Nottingham on 1 July 1918.

## Chapter 7: North American Imports

1. *Studies of Overseas Supply*, Hall, D., Wrigley, C. and Scott, J.D., pp.66–100.
2. Ibid, pp.19–31 and 102–16.
3. Ibid, p.99.
4. Ibid, pp.116–50 and 178–99.
5. The Democrats voted 236 to 25 in favour and the Republicans voted 135 to 24 against. Fortunately for Britain, the balance of the vote was 260 to 165.
6. Unfortunately, Arthur Purvis was killed in a plane accident in August and he was replaced by Morris Wilson.
7. *Studies of Overseas Supply*, Hall, D., Wrigley, C. and Scott, J.D., pp.2–46, 170–8 and 312–45.
8. Ibid, pp.150–69, 205–39, 253–83 and 293–311.
9. Ibid, pp.2–19.
10. Britain's dockyards and shipyards launched 523 destroyers, frigates, corvettes and sloops during the war, compared to the 99 American-built ones, which arrived towards the end.
11. 250,000 sailors would serve with the US Merchant Marine during the war and 185,000 sailors would serve with the Merchant Navy.
12. *Studies of Overseas Supply*, Hall, D., Wrigley, C. and Scott, J.D., pp.42–6.
13. The Soviet Union's Lend-Lease debt was written off in 1971; it had only paid off 7 per cent.
14. *Studies of Overseas Supply*, Hall, D., Wrigley, C. and Scott, J.D., pp.46–65.

## Chapter 8: Merchant Shipping


1. *Merchant Shipping and the Demands of War*, Behrans, C. Betty A., pp.1–41.
2. The gross tonnage is a ship's volume and it is used to decide what regulations and safety rules applied, while the net tonnage determines how much cargo space a ship has.
3. The ports of Valencia and Barcelona were heavily bombed.
4. *Merchant Shipping and the Demands of War*, Behrans, C. Betty A., pp.43–89.
5. They would become longer when the Mediterranean route was closed.
6. British supplies to France had replaced what it had been buying from Germany and Poland.
7. *Merchant Shipping and the Demands of War*, Behrans, C. Betty A., pp.91–152.
8. Ibid, pp.154–86.
9. Ibid, pp.188–200.
10. Ibid, p.198.
11. *Administration of War Production*, Scott, J.D. and Hughes, Richard, pp.139–50; *Factories and Plant*, Hornby, William, pp.47–51.
12. *Merchant Shipping and the Demands of War*, Behrans, C. Betty A., pp.250–307.
13. Ibid, p.263.
14. Ibid, p.285.
15. Ibid, pp.312–22.
16. Ibid, pp.328–77.
17. Now West Bengal and Bangladesh.
18. Britain alone had lost 8.3 million tons, or nearly 1,200 ships in 1942.
19. These liberty ships had a Structure Aft of Midships and the prefix SAM was at the start of their name. Many suffered from structural fractures in high seas and a handful sank.
20. *Merchant Shipping and the Demands of War*, Behrans, C. Betty A., pp.379–418.
21. Known as longshoremen.
22. The US armed forces wasted 9 million tons of supplies during the European campaign compared to 3 million tons lost due to enemy action.
23. Rapidly built which had their names were prefixed with SAM, which stood for Structure Aft of Midships.
24. *Merchant Shipping and the Demands of War*, Behrans, C. Betty A., pp.431–51.
25. Ibid, p.451.


## Chapter 9: The Factories


1. *British War Production*, Postan, M.M., pp.115–23, 152–63, 198–201; *Administration of War Production*, Scott, J.D. and Hughes, Richard, pp.251–8.
2. *British War Production*, Postan, M.M., pp.287–300; *Administration of War Production*, Scott, J.D. and Hughes, Richard, pp.100–103 and 184–212; *Factories and Plant*, Hornby, William, pp.54–8; *Labour in the Munitions Industry*, Inman, P., pp.117–22.

3.  Except for the battleship HMS *Vanguard*.
4.  The battleships HMS *Barham* in November 1941 and HMS *Prince of Wales* in December 1941. The battlecruisers HMS *Hood* in May 1941 and HMS *Repulse* in December 1941.
5.  *British War Production*, Postan, M.M., pp.287–300; *Factories and Plant*, Hornby, William, pp.51–2, 64–8 and 72–6.
6.  *Administration of War Production*, Scott, J.D. and Hughes, Richard, pp.97–100; *Factories and Plant*, Hornby, William, pp.68–72.
7.  *British War Production*, Postan, M.M., pp.58–66.
8.  The cost of degaussing at the start of the war was £2 million (nearly £80 million today); *Administration of War Production*, Scott, J.D. and Hughes, Richard, p.102.
9.  *Administration of War Production* Scott, J.D. and Hughes, Richard, pp.139–50; *Factories and Plant*, Hornby, William, pp.47–51.
10.  *British War Production*, Postan, M.M., pp.123–6 and 163–74.
11.  Ibid, pp.303–44.
12.  Ibid, pp.303–16.
13.  Ibid, p.323.
14.  Ibid, pp.326–32.
15.  They wanted both a pilot and observer because a lot of their work was reconnaissance.
16.  *Administration of War Production*, Scott, J.D. and Hughes, Richard, pp.358–62.
17.  *Factories and Plant*, Hornby, William, pp.395–404; *Design and Development of Weapons*, Postan, M.M., Hay, D. and Scott, J.D., pp.133–8.
18.  *Factories and Plant*, Hornby, William, pp.194–210, 215–7, 222–42 and 288–93.
19.  Ibid, pp.242–50.
20.  *British War Production*, Postan, M.M., pp.126–36 and 345–52; *Administration of War Production*, Scott, J.D. and Hughes, Richard, pp.258–69.
21.  The number of shells asked for was 35 per cent higher than the BEF used in 1918.
22.  *Factories and Plant*, Hornby, William, pp.77–91 and 134–54.
23.  Ibid, pp.121–34.
24.  *British War Production*, Postan, M.M., pp.183–93; *Design and Development of Weapons*, Postan, M.M., Hay, D. and Scott, J.D., pp.308–52; *Factories and Plant*, Hornby, William, pp.77–91 and 183–94.
25.  Newton, Chambers and Company factory was the largest tank factory in the country.
26.  Part of the Ford Motor Company.
27.  British War Production, pp.193–5; *Factories and Plant*, Hornby, William, pp.121–34 and 166–77; *Design and Development of Weapons*, Postan, M.M., Hay, D. and Scott, J.D., pp.324–8.
28.  *Factories and Plant*, Hornby, William, pp.154–66.
29.  *Design and Development of Weapons*, Postan, M.M., Hay, D. and Scott, J.D., pp.279–98.
30.  *British War Production*, Postan, M.M., pp.174–83.
31.  *British War Production*, Postan, M.M., pp.201–11; *Factories and Plant*, Hornby, William, pp.299–377.

32. Many had been made for France which had surrendered, so America was happy to sell them to Britain.
33. For example, the drill bits.
34. Just the cutting point of the tool is made from hardened steel, rather than the whole tool.

## Chapter 10: Expanding the Workforce

1. *Manpower*, Parker, H.M.D., pp.61–86.
2. Ibid, p.72.
3. *British War Production*, Postan, M.M., pp.145–52; *Manpower*, Parker, H.M.D., pp.87–116 and 212–25; *Labour in the Munitions Industry*, Inman, P., pp.201–208 and 428–38.
4. *Manpower*, Parker, H.M.D., pp.97–116.
5. The number was estimated at 72 workers for every 100 servicemen at the end of the First World War.
6. *Manpower*, Parker, H.M.D., pp.97–116, 135–49 and 180–9; *Labour in the Munitions Industry*, Inman, P., pp.208–15.
7. *Manpower*, Parker, H.M.D., pp.169–99; Labour in the Munitions Industry, pp.186–95.
8. *Manpower*, Parker, H.M.D., pp.200–11 and 226–52; *Labour in the Munitions Industry*, Inman, P., pp.195–201.
9. *Labour in the Munitions Industry*, Inman, P., pp.35–41.
10. *Manpower*, Parker, H.M.D., pp.372–91; *Labour in the Munitions Industry*, Inman, P., pp.68–78.
11. *Labour in the Munitions Industry*, Inman, P., pp.45–57.
12. *Manpower*, Parker, H.M.D., pp.334–48.
13. Ibid, pp.150–69.
14. Ibid, pp.158–60 and 299–314.
15. *Administration of War Production*, Scott, J.D. and Hughes, Richard, pp.170–2 and 179–83; *Labour in the Munitions Industry*, Inman, P., pp.82–101 and 125–54.
16. *Labour in the Munitions Industry*, Inman, P., pp.186–95.
17. *Manpower*, Parker, H.M.D., pp.97–116.
18. *Labour in the Munitions Industry*, Inman, P., pp.178–86.
19. *Manpower*, Parker, H.M.D., pp.318–30.
20. Ibid, pp.279–98.
21. Ibid, pp.349–71.
22. See the section on Coal Mining, in Chapter 4, The Fuel Industries.
23. *Manpower*, Parker, H.M.D., pp.472–9; *Labour in the Munitions Industry*, Inman, P., pp.78–81.

## Chapter 11: Industrial Relations

1. *Manpower*, Parker, H.M.D., pp.440–7; *Labour in the Munitions Industry*, Inman, P., pp.288–306.

2.  *Labour in the Munitions Industry*, Inman, P., pp.306–14 and 419–28.
3.  *Manpower*, Parker, H.M.D., pp.424–40; *Labour in the Munitions Industry*, Inman, P., pp.315–9.
4.  *Labour in the Munitions Industry*, Inman, P., pp.319–39.
5.  Ibid, pp.352–67.
6.  Ibid, pp.371–92 and 406–18.
7.  Named after The Right Honourable John Whitley MP. The idea was considered during the First World War but they only worked in government run establishment. The coal, steel and engineering industries rejected Whitley Committees.
8.  *Manpower*, Parker, H.M.D., pp.455–7 and 466–71.
9.  *Labour in the Munitions Industry*, Inman, P., pp.392–406.
10. *Manpower*, Parker, H.M.D., pp.459–66.
11. Ibid, pp.457–9.
12. *Manpower*, Parker, H.M.D., pp.411–23; *Labour in the Munitions Industry*, Inman, P., pp.258–87.
13. *Labour in the Munitions Industry*, Inman, P., pp.224–42 and 271–87.
14. *Manpower*, Parker, H.M.D., pp.411–23.
15. *Manpower*, Parker, H.M.D., pp.392–410 and 421–3; *Labour in the Munitions Industry*, Inman, P., pp.242–57.

## Chapter 12: The Blitz on Industry

1.  *The Defence of the United Kingdom*, Collier, Basil, pp.261–2.
2.  Known as Operation Loge and Operation Seeschlange.
3.  Known as Operation Seelöwe.
4.  *The Defence of the United Kingdom*, Collier, Basil, pp.263–75.
5.  Ibid, 276–7.
6.  Operation Gomorrah against Hamburg would inflict around 40,000 civilian casualties in July 1943.
7.  Ibid, p.277.
8.  The USAAF's B-17 bomber carried just 2,200 kilograms (4,800 pounds) of bombs, while the RAF's Lancaster bomber's normal bomb load was 6,350 kilograms (14,000 pounds).
9.  Ibid, 278–81.
10. *Factories and Plant*, Hornby, William, pp.203–8 and 285–93; *Labour in the Munitions Industry*, Inman, P., pp.215–22.

## Chapter 13: The War Ends

1.  *British War Production*, Postan, M.M., pp.371–83.
2.  Ibid, pp.383–6.
3.  *Manpower*, Parker, H.M.D., pp.256–72.
4.  *British War Production*, Postan, M.M., p.247; *Studies of Overseas Supply*, Hall, D., Wrigley, C. and Scott, J.D., pp.1–2.

# Index